Requirements-Led Project Management

Discovering David's Slingshot

Suzanne Robertson

James Robertson

✦✦ Addison-Wesley

Boston • San Francisco • New York • Toronto • Montreal
London • Munich • Paris • Madrid
Capetown • Sydney • Tokyo • Singapore • Mexico City

The publisher offers discounts on this book when ordered in quantity for bulk purchases and special sales. For more information, please contact:

> U.S. Corporate and Government Sales
> (800) 382-3419
> corpsales@pearsontechgroup.com

For sales outside of the U.S., please contact:

> International Sales
> (317) 581-3793
> international@pearsontechgroup.com

Visit Addison-Wesley on the Web: www.awprofessional.com

Library of Congress Cataloging-in-Publication Data

Robertson, Suzanne.
   Requirements-led project management : discovering David's Slingshot /
Suzanne Robertson, James Robertson.
      p. cm.
Includes bibliographical references and index.
ISBN 0-321-18062-3 (hardcover : alk. paper)
1. Project management. I. Robertson, James. II. Title.

TA190.R52 2004
658.5—dc22   2004010530

ISBN: 0-321-18062-3
Text printed on recycled paper
1 2 3 4 5 6 7 8 9 10—CRW—0807060504
First printing, August 2004

For our parents.

If we had to write the requirements for parents, we would have described them.

Contents

Foreword

Be Careful What You Wish For. You May Get It.

A common theme in folk tales is the story of a man who is given three wishes. After spending the first two wishes on a golden castle and a beautiful princess, and discovering the operations and maintenance implications of each, he is happy to spend the third wish getting back to where he came from.

This kind of story happens a lot in software development. Much of it is due to an overfixation in hurrying to get a set of requirements templates completely filled out by the Software Requirements Review deadline. The deadline is usually set very early by the upper management, based on such self-fulfilling logic as, "We need to hurry up and start coding, because we will have a lot of debugging to do."

This pushes the requirements analysts into a hurried activity to minimize such dysfunctional progress metrics as "percentage of incomplete requirements" so that the requirements can be signed off and the "real software work" can begin. As a result, the project gets locked into requirements for hasty and later-regretted wishes.

Suzanne and James Robertson have seen a lot of software projects fail in this way. They have seen it happen with teams misapplying the Robertsons' own requirements templates (named Volere after the Italian word for "to wish or want"), and have written this book in response. The book rightly emphasizes that the main purpose of the requirements activity is not template-filling. It is rather a *mutual learning activity* in which specialists from different areas and cultures try to fit *what people in a user culture need* to *what people in a development culture can produce*, subject to some *real-world constraints that people in an ownership and management culture need to live within*.

These real-world constraints lead to another important conclusion about software requirements.

> *It is not a requirement if you cannot afford it.*

A good example of this happened on a project I was involved in at TRW. A hasty requirements activity had locked the project into a commitment to a 1-second response time to user queries. This was based largely on marketing enthusiasm and some small-scale COTS product demos.

Belatedly, the designers found that the COTS products could only achieve a 2.5-second response time when scaled up to the customer's full workload. The best custom solution they could find carried a price tag of $100 million, as compared to the customer's real-world constraint of a $30 million budget.

Belatedly, the customer commissioned some prototypes. These determined that a 4-second response time was adequate for 90% of the queries, and that the COTS product could be used to provide an acceptable solution within the $30 million budget constraint. Fortunately, this was discovered before delivery, but only after 18 months and a lot of money spent on a design that had to be thrown away.

This experience leads to some further important conclusions about software requirements (and requirements for a system in general).

> *Don't lock yourself into a set of requirements until you're sure you have a design that will satisfy them.*

This is covered very well by the Robertsons in Chapter 11 on the need for strong overlap between requirements, design, building, and integration activities; and in Chapters 5 and 6 emphasizing the importance of early prototypes and simulations to validate requirements before committing to them. Also in Chapter 9, they emphasize the importance of "signing on" to requirements and solution commitments rather than "signing off" on a set of requirements templates.

> *Watch out for nonfunctional requirements (NFRs).*

The best design solution is often a discontinuous function of the NFR level, and you don't want to get caught in the wrong side of the discontinuity, as did our project in the 1-second response time, $100 million cost situation. NFRs are emphasized by the Robertsons in Chapters 6 and 11, and covered more in their previous book, *Mastering the Requirements Process*. Again, they require a lot of caution because:

A tiny change in NFRs can cause a huge change in the cost.

Just think. All it takes is changing one character from a "4" to a "1" in a 1000-page requirements specification to turn a $30 million project into a $100 million project.

In Chapter 8, the Robertsons advocate using function points to estimate the cost of the requirements activity. Note the restricted target of this estimate, as they are aware of the flawed notion advanced by overenthusiastic function point advocates that you can estimate costs from the requirements without thinking about the design. As we saw in the example above, one character change in a 1000-page requirements specification changed cost by a factor of over three. The big thing that changed was the design, which is the preferred basis for estimating costs.

Thus, when following the Robertsons' excellent guidance in Chapter 2 on developing a return on investment (ROI) analysis for your system and its requirements, it is important to recognize that:

- An ROI analysis is based on both benefit and cost estimates.
- Benefits are best estimated from the requirements, which tell you *what* the system will do for the users, and *how well*.
- Costs are best estimated from the design, which tells you *how* the system will be built (including the cost implications of using very high-level languages and using COTS, open source, or product-line components, none of which are included in the estimation formulas in Chapter 8).

That said, you'll find this book a treasure trove of experience-based guidelines and illustrative examples on how to get the requirements right on your project. These include guidelines and examples on treating the requirements as an investment activity in Chapter 2; getting the right people involved and understanding their cultures in Chapter 3; techniques for stimulating mutual learning and a shared vision among stakeholders in Chapter 4; the use of prototypes and simulations in Chapters 5 and 6; dealing with legacy systems in Chapter 7; and managing systems requirements, systems of systems requirements, and requirements processes in Chapters 9, 10, and 11. Each chapter concludes with a nicely balanced set of "What do I do right now?" and "What's the least that I can get away with?" checklists.

As a bottom line, the book does a wonderful job of lifting its readers from a focus on templates and objects to a focus on people's needs, capabilities, and ability to work together to achieve a shared vision of the requirements (and the design) for a system that will satisfy all their needs and constraints. I hope you have the opportunity to use its practices on your next project.

Barry Boehm

Overture

We explain how requirements and their successful management are inextricably linked to project success.

Through the years your authors have participated in and observed many projects, both successful and otherwise. A factor present in every successful project and absent in every unsuccessful project is sufficient attention to requirements. The "requirements," as we use the term, means having *knowledge of* the functionality and the qualitative properties the product must have, as well as constraints that affect the product.

It does not matter what the product is. Our clients in electronics, aviation, automotive, pharmaceutical, government, and software have all found the same thing: Requirements must be correctly understood before the right product can be built. Requirements are the way of communicating between the people who commission a product on behalf of anticipated users and builders of that product. The requirements are usually communicated in the form of a text document, a set of models, or both, according to the nature and needs of the particular project.

We believe it is self-evident you must know the requirements before being able to construct the right product and that many projects are aware of this even when they do not specifically practice it.

However, less awareness exists of the contribution requirements make to the managing of a project. Our experience is many project managers make less than optimum use of requirements.

For example, one of the outputs from the requirements activity is a context model. Requirements analysts build this model to define the precise scope of their study, then proceed to use it to determine the business use cases. But this is not just an analysis model—it contains enough information for a project manager to measure the size of the task and to

> 66 *Programmers and software engineers who dive into code without writing a spec tend to think they're cool gunslingers, shooting from the hip. They're not. They are terribly unproductive. They write bad code and produce shoddy software, and they threaten their projects by taking giant risks which are completely uncalled for.* 99
>
> —Joel Spolsky, *Joel on Software*

make accurate estimates of the needed effort. Similarly, the requirements analysts go through a process to identify all the stakeholders who have requirements for the project. By simply counting these stakeholders and looking at the requested interview durations, it is possible to schedule resources.

The project manager's intention is to deliver a product that satisfies (or perhaps enthralls!) the customer. We refer to this as a *project success indicator* and will discuss these in the first chapter. The requirements activity, as we set it out in this book, suggests you make use of project sociology analysis to ensure you have the right people on the requirements team, you use appropriate elicitation methods, you invent parts of the product (some of our most useful products are pure inventions), and add a customer value to each of the requirements. These are all major contributors to building a product to satisfy your customer, yet we sometimes see project managers short-change this activity in the hope of saving time to delivery. It never does save time and the product is always heavily (and expensively) modified before the customers find any use for it. Alternatively, the project manager who spends too much time on the requirements activity (yes, it can be done) is naturally wasting resources that can be better used elsewhere.

We aim to show you here how to effectively gather the requirements (Chapter 4), how much time you should be spending on your requirements (Chapter 11), and, fundamentally, whether or not you should be investing in building the product in the first place (Chapter 2).

Most important, we aim to show you the potential of requirements activity. Like David's slingshot, this relatively simple tool in the right hands can produce results far beyond its cost. We also hope it equips you to tame a few giants for yourself.

Development of Volere

Formalizing the link between requirements and project management has taken some time and many, many projects. We started toward this goal in 1995 when we posted the first edition of the Volere[1] Requirements Specification Template on our Web sites. The template is a framework for gathering and recording the different types of requirements-related knowledge. We wanted a formality for specifying atomic requirements, grouping them into business and product-related chunks and making

1. Volere (Vol-Air-Ray) is the Italian verb for "to wish or to want." We have used the word as the name for our work on requirements (template, process, tools, training, audits, and clinics). You can find more information at our requirements Web site at www.volere. co.uk.

them traceable throughout the project. We also wanted the flexibility of having requirements in a variety of forms and of choosing (according to the specific situation) when to gather detail, and how much. Since then, tens of thousands of people have downloaded the template. We originally developed Volere with software products in mind, but our requirements template and process have been adopted by people in projects as diverse as restoring old churches, designing motor vehicles, labelling pharmaceuticals, air traffic control, planning business procedures, and designing phones. After all, a requirement is a requirement regardless of whether it is for software, hardware, organizational procedures, consumer products, or anything else that someone wants or needs.

A requirement is a requirement regardless of whether it is for software, hardware, organizational procedures, consumer products, or anything else that someone wants or needs.

We have added the feedback from Volere users around the world along with our own practical experiences in consulting and teaching to develop and refine our approach. Part of the Volere approach is a generic process for gathering and communicating requirements. This is proving effective as shown by the thousands of organizations scattered throughout the world who are using adaptations of this process for their requirements gathering.

This Book

This book is about the contribution requirements make to the success of development projects. The book is intended for you if you are connected with the development of software or hardware or consumer products or services. You probably have the word "manager," or "leader" or something similar as part of your job title.

The book references some requirements-gathering techniques. We are not attempting to tell you how to perform these; we assume you already have some familiarity with them. When we talk about the requirements activities, we do so in light of how they contribute to project management, and project success. This book is about how to make better use of requirements and how to use the products of requirements as a management tool that contributes to project success.

During the course of this book we will show you

This is a book on how to make better use of requirements and how to use the products of requirements as a management tool that contributes to project success.

- How a quick cycle time can deliver more appropriate products.
- The most effective requirements process for your project.
- How to use the requirements as a way of discovering stakeholders and managing their involvement.
- The best way of progressively prioritizing requirements and managing expectations.
- How you can quantify customer value and concentrate on satisfying the most valuable requirements.

- How to manage requirements across multi-domain/scope/technology projects.
- How you can measure and communicate requirements progress.
- How you can use requirements as input to project management planning and decision making.
- How you can use requirements to communicate across business and technological boundaries.

The book also has insights for business analysts. However, it is neither an introductory book nor a techniques book. Our previous effort, *Mastering the Requirements Process,* is recommended if you are looking for a "how to" book on requirements analysis. In this book we are looking beyond the technicalities of the requirements process to justify the effort needed to discover requirements, to show how to get stakeholder commitment, to measure the effort needed, and to show you how to exploit the all-important links between requirements and project success.

Our intention is to provide practical ways of using requirements to contribute to your project's success. We feel we will have succeeded if your next project runs a lot more smoothly, your communication with stakeholders is more effective, you can react more quickly to changes, you can quantify the improvements, and you enjoy it more.

RESOURCE NOTE

Mastering the Requirements Process, by James and Suzanne Robertson, Addison Wesley, 1999.

Acknowledgments

When Michael Schumacher drove his Ferrari past the checkered flag to win his sixth Formula 1 world championship, he was alone in the car. However, as soon as he stopped the car, Schumacher rushed to embrace and thank his race director, engineers, and pit crew. He knew that without them and the other several hundred members of *Scuderia Ferrari* he would not even make it to the starting line. Though your authors are by no means claiming the talents of Schumacher, we do wish to acknowledge that, similarly, without help we could not have written this book.

Let us introduce you to *Scuderia Robertson*.

Perhaps our greatest influence through the years has been provided by our partners at the Atlantic Systems Guild: Tom DeMarco, Peter Hruschka, Tim Lister, Steve McMenamin, and John Palmer have all contributed their inspiration and experience to this book. John Favaro and Carol Dekkers provided valuable insights and technical assistance. Michelle Nyland of ETAS and Steve Howell of Jaguar have been sources of ideas and project common sense over the years.

Ian Alexander, Neil Maiden, and Joseph Schiefer reviewed drafts of the manuscript and gave us valuable input. We hasten to exonerate them from any errors that remain in this work. Your authors take responsibility.

We are grateful for the skills of our assistant, Sue Spurrell, in keeping our business running while we immersed ourselves in this book.

The team at Addison-Wesley has been especially patient and helpful. We acknowledge input and assistance from Peter Gordon, Bernard

Gaffney, Simon Plumtree, Karen Sellwood, Tyrrell Albaugh, and Elizabeth Ryan. Virginia Somma and Brian Wright of Stratford Publishing Services guided us skillfully through the editing process.

And we want to thank our clients for giving us the opportunity for demonstrating that our ideas work. We thank our students for challenging us and teaching us to be lucid when explaining these concepts. All of them have in some way contributed.

Thank you, all.

Suzanne Robertson
James Robertson
London, England

Requirements and Project Success

We discuss project success indicators. Although project success indicators are self-evident signals of successful projects, they are not always easy to positively influence. We refer to the chapters of this book that provide information on requirements activities that positively influence each of the indicators. We also suggest how your requirements activities can make your project more successful.

For more than a quarter century, the authors have participated in and managed software projects and many other types of projects including architecture, missile research, and business organization. We have witnessed many changes in technology, most of them innovative and beneficial, and a smaller number of changes in how technology projects are managed. We have observed in all projects the consistent connection between successful completion of a project and having a clear understanding of the project's requirements.

We have also observed the opposite: For all significant project failures, requirements were wholly or partly missing. Whenever a project team jumps directly into implementation (in the mistaken belief it saves time and effort because members "know" what is needed), it invariably leads to a delayed or cancelled result. "Build-first-ask-questions-later" projects significantly overrun their budgets and deliver less-than-optimum systems.

66 *The hardest single part of building a software system is deciding precisely what to build. No other part of the conceptual work is as difficult. . . . No other part of the work so cripples the resulting system if done wrong. No other part is more difficult to rectify later.* 99

—Fred Brooks, *No Silver Bullets*

Figure 1.1

The link between requirements and projects. Although requirements state what has to be built, they also reveal qualities that can and should be used to contribute to effective project management.

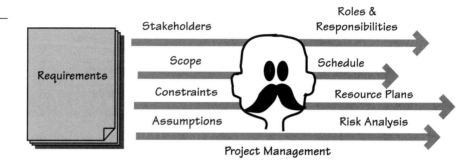

Figure 1.1 shows some of the relationships between requirements and project management. Your project exists to build some kind of product, and its requirements are a description of this product. However, to discover those requirements you need to talk to people with an interest in or knowledge of the intended product. We refer to these people as *stakeholders*. By defining stakeholders' roles and responsibilities project managers can allocate resources effectively and identify potential participation and communication problems.

A basic requirements practice is to have a precisely defined scope. This in turn provides the basis for accurate scheduling and change control. Constraints are a predetermined design or solution restriction, and we treat them as a type of requirement. Constraints indicate the organizational and technological factors that affect the solution and indicate the kind of resources needed. Your requirements specification should contain a section for assumptions, which the project team must make because of some uncertainty. In turn, assumptions are input to the risk analysis activity.

Project Success Indicators

Through the years, by observing our clients, participating in project teams, and listening to the wiser people in our industry, we have found successful projects do not occur by accident. Moreover, certain project characteristics indicate whether a project is likely to succeed. We refer to these as project success indicators (PSIs).

For example, one success indicator is that a product be correctly sized to meet project goals. This means the project team delivers the needed functionality and very little more. Additionally, the delivered functionality adequately supports the appropriate part of the user's organization. By meeting the indicator of correct size, the project team is successful because it has not spent any time building superfluous product.

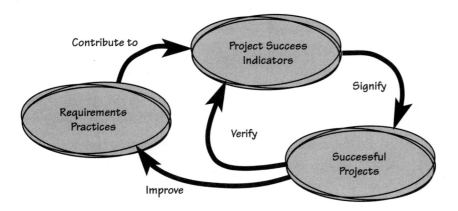

Figure 1.2

A number of observable indicators reveal the likelihood of a project being successful. During the course of multiple projects, we have observed require-ments practices that contribute to these PSIs. From successful projects we have learned to refine these requirements practices and thus to improve our chances of success indicators being positive.

How does a project team ensure it has a correctly sized product? The answer lies in the *requirements activity*. It is easier if we talk about *re-quirements practices,* which are the tasks or ways of thinking normally included in your requirements process (see Figure 1.2). For example, sup-pose you agree a correctly sized product is one of your PSIs. Then, you look for requirements practices that make a positive contribution this project success indicator.

In Chapter 2—Requirements Value we discuss how to put a business value on requirements. In Chapter 3—Project Sociology we explain how to ensure the right people are involved in the project. Then in Chapter 4—Learning What People Need we talk about correct elicitation: finding what is needed or not needed, and setting the context of the investiga-tion. Chapter 6—Requirements Simulations discusses how the use of simulations, scenarios, and prototypes helps get the correct size. And Chapter 9—Managing the Requirements covers requirements manage-ment and prioritization. Each of these requirements practices helps you implement only the most valuable requirements, those that give you the correct size for your product.

PSIs and Requirements Practices

We have discovered the existence of known and observable PSIs, as well as requirements practices that make a positive contribution to those suc-cess indicators. In this chapter we identify the PSIs, their associated re-quirements practices, and the chapters of this book that pertain to each requirements practice.

PSI 1: No Excessive Schedule Pressure

This PSI indicates success when you can:

- Precisely and progressively track and communicate the actual progress of the project against planned progress.
- Predict deviations from the plan.
- Quantify how changes affect project scope.
- Use requirements to improve scheduling—poor estimates, inadequate management, or poor anticipation of time-to-market demands are primary causes of an unrealistic schedule. In this case developers are forced to accept a schedule that results in poor-quality work. The team skips vital deliverables, erroneously thinking that doing so will save time.

Requirements practices for PSI 1 are described in the following chapters:

- 2—Requirements Value: Determining the worth of requirements and whether it is worthwhile investing in requirements or investing in the project.
- 4—Learning What People Need: Seeing how the context diagram clearly demonstrates the scope of the requirements effort.
- 7—Requirements for Existing Systems: Examining how to quantify changes to an existing system.
- 8—Measuring Requirements: Counting function points as a way of determining the size of the task.
- 11—Your Requirements Process: Building a requirements-knowledge model to define and quantify information to be collected.

PSI 2: On-Budget Delivery

Success indication means you deliver the product within the agreed tolerances of expected delivery time and/or financial budget. This implies delivery time and financial budgets are competently set and are used as goals for estimating and scheduling decisions.

The requirements practices for PSI 2 are described in the following chapters:

- 4—Learning What People Need: Using the context diagram to determine scope and to form the basis of the estimated effort.
- 7—Requirements for Existing Systems: Determining how to identify new requirements.
- 8—Measuring Requirements: Understanding function-point counting as an accurate method for determining size and effort for a task.

PSI 3: Lack of Creeping Requirements

A criterion for this PSI is fewer than 5% of requirements emerge after requirements are deemed to be complete. This percentage excludes requirements unknown because of changes in the law or in organizational objectives.

The requirements practice for PSI 3 is described in the following chapters:

- 3—Project Sociology: Getting the right people involved with the project to ensure scope and requirements are correctly identified in the first place.
- 4—Learning What People Need: Preventing out-of-scope requirements through better elicitation techniques.
- 6—Requirements Simulations: Focusing requirements on the correct product by extensive use of prototypes and other simulations.
- 7—Requirements for Existing Systems: Learning to recognize new requirements.

PSI 4: Control of Changes

You can recognize, quantify, negotiate, and integrate changes at any stage of a product's lifetime.

The requirements practices for PSI 4 are described in the following chapters:

- 4—Learning What People Need: Setting the context as a baseline for the work.
- 7—Requirements for Existing Systems: Monitoring requirements changes.
- 9—Managing the Requirements: Deploying requirements change management.
- 10—Requirements Meta-Management: Managing multicomponent systems; at any stage of its life a system might have a change that affects many other systems or subsystems.

PSI 5: Good-Quality Code

When the code is of high quality your team:

- Creates code that is practically error-free.
- Builds maintainability into the code.
- Excludes highly troublesome objects or modules.

Requirements practices for PSI 5 are described in the following chapters:

- 4—Learning What People Need: Getting the right requirements by enabling developers to write their code once, without having to constantly change it.
- 6—Requirements Simulations: Using prototypes, in addition to written requirements, to give developers a complete picture of what they have to build.
- 11—Your Requirements Process: Maintaining close contact between the requirer and builder through iterative development and short delivery cycles.

PSI 6: User or Customer Satisfaction

Success is normally indicated when you:

- Satisfy hands-on users with product functionality.
- Ensure users also like nonfunctional aspects of the product.
- Obtain a high usability rating from hands-on users.
- Create a product the customer considers valuable.

Requirements practices for PSI 6 are described in the following chapters:

- 3—Project Sociology: Getting the requirements from people whose knowledge is appropriate and respected means the product is what the organization needs.
- 4—Learning What People Need: Using appropriate requirements elicitation methods to increase the probability the product exactly matches the hands-on users' needs.
- 5—Inventing Requirements: Introducing innovation and imagination into a product, so it is accepted and liked.
- 6—Requirements Simulations: Using hands-on testing of prototypes to give users the chance to simulate usage and to correct their new product before delivery.

PSI 7: Completion, Not Cancellation

You run the project to its intended completion (with the exception of changed political circumstances, or some other extraordinary condition). Requirements practices for PSI 7 are described in the following chapters:

- 7—Requirements for Existing Systems: Recognizing and avoiding unnecessary new requirements

- 8—Measuring Requirements: Using proper counting methods and estimating practices to set realistic deadlines and expectations.
- 9—Managing the Requirements: Setting realistic and attainable project goals with concurrence of the stakeholders.

PSI 8: Correctly Sized Product

You meet PSI 8 when you:

- Deliver needed functionality and very little more.
- Provide in the product all functionality users need for the applicable part of their operations.

Requirements practices for PSI 8 are described in the following chapters:

- 2—Requirements Value: Knowing the value of the product to the organization to make sure the development team produces the appropriate product.
- 3—Project Sociology: Having people who know what is needed to ensure the proper product size.
- 4—Learning What People Need: Understanding the correct work scope to provide a better idea of what is possible and what is useful.
- 6—Requirements Simulations: Using various kinds of prototypes to determine the most useful product.
- 9—Managing the Requirements: Using requirements prioritization to control galloping requirements.

PSI 9: The Product Is Adding Value

You deliver a product that:

- Adds some functional value to the owning organization by reducing cost of operations, adding value in the marketplace, increasing customer revenue, or in some other way making a genuine contribution to the effectiveness of the organization.
- Has features that ensure it will sell well in a high-value marketplace.
- Does not simply rewrite a failing legacy product with little or no added functionality.
- Is more than just an integration of several existing pieces of functionality; it adds functionality or significantly improves existing functionality.
- Has a long life with a high return on investment.

Requirements practices for PSI 9 are described in the following chapters:

- 2—Requirements Value: Treating the project as an investment and determining its worth.
- 5—Inventing Requirements: Creating not simply what business users say they want, but adding something of value through invention and creativity.
- 6—Requirements Simulations: Demonstrating intended functionality via prototypes to enable correct decisions about the product's contribution to the organization.
- 7—Requirements for Existing Systems: Recognizing new requirements that add value.

PSI 10: Control of Configuration

You can:

- Smoothly integrate individual builds or versions into the operating environment, throughout the project.
- Successfully integrate commercial-off-the-shelf (COTS) components into the builds.
- Trace requirements from the business into the product and vice versa.

Requirements practices for PSI 10 are described in the following chapters:

- 9—Managing the Requirements: Controlling the assembly of various components through the art of change management.
- 10—Requirements Meta-Management: Dealing in a project with several subprojects or separate components being constructed at the same time; Chapter 10 discusses management problems of multi-component projects.

PSI 11: No Nasty Surprises

This PSI is met when you:

- Provide to the client both needed functionality and appropriate nonfunctional properties.
- Verify all COTS components work as expected.

Requirements practices for PSI 11 are described in the following chapters:

- 4—Learning What People Need: Enabling requirers to understand their requirements through appropriate elicitation techniques, and to concur with the requirements analysts as to what is needed.

- 10—Requirements Meta-Management: Ensuring when multiple technologies are used, all parts fit together and work as expected.
- 11—Your Requirements Process: Making the client constantly aware of what direction the product is taking through short release cycles.

PSI 12: The Product Conforms to the Product Goals or Company Vision

Success in PSI 12 is demonstrated when you:

- Deliver a product that fits well with the company product line or way of working.
- Demonstrate the goals of the project are met.

Requirements practices for PSI 12 are described in the following chapters:

- 4—Learning What People Need: Ensuring requirements are relevant through correct elicitation, setting the correct scope for the project.
- 9—Managing the Requirements: Setting measurable and testable goals.

PSI 13: Adequate Documentation

This PSI comes about when you:

- State requirements appropriately for the purposes of all relevant stakeholders.
- Make design and architecture documents adequate and understandable.
- Provide documentation that users find suitable to their needs.
- Provide requirements that are traceable.

Requirements practices for PSI 13 are described in the following chapter:

- 4—Learning What People Need: Correctly writing requirements to inform interested parties why the product is as it is.

PSI 14: Adequate Productivity

Adequate productivity means:

- Both management and the project team can demonstrate they are working as productively as is possible under the circumstances.
- The project team works at the average or better than established productivity standards for that type of project in that type of industry.

Requirements practices for PSI 14 are described in the following chapters:

- 9—Managing the Requirements: Using requirements to ensure that no inappropriate activities take place in the project; measuring the products of the requirements activity to monitor productivity and progress.
- 11—Your Requirements Process: Enabling the team to work at its optimum by implementing an effective requirements process and making the requirements process as effective as possible.

PSI 15: No Litigation

PSI 15 indicates success when:

- Nobody has sued, or is threatening to sue.
- You create conditions in which users are willing to work with the project team again, and vice versa; no internal feuds.

Requirements practices for PSI 15 are described in the following chapters:

- 3—Project Sociology: Having the right stakeholders involved (extremely valuable). Identifying the correct people to improve the chances of leaving yourself less susceptible to lawsuits.
- 4—Learning What People Need: Writing requirements correctly and unambiguously to reduce exposure to litigation. A correctly worded and formatted specification becomes the foundation of the contract.

PSI 16: Good Team Morale

PSI 16 is demonstrated when:

- Members are moulded into a solid, productive unit.
- Key team members are retained until completion of the project.
- Team members help one another, with no internal bickering or destructive behavior.
- Happy working relationships are created between the project team and the business users.
- Team members desire to work on other projects together.
- Other stakeholders express a full-term commitment to the project.

Requirements practices for PSI 16 are described in the following chapters:

- 3—Project Sociology: Finding the right people for the given scope of the project is essential to a happy project. Keeping people commit-

ted for the duration is necessary to avoid the negative impact of changing personnel mid-project.
- 5—Inventing Requirements: Introducing innovation and imagination into the end product, so it is accepted and liked by the project team.
- 11—Your Requirements Process: Keeping your team happy to have them working as effectively as possible. Short release cycles are a demonstrated way of keeping stakeholders enthusiastic.

PSI 17: No Misunderstood Requirements

PSI 17 is demonstrated when:

- The product matches stakeholders' expectations in all cases.
- Requirements analysts can communicate requirements to builders so the delivered product fulfills what the requirers want.

Requirements practices for PSI 17 are described in the following chapters:

- 4—Learning What People Need: Using effective elicitation methods to enable requirers to state requirements so the requirements analysts both understand the requirements and can provide feedback to demonstrate that understanding.
- 6—Requirements Simulations: Using prototypes and scenarios to enable requirements analysts to make practical demonstrations of the requirements. Eliminate misunderstandings before construction begins.
- 7—Requirements for Existing Systems: Understanding additional and changed requirements.

PSI 18: The Correct Process Is Being Used

When success is established under PSI 18:

- The project team and its management attest to happiness with the adopted process.
- Little time is wasted through activities that turn out to be unnecessary.
- Process is retained without changing on the fly to incorporate unexpected activities.

Requirements practices for PSI 18 are described in the following chapter:

- 11—Your Requirements Process: Crafting a requirements process to suit your organization and culture.

PSI 19: Testing Is Effective

This indicator is positive when you can:

- Involve testers early in the requirements process.
- Declare testing a success by both testers and developers.
- Reveal very few errors in any of the project's documents and inter-mediate deliverables in testing.
- Through testing, show the product is working with few fixes necessary.

Requirements practices for PSI 19 are described in the following chapters:

- 4—Learning What People Need: Writing a requirement to make it testable.
- 11—Your Requirements Process: Testing requirements to avoid corrupting any downstream process.

As mentioned before, PSIs point to a successful outcome for your project. However, having one positive indicator is not enough for a successful project. These are indicators for which most of them, or at least most of the ones relevant to your project, must be on the positive side of the ledger (see Figure 1.3). Our intention in this book is to demonstrate how good requirements practices contribute to project success indicators and the overall success of your project.

Obviously, project success requires more than effective requirements. The Software Engineering Body of Knowledge (SWEBOK) project—a joint initiative of the Association of Computing Machinery (ACM), Institute of Electronics and Electrical Engineers (IEEE) Computer Society, and the Université du Québec a Montréal—has identified ten knowledge areas that make up software engineering. They are

1. Software Requirements
2. Software Design

Figure 1.3

Think of the PSIs as a series of traffic lights. One green light on its own has little value, but to have many of them showing green means your project is likely to succeed.

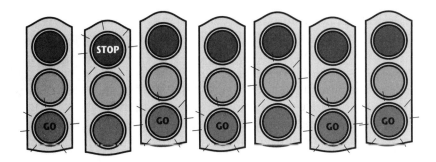

3. Software Construction
4. Software Testing
5. Software Maintenance
6. Software Configuration Management
7. Software Engineering Management
8. Software Engineering Process
9. Software Engineering Tools and Methods
10. Software Quality

Note the dependency of many of the knowledge areas on requirements. Design is crucial to get a working product, but the designer cannot design a successful product unless the requirements are well understood. The same applies to construction: Most programmers are skilled in their craft and can construct the correct product, assuming they are given the correct requirements. Testing is testing against the requirements. The testers can only determine the product is working correctly if they have a suitable definition of what "correct" is. And if you look through the rest of the knowledge areas, you see a link, sometimes a strong link, to requirements.

Apart from knowledge, some personality attributes make for successful project leadership and usually successful projects. Being a good communicator, having the respect of the project team, being adroit at navigating the organizational minefields are all part of successful project management. These desirable attributes are a little outside the scope of the book. Instead, we concentrate on the requirements aspect of projects, and show you how you can use requirements to improve PSIs and to steer your project along the road to success.

Effective Requirements

Requirements are the foundation for almost all systems development activities to come. They are like an architect's plans for a building: If the plans are wrong, the builders will construct the wrong building. But an architect's plans can only be correct if he has gone to the trouble of finding out exactly what the building owner wants, and the building's intended use.

> *If your software does not have to meet requirements then I have some software at home that you can use.*
>
> —Anonymous

We are using the term requirements to mean more than the requirements specification document. Most of the effort does not go into the writing of requirements, but into *discovering* them. This discovery process is often seen by many project managers as too laborious, too time consuming, or too difficult to undertake. Deep-seated cultural reasons often exist for this reluctance to devote time to requirements. This is especially true in the software industry in which progress is traditionally measured by the amount of code written.

If your requirements are intangible, inconsistent, or imprecise, it becomes very difficult to justify spending time on them. However, if you can make your requirements measurable and communicable, you are in a good position to quantify the advantages. Quantification means you can demonstrate how *not* investing in requirements flies in the face of reason, statistics, and real-world project experience.

So let's look at some effective requirements practices. These are expanded and expounded throughout the rest of the book.

Setting the Correct Scope

> *There is no use working on anything else until boundary-elements closure can be obtained. If it can't be obtained, there is no better option available than project cancellation.*
>
> —Tom DeMarco and Tim Lister, *Waltzing with Bears: Managing Risk on Software Projects*

The first characteristic of good requirements is they specify the correct scope. Too often we hear of projects suffering from "scope creep," or of someone building the wrong product because analysts studied the wrong part of the business area. Good requirements practice mandates scope of the project and scope of the product (different scopes) are both clearly and unambiguously defined.

The foregoing may sound good and be easy to state, but your practice must include some form of scope diagram for both project investigation and the product to be built. Textual descriptions of scope can never be precise enough. Scope needs to be described in diagrams backed up by textual descriptions of the interfaces and adjacent systems; they must not be open to any false interpretation or misrepresentation.

Figure 1.4 shows how the scope of the project is defined using a context diagram. The central process is the work, not just the anticipated product, to be studied. The data flowing to and from the work represents the outputs, and hence the responsibilities, of either the work or the adjacent systems that surround the work. The definition of the input and output flows—to the level of business data elements—provides the basis for agreeing upon the size of the requirements investigation.

Having Well-Defined and Testable Goals

A project goes nowhere unless the project team knows where it has to go. Goals are a steering mechanism for the project. Without measurable goals it is too easy to spend time on subjects that are low priority or irrelevant . . . or it is too easy to miss subjects that are vital.

A goal is both clear and testable. That is, everyone concerned with the project can tell whether a goal has been reached. A clear goal means the project team knows the requirements on which to spend time and those that can be discarded because they do not contribute to the team's goals.

Releasing the Product in Short Cycle Times

Discovering requirements should not force you into a waterfall process. That is, it is not necessary to write all requirements specifications before

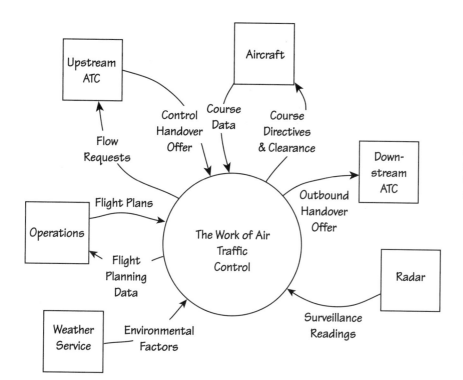

Figure 1.4

An example of a context diagram showing the scope of the work to be studied. The flows to and from the work will be defined using a data dictionary or some other way of specifying their precise data content.

starting to build. By waiting for all the requirements, you almost certainly create a long lag between requirements gathering and when something appears on the desktop or in the hands of your users or consumers.

This hesitancy typically discourages participation in the requirements process as requirers receive no feedback on the work they have put into supplying the requirements. Further, your business analysts have more difficulty gathering the requirements. If stakeholders think they will see no return on their requirements contributions for 12 months or more, they are unlikely to put their hearts into participating with the business analysts (see Figure 1.5).

Testing the Requirements

A requirement that cannot be tested is not a requirement. When you have a requirement along the lines of "the product shall be user friendly," you must find a way of making it testable. Keep in mind that the requirement may be correct according to whoever originated it, but not stated in a measurable way to make it testable. Good requirements practice entails you test requirements to ensure they are within scope, testable, not frivolous, and meet whatever other quality measures you implement. Always test requirements before making them part of the specification.

Figure 1.5

The release cycle should be short. What is short varies depending on the complexity of your project sociology, but we suggest somewhere between two weeks and three months between releases. These lengths of time enable people supplying the requirements to get frequent feedback on their contributions. People can thus also see the product in its embryonic state and make necessary corrections before it becomes too difficult to do so.

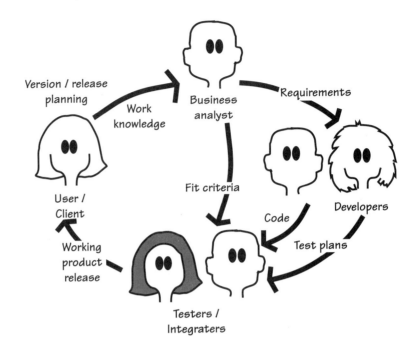

Any requirement that cannot be tested is not a requirement.

Good requirements practice also means you write your requirements to include a fit criterion. A fit criterion is a measurement of the requirement that enables testers to precisely determine whether the solution meets, that is, fits, the requirement.

Having the Right People Involved . . . and Committed

Requirements come from people. The requirements analyst works with users, subject-matter experts (SMEs), management, usability experts, outside suppliers, and many others to find the requirements for the optimum product. Only by having people with the appropriate knowledge participating in the project can the analyst find the right requirements. Projects that have the wrong people, or not all of the right people, rarely come up with the right requirements.

Controlling Requirements Creep

Requirements creep refers to requirements that enter the product after the requirements process is finished. It also refers to the seemingly never-ending stream of requirements that appear to be way beyond the original goal of the product. Effective requirements practice includes a well-defined and unarguable scope, along with a test for relevance of all requirements. Good requirements practice also includes prototyping and user involvement as a way of controlling requirements creep.

Ensuring the Product Adds Value to the Organization

Organizational value added is not normally considered as a requirements activity, but we believe successful projects have the objective of delivering a product with tangible and measurable benefits to the organization. Does the product carry out some necessary task that no other product does? Is it producing information or services in which the user has expressed high interest? All these are determined during the requirements process.

If the product is a commercial product for sale, it must display a differentiation to the intended buyer. Again, the requirements gatherers have to study the proposed work area to ensure their product delivers tangible benefits.

Declining Doomed Projects

If you have a positive reading for most of the PSIs, then barring meteor strikes or plagues of locusts, your project will likely succeed. The converse is also true: In the absence of mostly positive PSIs, your chances of success are small indeed.

Usually good requirements practices have a beneficial effect on the entire development process.

Good requirements practice includes an initiation activity—we refer to the initiation activity as "The Blastoff"—in which you determine or confirm scope, goals, and stakeholders. If key stakeholders cannot reach a consensus on these three items, the likelihood is the project will not succeed. You should also consider project feasibility, stakeholder support, and resource availability.

All the above qualities contribute to a conscious go/no go decision. It's straightforward: if you do not have the necessary positive indicators, then your project is seriously disadvantaged. There is very little point carrying on beyond this point as the outcome is predictable and expensive.

No shame exists in cancelling a doomed project. But it *is* shameful to proceed with a venture in which failure is practically guaranteed *and* valuable resources are used up. Plenty of other projects exist that can well use the resources.

This book discusses the requirements part of your project. We realize requirements activity does not exist in a vacuum, but moves in step with other activities of a project. The actual gathering and verifying of requirements has an influence on surrounding activities. For example, requirements activity changes current work by delivering a new product for that work. Additionally, the way people work affects requirements activity by guiding analysts as they gather their requirements (see Figure 1.6).

Figure 1.6

Your requirements process is a set of interconnected pieces all working in harness. As we progress through the book we will discuss these issues.

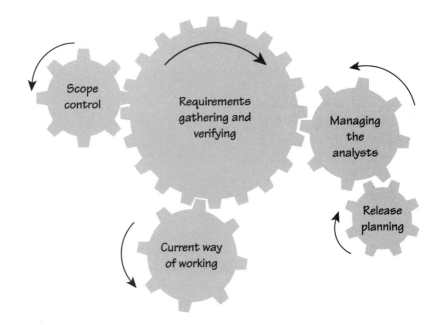

Naturally, the more effective the requirements activity, the more progress can be made on the project. Usually good requirements practices have a beneficial effect on the entire development process.

What Do I Do Right Now?

Start with the idea that requirements, identified correctly, are a major contributor to project success. Look through the PSIs and consider which of them are most applicable to your projects. Alternatively, consider which of them were lacking in your previous project.

Consider adopting requirements practices aligned with your contributing PSIs. Accordingly, consider how to monitor the effect of these practices—counting lack of repair, value of increased customer satisfaction, and so on.

As you work your way through this book and read about managing the various parts of a good requirements process, keep in mind you need to monitor and control the adoption of changes to the way that you run your projects. A need exists to be able to measure the effects of changes and the effects that these changes have on your delivered product.

We suggest you start with parts of the book that best match your identified project problems (PSIs with a negative measure). The only constraint is Chapter 11—Your Requirements Process may not make much sense without having read some of the other chapters first.

What's the Least I Can Get Away With?

Recognize that building the right product is the fastest and cheapest way to work. Then consider the main negative contributor to your project expense. By this we mean the cost of fixing the product after delivery, the cost of lost opportunity, the cost of cancelled projects, and so on.

Then consider the PSIs we outlined earlier in the chapter, and which of them most closely connect to the negative costs of your projects. Then consider adopting requirements practices that can remedy the identified PSIs. Keep in mind this is a quick fix, and you can get a longer-term benefit by adopting more of the requirements practices.

Requirements Value

Whenever we make an investment—some stocks, a new car—or do some work, we like to think we get something in return for the money or effort expended. In this chapter, we look at your investment in requirements and what you can expect in return. And though all men may be considered equal, all requirements are not. Some requirements are crucial to the product, while others are gold-plated luxuries. We discuss how business people and requirements analysts can determine how much to invest in requirements, by focusing on the value of requirements to their organization.

An Investment Story

Amelia's parents have decided move to Australia. A week before they leave, Amelia's parents call Amelia over and tell her the camera shop they have been running for the past 20 years is all hers. "It's not the greatest camera shop in the world," they tell her, "it has been losing a little bit of money for the last few years, but we kept it going for your sake. We are sure you can turn it around. Here are the keys and the lease for the shop. We're off now. Be sure to write."

Amelia looks at *her* shop. "A little run down," she thinks, "but the location is good. The main problem is Mom and Pop have not kept up with the times. Perhaps if I update things a little it will work out for me."

> "Improved software practices provide returns ranging from 300% to 1900% and average about 500% . . . The reason for these exceptionally high returns is . . . improved practices [that] have been available for decades, but most organizations aren't using. Risk of adopting these practices is low; payoff is high."
>
> —Steve McConnell, *Professional Software Development*

Figure 2.1

Amelia has to decide
whether or not to
invest in the camera
store. Her thinking is
not unlike deciding
whether to invest in
requirements.

Amelia is now faced with several investment choices (see Figure 2.1):

1. Take over the store and continue to run it exactly as is.
2. Take over the store and invest in it. This means updating the image, putting emphasis on digital photography, and buying equipment to give digital customers full service.
3. Make minor changes hoping the changes will attract enough customers to keep her head above water.
4. Walk away.

The first option gives Amelia no apparent risk in that she invests no money of her own, and thus will probably steadily lose money over time. So "business as usual" appears not to be a good strategy for her.

If she chooses option 2, she has to borrow heavily and invest in the store and particularly in digital photography. The track record of other stores doing this seems good, and the market for a good, modern camera store in this neighborhood is buoyant. Choosing this option, the next question for Amelia is how much to invest. She might plunge in heavily and turn the store into a complete digital imaging center, in which case the return on investment (ROI) will be longer term. Or invest just enough to make this a popular store for people looking for the latest piece of cool photographic technology. The lighter investment will see returns earlier, but the long-term gain will be less than if she makes the deeper investment.

Option 3 is bland. Amelia knows she will not make a lot of money from the store if she follows this route, but the investment amount is low and she feels good about being able to repay the loan.

Option 4 has a complete lack of risk. She invests nothing and gets nothing in return.

This is not a book about camera stores. It is about requirements and project success. However, Amelia's choices are concerned with investing in something to make it more valuable. Requirements are the same: You are investing in the requirements part of product development to end up with a more valuable product *and* get it less expensively. We aim to show you how investing in the requirements part of your project should be seen and treated the same as if you were investing in property, bonds, stock shares, or anything else that has the potential to give you a positive return on your investment.

Investing in Requirements

Let's return to the allegory of Amelia and her camera shop. She has several investment choices. The first is business as usual. The parallel for you is continuing to do whatever you are doing in the requirements field today. Nothing ventured, and nothing will be gained.

Her second choice is to invest in the store, bring it up to date, install modern equipment and sell modern cameras. This might cost her some money but is probably the best way for her to make money in the long run. For your project environment, the analogy is to invest time and effort in improving the way you discover and communicate requirements and reaping the reward of better products and cheaper delivery.

Amelia has two other options. She can tinker with the store. A minimal "Band-Aid" approach might be acceptable if she thinks the store is incapable of producing more value. However, it will probably not yield much. Nor can you expect a "Band-Aid" approach in project development work to yield substantial returns.

Her final choice is to walk away. For Amelia, walking away may be the right choice depending on the business climate for camera stores. In your case, however, given the increasing evidence of the positive effect of good requirements on project success, this is the equivalent of management's head in the sand.

In this chapter we give you some ways of justifying, determining, and managing your investment in requirements. You can, and should, look at your investment in requirements as you would look at any other investment.

You are investing time and effort in improving the way you discover and communicate requirements, and reaping the reward of better products and cheaper delivery.

- How much are you willing to invest?
- What is the ROI?
- What is the time for ROI?

- What are the risks?
- Should you invest at all?

The last question is perhaps the most pertinent for requirements. In our experience, several reasons exist for investing in requirements.

1. To build the right product.
2. To shorten the delivery time.
3. To find the right product for the long-term operational or sales success.
4. To take advantage of the products of requirements engineering to help guide the project by making more informed decisions.
5. To discover a better product.

Killer requirements turn out to be wonderful business assets and produce a huge return on their investment.

We address each of these reasons in this chapter, but first let's consider the least-cited reason for investing in requirements:

To discover a better product.

Investing in requirements means investing the time, effort, and skills to discover the requirements correctly. The careful gathering of requirements always results in an inspirational leap forward for the product. The collective effort of the interested stakeholders produces the "killer requirement," something considerably more than routine automation of an existing task.

These killer requirements turn out to be wonderful business assets and produce a huge return on their investment. For example, requirements that enabled customers at Amazon.com to write their own reviews gave customers a feeling of participation and belonging to the site; people kept coming back for more. Another great Amazon requirement was to make ordering as simple as possible. When requirements analysts had defined "as simple as possible," Amazon invented 1-Click and customers loved it.

66 On FedEx.com we're averaging more than 2.4 million tracks per day and each one of those transactions averages just under a nickel. We're saving about $25 million a month. 99

—Robert Carter,
CIO of Federal Express,
Fast Company, April 2003

Federal Express, UPS, DHL, and others invested in a requirement they discovered from their customers. Customers wanted to track their shipments online. The couriers spent millions to satisfy this requirement, and so far it is proving to be a very good investment. FedEx calculates each telephoned tracking request costs FedEx about $2.30. FedEx receives about 100,000 calls per day. The Internet alternative is far cheaper and has produced some stunning savings in ongoing operational costs.

As another example, FedEx has recently added InSight to its services, which enables customers to track inbound shipments without needing to know who is sending them. Nor do they need to know the tracking number. So far, InSight is proving popular with clients who wish to plan their production for incoming shipments of materials.

Building the Right Product

Building the right product means finding what is really needed, and not just what people say they want. It also means getting it right the first time, and not having to drag through the long repair activity that many projects suffer. Requirements gathering is about finding this right product and specifying it unambiguously to the developers.

Shorten Delivery Time

Shortening delivery time might seem at first glance to be a surprising reason to invest in requirements. However, our clients consistently find that by including a thorough requirements activity in their development cycles, they deliver the right product sooner. Requirements have value because they enable the builders to concentrate on developing the product instead of guessing about missing or ambiguous requirements, then having to retrace their steps and undo incorrect interpretations. When the builders do not receive the correct specification, programmers spend at least half the project budget in post-implementation correction. This is not only expensive but very frustrating to the client and business users waiting to deploy the finished product.

Requirements have value because they enable the builders to concentrate on developing the product instead of guessing about missing or ambiguous requirements, then having to retrace their steps and undo incorrect interpretations.

Linking Requirements to Managing

Requirements activity includes several deliverables we have found invaluable in the management of projects. For example, it includes building a context model. From the context model, we count function points to accurately measure the size of the work to be studied. We also advocate you use the context model to identify business use cases. Then use these as a collection unit for gathering requirements.

We know plenty of managers who use the status of business use cases as their way of measuring progress. The identification of stakeholders gives you a way of assessing the willingness of the people whose participation you need. This alone can serve as a reliable indicator of whether or not to proceed.

We will discuss this area more fully in Chapter 9—Managing the Requirements. For more on context models and business events see Chapter 4—Learning What People Need.

Return on Investment

The simple way to look at the ROI is the net gain from the requirement divided by the cost of discovering, verifying, building, and operating the requirement:

$$\% \; ROI = \{(benefits - costs) \, / \, costs\} * 100$$

Suppose you discovered and implemented a requirement for your Web site to recognize long-term customers and award them loyalty discounts. Then you find out orders from the Web site are up 5% because of these loyalty discounts. Let's say the cost of finding the requirement is $1,000, the cost of implementing it is $100,000, and the profit to the business because of the increased orders from that requirement is $250,000 in the first year. Assuming the correct requirements are implemented as specified, the ROI of the requirement (147% in the first year) is pretty good.

It would be very difficult, and time consuming, to establish the cost of a single requirement. As we progress, we will look at "units of requirements" (product use cases, business use cases, tasks, products) we can measure. Similarly, the benefit can be a saving as a result of installing the requirement or income generated by the requirement's existence.

Investment Risks

Any reasonable investment advisor, and most investment advertising, cautions you about risk. The following are some of the risks related to investing in requirements:

Our SAP project had built a budget for the development work being done this year for our SAP installation into Dublin, Ireland. We have only had to spend 53% of those dollars. Why? A more thorough job of requirements development was performed, resulting in the employment of less programming contractors.

—John H. Capron,
Worldwide Systems
Technology Manager, IBM
Enterprise Systems Group

- Not knowing the requirements
- Putting too much effort into requirements
- Being too formal with the requirements and the specification
- Being too casual
- Becoming bored with the requirements process

Risk, as we use the word here, is a potential problem. In project management terms, it means you have to be aware of risks, the likelihood of a potential problem becoming an actual problem, and the impact if it does. If the likelihood is slight, then the best course of action may be to proceed, monitor the risk, and act only if the problem manifests itself. On the other hand, if the risk is considerable and the consequences dire, then the obvious action is to implement preventive measures.

DeMarco and Lister[1] define risk as "a weighted pattern of possible outcomes and their associated consequences." The risks that you face in project work fall somewhere between "slight" and "considerable." Let's look at them and consider the appropriate response.

1. DeMarco, Tom and Tim Lister. *Waltzing with Bears: Managing Risk on Software Projects.* Dorset House, 2003—*Practical strategies on how to recognize and monitor risks. The writers focus on risks common to software projects but their techniques are applicable to any type of project.*

Risk of Not Knowing the Requirements

This risk must always be considered serious, as it is impossible to build the right product if requirements are unknown. Note the requirements need to be *known*. The builders can know them without having them in writing; undocumented requirements are acceptable in some circumstances. However, it is extremely unlikely the builders can know the requirements if they have not studied the work area into which the product is to be deployed.

From our experience, about 60% of software errors are requirements errors. Thus, not knowing the requirements is, by most people's definition, a considerable risk. As with any other risk, you can calculate the impact of poor or missing requirements. If the unknown-requirements risk becomes a problem you attribute the cost of rework, debugging, error correction, complaint handling, lost customers, and delays while the product is made right to lack of awareness of the requirements.

About 60% of software errors are requirements errors.

For strategic products, the impact can threaten the health of your organization. If the product is in any way medical, it can threaten the health of your customers. In any event, you need to assess the impact along with the likelihood of the risk manifesting itself as a problem.

Risk of Putting Too Much Effort into Requirements

This one might seem strange coming from people who make their living consulting on requirements projects. However, it has been our experience that some organizations specify requirements that have already been specified in some other form. The object of the requirements activity is to ensure the right product is built. However, it must only specify requirements that are not already known to the builder of the product.

This risk is usually greatest in organizations that have an inflexible development process. Analysts are forced to grind out the requirements specification and perform whatever else is ordained merely to satisfy the process itself. The risk manifests itself as a delay in building the product, as well as in the dissatisfaction of people involved in the project. Further, builders spend extra time wading through extraneous documentation generated by an inflexible development process.

A balance exists between not putting enough effort into the requirements activity, and putting in too much. You have to assess the skills and knowledge of the builders and determine if the requirements analysts are feeding them what they need or more than they need.

Risk of Being Too Formal with the Requirements and the Specification

You do not have to write down all requirements as atomic statements, provided you have some other way of communicating them and provided this other way of communicating serves as a record of the requirements. For example, if you have a set of process models supported by process specifications, a data dictionary, and a data model, then these models may be sufficient specification of the functional part of the product. If the models are rigorous, little is gained by writing out each functional requirement.

Alternatively, you may have fully specified a product use case. This specification includes the preconditions, the exit criterion, a description of the process, and the actors. Provided the use case is relatively simple, this specification alone may suffice as functional requirements.

Please bear in mind neither of the above alternatives specifies the equally important *non*functional requirements. These are the properties or qualities the product must have. The alternatives mentioned deal only with functional aspects of the product.

Factors that help to decide the necessary degree of requirements formality are:

- Degree of hierarchy and politics
- Fragmentation of knowledge
- Geographical distribution of stakeholders

If you have several levels of management and the requirements must be reviewed at all levels, you need consistent formality. If requirements knowledge about a particular subject is scattered among several people, you need formality; otherwise, you waste a lot of time dealing with inconsistent interpretations. When stakeholders are located in different offices, buildings, cities, or countries, then you need more formality to avoid misinterpretations and wasted time.

Risk of Boredom with the Requirements Process

This investment risk applies to projects in which you determine the requirements by communicating with business users. The business users are giving you their time in the expectation they will eventually get a suitable product. Business users generally feel the time they spend with analysts is time away from their own work. You need to give them something in return for their time, and give it quickly and often, so they do not become bored and discontent with the requirements process.

The boredom risk manifests itself in the behavior of business users participating in the requirements process. They believe they are contributing, but because they lack feedback or because the projected delivery of the product remains so far away, they enter into a robotic-like style of participation. Their answers sound good, but are often intended to get the analysts out of their office.

Practical ways of avoiding the boredom risk are to give feedback on the requirements the user has contributed and to implement early and frequent releases of the product or simulations of the product. Only when the business users (and for that matter the project team) can see the results of their requirements effort do they fully understand the benefits of spending time with the business analysts. By firmly and continuously establishing the requirements-to-product connection in the business persons' minds, you address their reluctance to participate in your project.

Only when the business users (and for that matter the project team) can see the results of their requirements effort do they fully understand the benefits of spending time with the business analysts.

What to Invest In?

There are always more possible investments than time or money available. We find some products make better investments depending on the time needed to realize a return. Figure 2.2 summarizes this idea.

A *strategic product* is one that adds value to your organization by providing a service or product not currently provided. Further, it provides some long-term market or operational advantage. For example, at the time of writing airlines are converting to e-tickets. This is a strategic product as it enables passengers to interact differently and may eventually significantly reduce the cost of check-in.

At the time of writing, Apple has become very successful with its on-line iTunes Music Store. The millions of songs sold through this site have added considerably to Apple's revenue stream. This product is strategic: Though it is not part of Apple's core (no pun intended) computer and software business, it is a logical add-on to its digital lifestyle approach.

Infrastructure products on the other hand are changes more than additions and are intended to make some internal process run more smoothly

Figure 2.2

This model helps to manage expectations of ROI. High investments in a strategic product usually result in a quicker ROI than the same amount invested in an infrastructure product. This does not necessarily mean it is better to invest in strategic products, only that expectations for return on investment are different and should be recognized as such.

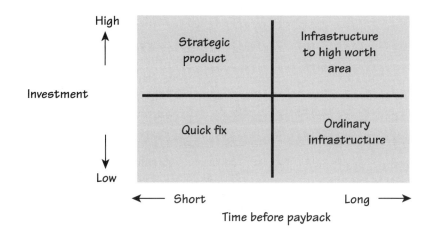

or at a reduced cost. For example, when you changed to using barcode scanners in the warehouse to perform inventory, that was an infrastructure change. When you abandon barcodes in favor of radio-frequency identifiers, that will be another infrastructure change. You do not sell infrastructure products (unless you are a vendor of ERM or CRM or similar kinds of software), and infrastructure products do not generate revenue.

Think of an infrastructure product as something you build (or buy) to use.

Returning to Figure 2.2, suppose you are a bank. Let's say a strategic product for you is a new type of bank account intended to attract a type of customer you do not have at present. Your investment is probably high but you expect to realize a high return in a short time.

Continuing with the banking analogy, suppose you make enhancements to your Internet banking so your customers can pay any bill using the Web site. This shows on the diagram as *infrastructure to a high worth area*. Your investment is high (to enable paying *any* bill is expensive), it is likely your return will be longer term because you are providing a better service and it may take people a while to realize it. After all, paying bills is not uppermost on most people's wish lists. (As an aside, if you could produce a product whereby people did not have to pay their bills at all, that would be a strategic product, and the payback would be quick and spectacular.)

You can have a low investment and get a fast payback from doing a *quick fix* like making corrections to something that is not currently working. You might also make an enhancement to the *ordinary infrastructure* that bank employees use to order stationery. The payback is longer term: While the bank infrastructure works better for the employees, it is not a high-worth area that adds value to your organizational purpose.

To Invest or Not to Invest

John Favaro is a software consultant who works in Italy. His brothers work in management consultancy in New York and Chicago. Despite the geographical separation, they have managed to combine the well-established principles of strategic investment management with investment in software products. They have used the Market Economics and Competitive Position framework to explore two factors to consider when making an investment decision: *worth* and *competitiveness*.[2]

2. Favaro, John and Kenneth. "Strategic Analysis of Application Framework Investments," *Building Application Frameworks: Object-Oriented Foundations of Framework Design*, edited by M. Fayad, R. Johnson. John Wiley & Sons, 1999—*Combines John's software knowledge with Kenneth's strategic investment knowledge and provides background on the principles of bringing together strategic investment principles with the investment in software.*

Worth

Worth is about identifying the value you place on your area of investment—the market in which you might invest. For example, before Amelia decides whether to do anything about her inherited camera shop, she must decide if it has any worth to her. That is, does she really want to run a camera shop? Does she intend to become a writer, say, and a camera shop has no worth for her? On the other hand, if she dearly wants to carry on her parents' work, or she sees the shop as a great way to make her living and feels the photographic market is lucrative, then she may place a high worth on it.

Next consider competitiveness. To attract customers, Amelia will have to give her shop features, or provide services that attract potential customers. If her shop sells a better range of cameras, or sells them more cheaply, or provides printing and uploading services unavailable in other shops, she increases her competitiveness.

We can ask the same two questions—worth and competitiveness—to assess investment in requirements.

Your product (regardless of whether it is a consumer product, a piece of software, or a service) will be deployed in a work area. Bear in mind a work area is either a part of your own organization or an external market for which you are developing products. The work area may be accounting, research and development (R&D), marketing, engineering, or almost anything else.

The question is, what is the worth to the organization of that work area? For example, the pharmaceutical companies place a high worth on R&D. If they do not come up with a breakthrough drug every few years, sales decline as generic products start to encroach on sales. If you are an investment broker, the trading part of the business has a high worth to you as the source of your revenue stream. If you are in the retail business, the supply chain—having the right goods available for sale at the right time—is a high-worth work area.

Look at your organization and possibly speak with your upper management to find what they find worthy. The answer by the way is not "profitability"—profitability is a goal, not a work area. But it is a useful answer. Now ask what parts of the organization contribute most to the profitability of the company. Also ask what work areas have the most value in meeting company goals. This question is all about investing in good work areas or markets: those where the money is.

> *Worth is about identifying the value you place on your area or investment. The question is about investing in good work areas or markets—those where the money is.*

Competitiveness

Next, competitiveness. Consider the differentiation and cost position of the product in question. Differentiation does not merely mean different.

Differentiation is to do with your customers' or your users' perception of your product.

(It's easy enough to have a different product—just paint it yellow.) Differentiation refers to the perceived improvement of the new product. In other words, do consumers believe the new product makes some tasks much faster, or makes the work cheaper or easier? Or does it enable external customers to look up their own accounts and save internal clerks from doing it? Does it provide some new quality customers value? Or can it provide some advantage—streamline operations, reduce costs, comply with the law, etc.—that has value to the project sponsor?

For software for sale, differentiation means the improvement or benefit offered by your product over your competitors'. Think about the advantage to the consumers if they buy your product instead of someone else's.

Differentiation is all to do with consumers' perception of your product. If the consumer is willing to pay more (or alternatively the price stays the same but more people are willing to buy it), you have achieved differentiation.

The other aspect of competitiveness is economic cost position. Can you produce the same product with a better cost advantage? For instance, Amelia can go through an analysis to see how to run her shop to obtain an advantaged cost position. Maybe if she outsources the photo lab instead of having her own in-house printing, she can offer prints at lower cost than the competition.

We strongly suggest some combination of project sponsor, intended buyer, and operational user evaluate competitiveness. Unless you are a very unusual project manager, you tend to overestimate the differentiation and underestimate the cost of your product. After all, it's your project and you want it to be seen as valuable. You need a more objective assessment of competitiveness than you can normally provide by yourself.

Figure 2.3 looks at the desirability of investing. Note that if your organization is building products or services for sale, then the "worth of work

Figure 2.3

The vertical axis shows the worth of the work area relevant to the delivered product. The horizontal axis is the degree of competitiveness, improvement over the existing or competing product, the proposed product delivers. This graph is adapted from work by John and Ken Favaro.

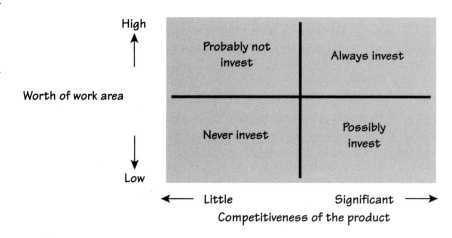

area" scale should be replaced by "Attractiveness of the market." Is it a high-yield market with good margins and high demand—video games, software, DVDs? Or is the market soft and unattractive with low margins and unprofitable sales?

The obvious project that warrants investment is building a product likely to be deployed in a work area that has a high worth to the organization, and the proposed product is more competitive (produces increased profits) than its predecessor or competition.

When the product is to be used in a work area of high worth but the product has low competitiveness, investment is not advisable. From the point of view of investing in a product for your own organization, people working in the high-worth area are probably bright (look at your own organization to see where the best and brightest work) and you will not gain by giving them a product that provides little competitive advantage.

From the point of view of an external market, a company in a bad competitive position is likely to be unprofitable even in a market where the average participant is profitable. For example, suppose that Amelia assesses that the Internet photo printing market is highly attractive. However, she is horribly disadvantaged competitively because she only has a 56Kb dialup telephone line and an old desktop printer for printing photos. Even in this profitable market, her competitive position makes it inadvisable for her to invest.

The product that offers significant competitiveness in the low-worth work area is a better investment, as it may make some noticeable difference to that area—perhaps enough for the area to become more valuable to the organization.

You can consider this from the point of view of an external market. Suppose Amelia wants to invest in running photography classes. Her analysis shows the average camera store does not make money in this market. However, she has a huge competitive advantage because her uncle, who is a famous photographer, is the teacher. So everybody comes to her store's class and she's the only profitable participant in an otherwise unprofitable market.

Regardless of whether you are analyzing an investment in an internal work area or an external market, competitive position generally carries more weight than worth of the work area.

Regardless of whether you are investing in an internal work area or an external market, competitive position usually carries more weight than worth of your work areas.

Investing in Requirements

Having determined it is advisable to invest in a product, you must now make the same decision about whether you will invest in gathering requirements for that product. Given that requirements accelerate the delivery of the product, the answer is generally yes, but there are degrees of

Figure 2.4

If you invest zero effort in requirements, your chance of success is also zero. Probability of success rises as you invest more and more in requirements. The maximum amount you can invest is close to half of your project budget.

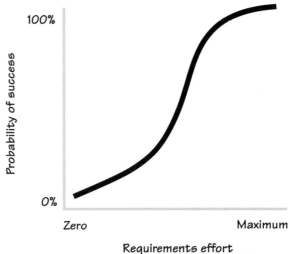

No successful projects result from activity in which no effort was devoted to requirements. . . .

requirements gathering. The effort you put into your requirements activity, and the formality of the requirements specification, should be varied to suit the project.

Figure 2.4 looks at the probability of success for your project measured against the effort put into requirements. No successful projects result from activity in which no effort was devoted to requirements, so we start at zero effort/zero chance of success. After that the probability of success rises as the requirements effort increases. However, at some point extra effort brings less incremental improvement in the success probability. The inference of this is that the requirements effort to be expended in the project is not automatically the maximum, but should be selected by considering the project's variables.

For large projects, the decision is always to invest in requirements and to budget for an extensive requirements activity. The magnitude of the requirements effort usually depresses project managers, but the ROI is huge. Without a proper requirements activity, likelihood of failure is high, and cost of failure is also very high. Large projects always make the headlines by cancelling when it becomes obvious to all concerned the project cannot deliver. And almost always, at the time of cancellation, too much code exists and too few requirements.

Conversely, if your product is very small, a better chance exists for developers to successfully guess some of the requirements. The cost of failure here is not too large, as requirements errors can be corrected relatively cheaply.

Similarly, for an infrastructure product, the requirements are better known to the analysts and the developers, and subsequently a less formal requirements effort is needed. The ROI for requirements for an infra-structure product is less than on strategic products, but still significant.

The worth of the work area also comes into consideration. For high-worth work areas, the cost of failure is high, usually because of lost op-portunities to that work area. The cost of lost opportunities alone makes it worthwhile investing in requirements.

For strategic products, always invest in the requirements. The risks of a strategic product are far higher; in some cases organizations are betting their future on the success of the project. The cost of failure is thus ex-tremely high, and the likelihood of failure without good requirements is also very high.

For strategic products, always invest in the requirements.

We always advise our clients, before deciding to invest, to take into consideration the value of the resources that the project will use. If the project uses valuable resources (assuming all resources are not equal) then failure is expensive as these resources can be used elsewhere.

The final consideration whether to invest in requirements is the in-evitable question of how close is the deadline? Apart from trivial prod-ucts, delivery is always fastest when developers have an intimate knowledge of the requirements. Always.

Size of Requirements

In Figure 2.2 we use "Investment" as an axis of the diagram. This refers to the amount of the investment that you are about to make. The invest-ment amount can be an amount of money or an amount of effort. Alter-natively, you can also think of the size of the business area you are about to study.

When you think of an investment amount, an obvious correlation oc-curs between effort and money. But also a relationship exists between the size and complexity of the work area (or product) and the effort needed to determine the requirements. In Chapter 8—Measuring Requirements we talk about measuring the size or functionality of the work area.

The amount of investment follows the size of the task. But it can be re-duced by factors such as:

- The experience of the analytical team
- Availability of the stakeholders
- Experience of the stakeholders
- Extent of the documentation of current work
- Existence of reusable requirements
- Skill and involvement of the testing team
- A template that has been customized for the organization
- Other factors unique to your organization

The point we wish to stress is you must know the size of your investment before proceeding. When we talk about the value of requirements we are really talking about ROI. Naturally, it is crucial you know with a fair degree of accuracy how much you have to spend before calculating any return.

The Value of Requirements

We have discussed the idea of investing in requirements, and thereby the project. As a requirement is a demand for something to be built, we also discuss the idea of whether it is worthwhile investing in building a solution to a requirement. In *Mastering the Requirements Process,* the authors referred to collecting the requirements as "trawling."

Trawling is a peculiarly British word that refers to deep-sea commercial fishing. The boats, or trawlers as they are known, use large nets, sometimes incredibly large, to drag through the oceans for their catch. The idea of running a net through the ocean for fish is analogous to dragging a metaphorical net through the organization to gather up requirements (see Figure 2.5). By using a net, a fisherman catches species of fish other than what he wants. Similarly, the diligent requirements analyst dredges up not only trivial or low-value requirements but also more requirements than can be built in the time allowed.

Not all requirements are of equal value to the organization. This makes it worthwhile to consider the value of each requirement before deciding whether or not to build it. We refer to this as *customer value,* with the inference that you ask your customer, "How important is this requirement to you?" Keep in mind if you ask a customer to grade a requirement as high, medium, or low, the customer will tend to grade almost all the requirements as high importance. Such is human nature—if I tell you

Figure 2.5

Trawling for fish has similarities to trawling for requirements.

that everything is of high importance then I believe I will get more of my requirements implemented regardless of their importance.

Another thing that fights against grading a requirement as high, medium, or low is the expectation embedded in the term "requirement." If I call something a requirement the implication is I definitely need you to give it to me. Within systems engineering we have a different meaning for the term—in fact, it would be more accurate to talk about *wishes*.

A requirement is something somebody wishes to have implemented but no guarantee exists it can be implemented until we know all the requirements and can determine which ones can be implemented within the constraints. Given this reality, it makes sense to make requirers aware they will need to make choices and to provide them with a mechanism for considering choices early.

> *A requirement is something that somebody wishes to have implemented but no guarantee exists it can be implemented until we know all the requirements and can determine which ones can be implemented within the constraints.*

We have adapted William Pardee's idea of *customer satisfaction* and *customer dissatisfaction*[3] as a way of helping people to consider the relative importance of their requirements.

Pardee suggests you ask two questions about any requirement:

1. "On a scale from 1 to 5 how satisfied will you be if I implement this requirement?"—where 1 means you don't particularly care whether the requirement is implemented and 5 means you will be extremely pleased if it is. (The scale of satisfaction.)
2. "On a scale from 1 to 5 how dissatisfied will you be if I do not implement this requirement?"—where 1 means you are unconcerned if the requirement is not part of the product and 5 means you will be extremely unhappy. (The scale of *dis*satisfaction.)

The idea behind Pardee's thinking is that if your customer has a large-enough continuous scale, he can give you a more accurate indication of importance. The notion of having two scales is even more helpful. For example, the customer considers some requirements to be natural or part of the existing system, and thus the customer sees no reason why they would not be contained in any future product.

In the situation of "natural requirements" the satisfaction rating is likely to be low: The customer is not going to get excited if you deliver something already there. However, if you do *not* deliver the requirement, dissatisfaction is likely to be high. Conversely, if a customer considers a requirement to be a trivial piece of gold plating, it will garner a low dissatisfaction rating.

RESOURCE NOTE
At www.volere.co.uk you can download the Volere Atomic Requirement Template, which shows requirements attributes including customer satisfaction and customer dissatisfaction.

---

3. Pardee, William. *To Satisfy and Delight Your Customer.* Dorset House, 1996—*Contains many good ideas in the area of managing customer expectations. The notion of customer satisfaction and customer dissatisfaction is a useful tool for prioritizing requirements.*

We have found Pardee's way of measuring satisfaction and dissatisfaction superior to the commonly used scale of "must have, nice to have, fit it in if you get time."

A simple way of determining the future of a requirement is to add the satisfaction and dissatisfaction scales. Any requirement that has an aggregate score of four or less should not be implemented. Then, starting with the highest aggregate scores, implement as many requirements as you can in the allowed time. However, to make your implementation decision, weigh the customer value against the cost of implementing the requirement. In other words, just because a requirement has high customer value does not necessarily mean it will be possible to implement it. In Chapter 9—Managing the Requirements, we discuss the subject of progressive prioritization and prioritization techniques.

Reusing Requirements

Think of the requirements you gather as business assets.

You are considering investing in requirements with the objective of a payback on investment. A final consideration is whether the requirements have a value after they have been used on your current project. To put that another way, can you think of the requirements you gather as business assets? They deliver a further payback on your investment when you recycle them on subsequent projects.

You are probably not reusing only one or two requirements—no justification exists for doing so. However, if we look at the idea of clusters of requirements, then reuse becomes much more viable. Earlier in this chapter we mentioned the idea of clusters, or units of requirements (work context, product context, business use cases, product use cases, functional requirements, nonfunctional requirements, constraints) as an investment vehicle. Figure 2.6 identifies these units of potentially reusable requirements and the associations or relationships among them.

Requirements reuse depends first on the ability to identify reusable requirements, and second on having requirements reuse as part of your requirements process. Our experience shows many projects have significantly overlapping requirements. By abstracting and looking at the functionality, and for the moment ignoring its subject matter, we have been able to identify whole clusters of requirements in which simple subject-name changes have yielded significant portions of a functionally correct specification.

Our experience is that many projects have significantly overlapping requirements.

We have also learned many projects can save considerable time by intentionally looking at existing requirements documents. The analyst trawls through existing specifications looking for requirements that can be reused. It helps to ignore the names of the objects being manipulated, and concentrate instead on the abstract functionality.

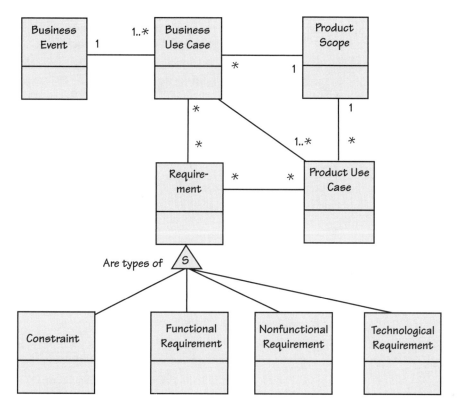

Figure 2.6

This class model shows units of requirements that are potentially reusable. The * indicates that many instances exist of the entity at that end of the association. For example, a *Product Scope* may have many *Product Use Cases,* but the latter belong to a single *Product Scope.* The triangle shows that *Functional Requirement, Nonfunctional Requirement,* and *Constraint* are all types of requirements.

Identifying Reusable Requirements

Even if you have not been consciously producing reusable requirements, you are sure to have many potentially reusable requirements already existing in your organization. The chart shown in Figure 2.7 suggests some of the places you might find them. Use it as a checklist to help take advantage of reuse opportunities.

For example, the checklist identifies a dozen potential sources of reusable functional requirements and six potential sources of constraints. There will be others within the documents and models produced by your organization. The chart can help you get started. Your organization should update the list when discoveries take place, for the benefit of future requirements projects. The more consistent your requirements deliverables, the more likely you can reuse them as requirements on another project.

Your Process for Reusing Requirements

The best advice we can give you is to start each of your projects with a stock-take and use potentially reusable components as a starting point.

Figure 2.7 This chart summarizes potentially reusable requirements components along with suggestions for where to find them. Its intended use is as a checklist of reuse opportunities. The more progress you make toward formalizing reuse, the more consistent items in the *Where to Look* column will become. You should update the chart with places from your own environment.

Where to Look	Reusable Requirements Components							
	Work Context	Business Event Response	Product Context	Product Use Case	Functional Requirement	Nonfunctional Requirement	Constraint	Design Requirement
Project Goal Descriptions					×	×	×	
Work Context Model	×	×			×			
Business Task Descriptions	×	×			×	×	×	
Business Process Models	×	×			×			
Business Scenarios	×	×			×	×		
Business Data Models	×				×			
Requirements Process Patterns	×	×			×			
Requirements Data Patterns	×	×			×			
Product Context Models			×					
Product Use Case Models			×	×				
Product Scenarios			×	×	×	×		
Product Sequence Diagrams			×	×	×	×	×	×
Product Class/Data Models					×			×
Atomic Requirements Definitions					×	×	×	×
Technical Architecture Models							×	×
Design Patterns							×	×

This does not have to turn into a bureaucratic process. It simply means spending some time (maybe a few hours) looking around before starting detailed work. We suggest drawing a quick work context diagram of your project. Then within this scope look for potentially reusable requirements components using the chart in Figure 2.7 as a guide. The questions to ask are:

- Does the component contain any of the same data bounded by the interfaces on my project's work context diagram?
- Does the component refer to any of the adjacent systems mentioned on my project's context diagram?
- Does the component contain any business rules that contribute to my project's goals?

For each of the potentially reusable components you identify, consider whether it will save you time by giving it the *essence test* (see Figure 2.8). This test asks what percentage of the component exists because of essential business rules versus what percentage exists because of a particular solution to meeting the business rules.

For example, one of us, Suzanne, undertook a project with an insurance company. The project team wanted to reuse the business data model. However when we applied the essence test we discovered that it was a business data model in name only. It had been partitioned according to a particular database implementation technology and contained many attributes such as keys and pointers that existed because of the implementation.

Because of that unique implementation, the model was very difficult to reuse: Business requirements data (claims, premiums, policies, bonuses, rates) were extremely fragmented and confused as a consequence of the number of implementation attributes. It was quicker to start from scratch—this annoyed the business experts because we had to ask them questions the other project group had already asked. If the

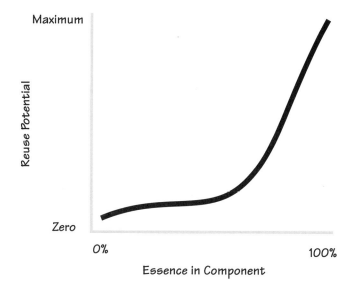

Figure 2.8

The essence test evaluates the percentage of the content of a component related to the essential business within the domain. The higher percentage of essence, the more likely the component is reusable.

business data model had truly been a specification of business requirements rather than a specific implementation, we could have reused the business knowledge it contained.

Components containing less than 60% of essence are probably going to be too implementation-specific for reuse. You would spend too much time removing the implementation details and reorganizing them so you could figure out their meaning in terms of the business requirements. For more on how to discover the essence of a system, please read *Essential Systems Analysis* by Steve McMenamin and John Palmer.[4] Also, please refer to Chapter 4—Learning What People Need, which contains more on essence.

The approach of considering requirements reuse at the start of a project leads you toward treating requirements as continuing business assets rather than things that only apply to one project.

What Do I Do Right Now?

A number of the project success indicators (see Chapter 1) are affected by requirements value:

- No excessive schedule pressure
- Correctly sized product
- Product adds value to the organization

Determine the value your project adds to your organization and the value requirements add to your project. According to studies carried out by the Standish Group, about three-quarters of software projects deliver late or not at all. The main three reasons are lack of user input, incomplete requirements, and constantly changing requirements. These handicaps are eliminated, or significantly reduced, by a competent requirements process.

So long as your project is not trivial, you are going to invest in requirements. However, the adroit project manager takes into account the uniqueness of the project and the degree of fragmentation of information and people, then determines how much effort needs to be expended on requirements.

Estimate the effort needed by measuring the work area to be studied. We suggest function points as an effective way of doing this. From the

---

4. McMenamin, Steve and John Palmer. *Essential Systems Analysis*. Yourdon Press, 1984— *This classic work explains the difference between the implementation and the real problem (referred to as the essence). Full of examples on how to arrive at the essential view of a system and thereby understand the real requirements.*

size of the work area—or product if that is what you measured—determine the amount of requirements analysis needed. Capers Jones of Software Productivity Research puts the U.S. average cost of installing a function point at $1,000. Requirements activities should consume between 30 and 50% of that cost. We discuss function point counting in Chapter 8.

Adjust this number by the nature of the project—infrastructure, strategic, large, small, and so on—to determine whether your requirements activity is going all out to produce an absolutely complete requirements description of the product, or whether the risks involved in doing less than the maximum can be tolerated.

What's the Least I Can Get Away With?

A little bit of honesty. After you have read this chapter, ask yourself:

- Does the product I am about to build add value to the organization?
- How do I know it will add value?
- Does my project contribute to the overall goals of the organization?
- Is the project worth investing in? Does it create a product that has significant competitiveness for a high-worth work area?
- Do I know what it costs to discover the requirements?
- How do I know the costs? (If you are guessing, then you are doing less than the "least you can get away with.")
- What is my break-even point—when the cost of reworking the product is less than the cost of investing more in the requirements?
- What return do we expect on the investment, and when?
- Have I honestly considered the risks associated with this project?
- Are there any risks that require some preventive actions?
- Do we already have some requirements that are reusable by this project?

These questions may seem obvious, but to start a project without having satisfactory answers for all of them is flirting with alligators.

Additional References for Requirements Value

The following sources, in addition to those already referenced, have useful information on requirements value.

- Favaro, John. "Managing Requirements for Business Value." *IEEE Software*, March 2002—*Discussion of the value of reusing requirements and the advisability of involving business strategists in the process.*

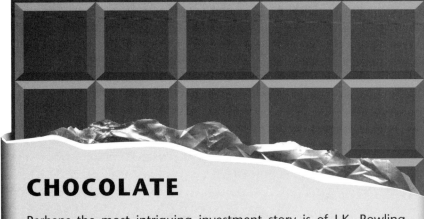

CHOCOLATE

Perhaps the most intriguing investment story is of J.K. Rowling, renowned author of the Harry Potter stories. Her investment was the time, and not-especially encouraging time, she spent writing the first of her Harry Potter books. Unemployed at the time, she was living in a mouse-infested flat in Edinburgh when she started writing. It is a tribute to her belief that her investment in writing was not going to be wasted, as reports suggest that 14 publishers rejected the manuscript before Bloomsbury Publishing paid her the equivalent of about $4,000 to publish *Harry Potter and the Philosopher's Stone* in June of 1997.

Today the five Harry Potter books have sold 250 million copies, and on the day we write this, J.K. makes her debut on Forbes magazine's billionaire list.

A good investment of effort.

- McConnell, Steve. *Professional Software Development.* Addison-Wesley, 2004—*McConnell's words on return on investment are alone worth the price of this excellent book.*
- Thomsett, Robb. *Radical Project Management.* Dorset House, 2002— *Packed with tools and hints for making project management decisions in a changing environment.*

Project Sociology

In several decades of project experience, we have never seen a project fail for technological reasons. It has always been human failures that have caused otherwise good projects to grind to a halt. Project sociology is about getting the right people into the mix, ensuring their skills and knowledge are appropriate to their roles, and keeping them involved throughout the life of the project.

What Is Project Sociology?

A project team becomes dysfunctional if it is composed of the wrong people, or the wrong mix of skills, or indeed missing skills. A project's sociology is the society (the stakeholders) of the project. To understand project sociology we need to understand the human beings involved in the project, why they need to be involved, and what level of commitment is necessary.

We can best explain project sociology by looking at other human societies or collections of human beings connected by a common interest. A ready-made example is the family (see Figure 3.1). Individuals in a family are different—each has his or her own preferences and attitudes—and yet the family, as a unit, works. Granted tensions and differences exist, sometimes arguments, but the underlying basis of the family means that unless there are genuinely extraordinary circumstances—Mother runs off with the repair man, Father leaves to join the Foreign Legion—the family functions as a team.

A family is a collection of individuals, and as family therapist Lynn Hoffman points out, something gives them a shared objective, some *good* or *product* they all want. The pursuit of this good makes families relevant,

66*Man was formed for society.*99

—Sir William Blackstone,
*Commentaries on the
Laws of England*

Figure 3.1

A family is a collection of individuals with an "orderly access to intimacy," and a shared objective.

and by the way, it makes project teams relevant. Many of the things you get by belonging to a family, such as economic advice, child rearing support, guidance in learning, and so on, can be satisfied by other institutions in society. However, Hoffman points out one thing that is special to the concept of a family: *an orderly access to intimacy.*

Kai Erikson expressed the same idea in a different way. He said the family provides a *social envelope* comprising things like familiar objects, people, customs, jokes, furniture, time events, places, obligations, houses, and so forth (see Figure 3.2). This social envelope provides the ingredients for the intimate binding within a group of people.

Think of the peculiar customs of your own family. Your family likely has a vocabulary of its own that is all but impenetrable to outsiders: The family dog is *barkative*, Dad is *maungy* because his team lost, and one family we know eats *gay bread*. If your family does not have a special language, then it has jokes, customs, manners, and observances that make your family unique, and to bring you together in the sharing of this intimacy. However, the social envelope is not just a superficial aspect of family life. Erikson points out it is "as important for individual survival as amniotic fluid is to an unborn child."

> 66 *The social envelope is as important for individual survival as amniotic fluid is to an unborn child.* 99
>
> —Kai Erikson

Through the years, we have been members of many project teams and have observed many more. A characteristic of all successful teams is the sharing of jokes, customs, sayings, space, food, and many of the things that are common to a closely knit family. Erikson's social envelope seems to be the ideal foundation for examining how people relate to each other when brought together to work on a project.

One characteristic of all successful teams is the sharing of things that are common to a close-knit family.

In our project work we have often observed the social envelope's contribution to overcoming individual differences and getting members of a project group to work together. We would not go so far as to say you should treat your project team just like a family, but some aspects of the

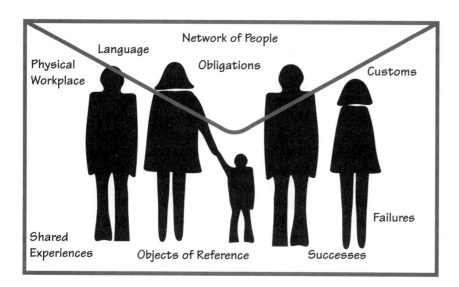

Figure 3.2

The social envelope contains the special customs, places, objects, events, obligations, and so on that provide access to intimacy between a group of people.

family social envelope make for better project teams as well. Let's introduce aspects of the social envelope as a way of establishing some common good and sense of belonging to a unit.

Doing so can be very simple. On one of our projects we found we had inherited a fairly disparate and dispirited group. The team was housed in a larger open-plan area surrounded by other unrelated teams. There was very little team spirit or sense of belonging to a unit. In our first few days we noticed people used an inordinate number of clichés when they spoke, and we decided to introduce fines (see Figure 3.3).

It cost a penny for any team member uttering one of the listed clichés—we taped up a large chart with the offending words—and one member quickly volunteered to be the bearer of the collection box. During meetings or normal office conversations, people became very adept at pointing out other people's offenses, and rattling the collection box under their noses. It became a point of honor to pay up promptly for any cliché transgression.

It was a joke, but a joke shared only within our team. The most pleasing part came when a member of another team asked if he could borrow the collection box as he had another team using clichés. He was told "Sorry, it's only for our team." This simple, maybe even silly, custom had contributed to our social envelope. From that point we encouraged other customs that reinforced the team's sense of belonging to a unit. The collection box, enhanced by an intrateam sweepstakes, was later used to take the team to dinner at Christmas, thus further reinforcing the social envelope by dining together.

> ❝Intimacy in organizations starts with a commitment to get to know people behind the mask of their job title, role, or function. Members of an intimate team know each others' preferences and predilections.❞
>
> —Peter Senge, *The Fifth Discipline Handbook*

Figure 3.3

Team members were fined for using clichés. They quickly learned to enjoy the joke and the intimacy of the practice.

Basically, it's a multi-phase expanded collaborative customer-centric solution, like in an enterprise eBusiness situation....

1¢

Who Are the Stakeholders?

Let's consider the people you need to meld into a working team for your requirements project: your stakeholders. A stakeholder is anyone who has an interest in the project. This interest is not limited to people who build the product or the people who use the product, nor does it require a financial stake in the product. Stakeholders are all the people who are affected by or have some effect on the product. In other words, anyone who directly or indirectly influences requirements for the product.

Stakeholders might be people whose advice and opinions affect the success of the product, people who set standards to which the product must adhere, people whose work has an interface to the product, people whose technical knowledge is needed to make decisions, people who can influence how others view the product, and many more.

A stakeholder is anyone who directly or indirectly influences requirements for the product.

As stakeholders are people who provide the requirements for your product, it is crucial they all make their best contribution. We suggest that you think about the social envelope as it applies to your stakeholders, because the benefits of having them all feel they belong to something special cannot be attained without embracing it. You cannot pay people to think this way, just as you cannot force them. They have to believe in it for themselves.

When we are on consulting assignments, we make a point of talking to as many stakeholders as possible. We try and find if they are all signed on to a common goal, and if they all have the same objective. It is surprising how often we discover, either through willful actions or just plain misunderstanding, stakeholders heading in different directions. Our intention is not to point fingers at those who choose to march to the beat of a different drummer, but to ensure as much as possible all stakeholders have the same understanding of what they are trying to achieve. Only when they know the objectives can they decide if they want to be part of the team.

Also, while considering your stakeholders, how much turnover do you see? Low turnover is a solid indication your team members feel they belong in the same social envelope. The social envelope also means that your team believes it is unique, and is better in some way than other teams in the organization. More important, stakeholders share a belief the product is important and they are determined to make their best contribution to its success.

Knowledge, Role, Person

Some stakeholders are easier to discover than others, and sometimes they are just plain obvious. Others take some effort to find. We have found that the trinity of Knowledge/Role/Person helps us to find some of the more elusive ones.

The questions asked in Figure 3.4 illustrate the three questions—knowledge, role, person—that help identify stakeholders. *Knowledge* refers to the category of knowledge needed for the product's requirements,

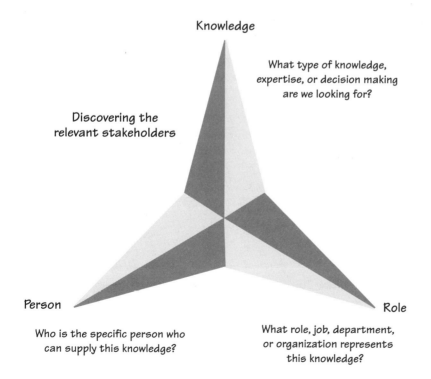

Figure 3.4

The trinity of questions about type of knowledge, functional role, and person's name helps to find relevant stakeholders and also to discover where a shortfall of stakeholders exists.

which is indicated by product subject matter and requirements types in your specification template. We use the term *role* here as we find job titles can be misleading and often cover more than one role. For role we are looking for the organizational responsibility for the needed knowledge. *Person* is simply the name of the individual or individuals who can supply the knowledge or requirements.

For example, let's start with the knowledge question. Suppose your project is to build a financial system to be used by clients on the Web. Naturally, there are security requirements. Then ask "Do I know the person who has security knowledge?" If so, include that person as a stakeholder. Otherwise ask, "What organizational role is responsible for security?" Having located the role—say your organization uses an outside firm of security consultants—then ask for the person, or people, who the security consultants intend to assign to your project as source(s) of security requirements.

We have found this approach useful when the organizational structure is either difficult or unknown. Similarly, we use it when we know job titles, but do not know who the people are or what they know. Conversely, we have used the triangle to eliminate stakeholders who are not relevant to the project, as well as discovering where knowledge or commitment gaps exist.

Keep in mind when you do identify stakeholders, you must get their agreement they are prepared to be stakeholders, and you must include them in your extended social envelope.

Stakeholder Types

Figure 3.5 summarizes the different types of stakeholders, each of which makes different contributions to the project. Let's look at some of these.

Core Team

The core team, probably what you refer to as your project team, produces the product. They can have titles like project manager, program manager, developer, business analyst, key business people, marketing specialist, product manager, release manager, R&D specialist, designer, tester, or programmer. Some members of the core team have business/subject matter/domain knowledge and some of them have technical skills. Team composition varies from organization to organization, and within the organization, depending on the nature of the product to be built.

The core team discovers and writes the requirements.

The core team is charged with discovering and writing the requirements. The team ultimately decides the requirements and ensures the product conforms to those requirements. This is a full-time task. Others

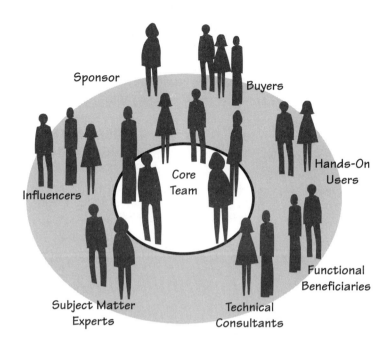

Figure 3.5

Different stakeholders make different contributions to the project. The core team works on the project on a day-to-day basis. The peripheral stakeholders have requirements for the product, but their participation is on an "as needed" basis.

contribute requirements, but are not considered part of your core team. Let's look at some of them.

Sponsor or Client

The sponsor, or executive sponsor, has organizational responsibility for the project. The sponsor may be paying for the development because it comes from the sponsor's budget, or the sponsor may be the person who makes the final decision on whether the product is acceptable. The sponsor can also be the one who decides on project resources.

The sponsor has organizational responsibility for that project, and is usually paying for it.

The role of sponsor is often referred to as the *client* role, particularly when the individual is responsible for the financial investment necessary to do the project. You can also refer to this role as product manager or program manager, depending on your organization. Keep in mind that this is a *role,* not a job title.

The above description of sponsor or client may seem wide, but our experience shows sponsors have differing responsibilities in different organizations. The important point is that without a sponsor your project will be shortlived. Without someone to sign the checks or to say "I am organizationally responsible," your project has little chance of succeeding. A responsible individual is especially important in government or large-company projects in which organizational responsibility is sometimes very hard to determine.

The sponsor also helps the project with problems outside the power of the project manager. On one of our projects in England we found members of the team were scattered throughout several buildings. We commented on the adverse effect this was having on the members' ability to communicate with one another. We were able to prevail on the sponsor who talked to other managers, and who was then able to find a vacant Nissen hut[1] on the organization's grounds. He did the necessary politicking to have it allocated to the team. Though it was fairly basic accommodation, it did the trick. The team was together, team members could talk to one another, and they could get their work done. Such a positive result would not have occurred without the sponsor's organizational influence.

The sponsor usually has to take the view of the entire organization and embrace other projects, whilst your project team is naturally looking at situations from the perspective of their particular project. The goals of all projects have to mesh, as do the context models of all projects. (See Chapter 4—Learning What People Need, which describes how the context model determines project boundaries.) Similarly, the sponsor is someone who makes it possible for the project to flourish in the organization and who ensures it remains relevant when changes occur in the organization.

Buyers

Buyers buy the product and use it for their work. Your task is to identify the buyers and the requirements they consider important.

Buyers buy your product and/or use it to do work. Buyers (also known as customers or consumers) play an important role project managers need to identify and understand. Buyers ultimately decide whether to pay for your efforts—they can be individuals who decide to buy a new piece of software or a new hi-fi system. They can be people in an organization who decide to commit part of their department's budget to buying a new piece of communications software or a new personal organizer for their staff.

Money does not necessarily change hands; instead, a buyer can be someone who influences whether a product is adopted by an organization, as shown in Figure 3.6. For example, suppose you are building a product to help children learn mathematics. The children's teachers are not making the decision whether to spend money on the product—the school boards have already decided that. The teachers are buyers in the sense they decide whether to instruct pupils to adopt the product as part of their lessons. If the teachers "buy into" the product it is likely to be more successful in its subject-matter market.

---

1. "Nissen hut" may not be a term known to many U.S. readers. It's a WW2 army building a little like a corrugated water tank, cut in half vertically and laid on its side.

Figure 3.6

The buyer is who you have to persuade to pay for your product. Have you understood the buyers' needs, prejudices, opinions, and work well enough for them to part with their money?

Part of understanding your project's sociology is to identify the buyers: people who can be influenced to pay for the product or people who will introduce your product into their workplace or home. Your task is to identify these people and to discover the requirements buyers consider important.

Hands-On Users

Another important consumer role is played by people who have direct contact with your product to achieve some specific task. These people are normally referred to as *users* of the product. For example, a user is the person making a withdrawal at an automated teller machine (ATM), or an air traffic controller looking at a radar screen, a nurse monitoring heartbeats on a screen, a patient to whom your device is attached, a bank clerk sitting at a computer to make an interbank transfer, a software designer using a tool that records and evaluates a design. Hands-on users rarely have a wide view of the product. Instead, they have requirements that relate to how the product specifically affects them.

In order to discover user requirements you need to have some understanding of the users themselves. You are interested in things such as:

- Subject-matter experience.
- Technological experience, good and bad.
- Intellectual abilities—Would you build a different product to be used by Ph.D. engineers as you would for untrained members of the public?
- Awareness of the project purpose.
- Attitude toward the job.
- Attitude toward technology.
- Education.
- Linguistic skills—You cannot assume all people read and express themselves as well, or in the same way, as you do.

- Age—Older people have different life experiences from young people and may not adapt as quickly to completely new concepts.
- Gender—Men and women may have different perceptions.
- People with disabilities—blind, deaf, nonreaders.
- People who do not speak the home language.
- First-time or experienced users.
- People who might be angry, frustrated, or in a hurry.

It is apparent the better your knowledge of your hands-on-users, the better equipped you are to build a product that fits into their way of working and their perceptions of their work.

Subject-Matter Experts

Subject-matter experts (SMEs) are people or organizations whose knowledge is necessary or beneficial in order to discover the requirements. These are not necessarily people with knowledge of your particular product, rather having knowledge of your subject matter. SMEs are often found outside your organization. They are often consultants who come and add their knowledge of logistics, banking, ticketing, process control or whatever you need.

For example, we have used airline consultants, banking experts, finance professionals, and frequently lawyers as subject-matter experts. We remember fondly a project for the Polish State Railways in which they used the services of SMEs from both British Rail and the French SNCF. Although they had little knowledge of how the Poles ran their railroads, the SMEs' knowledge could be applied to almost any product built to support the running of any railroad.

Some organizations employ their own SMEs. These are usually larger organizations that build enough products in the subject-matter area to warrant keeping SMEs on staff. But whether your SMEs are internal or external to your own organization, they need to be identified and notified of your project's demands on their time.

Technical Consultants

Usually a project has need of technical knowledge in addition to that of the core team. The network consultant, an e-commerce expert, a system software expert, a configuration-management expert, a hardware supplier, a usability expert, information experts, are all examples of technical specialists whose knowledge and skills may be needed by the team at some stage of the project. You should also include operations and maintenance people who run and support your product when it goes into production. Consider safety specialists if your product is to be deployed in the public arena and possibly even emergency services. Inspectors who maintain standards or laws with which your product must comply are also potential technical consultants.

Influencers

Influencers generally reside outside your own organization. They are people or associations that have opinions or rules you need to consider. For example:

- Professional bodies—Do any professional bodies exist in your industry that have rules, standards, or expectations?
- Public opinion or special interest groups—Are there any special opinions that have an effect on your product?
- Other organizations within your domain or industry having some expectation of your product.
- Police—We once had a police force ask us not to use fingerprints as identification for ATMs: They feared the amputated fingers of wealthy people would become valuable to criminals.
- Governments sometimes have agendas that encourage or discourage your product.
- Cultural interests—It is surprisingly easy to offend, and it is crucial to understand the culture in which your product appears.
- Adjacent systems—Think of people or organizations adjacent to your study; adjacent systems appear on your work context model.
- Competition—Products in competition with yours influence the success of your product. Do competitive products have characteristics buyers will expect from your product?

Influencers generally reside outside your own organization. They are people or associations that have opinions or rules you need to consider.

Finding the Stakeholders

It helps you to find the relevant people for a project if you maintain a checklist or analysis of likely stakeholders. (You may download the stakeholder analysis spreadsheet from www.volere.co.uk and use it as the starting point for your own checklist.)

Of course not all types of stakeholders are relevant for all types of projects. Stakeholders you need to emphasize are influenced by factors such as whether you are building an information technology system, or embedded software, or a consumer product, or making a change to an existing product.

An effective way of identifying your stakeholders is to build a stakeholder map for your project. The following sections look at some examples of stakeholder maps.

The stakeholder maps we have most recently developed combine our work on project sociology, our stakeholder analysis spreadsheet, our early stakeholder maps (see Figure 3.5), and our collaboration with Ian Alexander. Ian came up with the metaphor that project sociology is like layers of an onion with the product at the center surrounded by specific stakeholders in each layer; he continues to develop the onion model.[2] For more on Ian Alexander's work, visit http://www.scenarioplus.org.uk.

Stakeholder Map for an In-House IT Project

Figure 3.7 is a stakeholder map for an information technology project showing where to look for potential stakeholders and which stakeholder roles are most relevant.

Figure 3.7

This stakeholder map is for a project that builds a software product for in-house use.

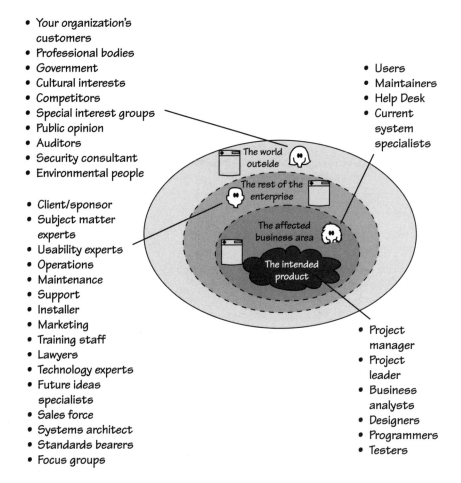

- Your organization's customers
- Professional bodies
- Government
- Cultural interests
- Competitors
- Special interest groups
- Public opinion
- Auditors
- Security consultant
- Environmental people

- Client/sponsor
- Subject matter experts
- Usability experts
- Operations
- Maintenance
- Support
- Installer
- Marketing
- Training staff
- Lawyers
- Technology experts
- Future ideas specialists
- Sales force
- Systems architect
- Standards bearers
- Focus groups

- Users
- Maintainers
- Help Desk
- Current system specialists

- Project manager
- Project leader
- Business analysts
- Designers
- Programmers
- Testers

The world outside
The rest of the enterprise
The affected business area
The intended product

2. Alexander, Ian and Suzanne Robertson. "Understanding Project Sociology by Modelling Stakeholders." *IEEE Software*, January 2004—*Explanation of how to use stakeholder templates and maps to identify stakeholders and maintain their involvement.*

The intended product lies at the center of the map. For an IT project usually some idea exists, although it may be fuzzy around the edges (indicated by the cloud symbol), of the intended product. The core team (project manager, analysts, designers, testers . . .) has responsibility for removing fuzziness from the intended product by discovering relevant requirements and defining the product. In order to do this the team needs to discover the requirements of the stakeholders in the second ring, that is, those who work in the *affected business area*. The people who have a hands-on connection with the product typically have requirements that relate to their day-to-day jobs.

The third ring contains stakeholders who are part of the *rest of the enterprise,* but who do not necessarily have a direct connection with the product. These stakeholders know requirements pertaining to the overall business reason for the product.

The fourth ring is the *world outside* your organization. The stakeholders here are other organizations whose knowledge might have a positive or negative effect on your product. Although they may not regard themselves as stakeholders, they are nonetheless a source of requirements. Failure to consider their expectations can have a harmful effect on the success of your product.

Stakeholder Map for an Embedded System

Compared with an IT project, a project building an embedded system starts with a more precise understanding of the product boundary. Suppose the *intended product* in Figure 3.8 is a controller for part of a vehicle's electrical system. Then, perhaps requirements for the internals of the product are reasonably straightforward. But many other requirements are related to *the remainder of the client's product*: other components (mechanical, electrical, and software) that make up the electrical system.

Stakeholder Map for a Consumer Product

When the product is a consumer item such as a new type of vacuum cleaner, a television set, a telephone, and so forth, the boundaries of the intended product are often uncertain at the inception of the project. This is shown in Figure 3.9.

In this case the stakeholders are sources of ideas for the product. They are also the people who can make those ideas into reality. In the figure the world outside contains stakeholders who may (if we get it right) buy the product. Other stakeholders include those whose rules, regulations, or attitudes can affect the success of the product.

Figure 3.8

When the product is an embedded system, you can avoid missing requirements by paying careful attention to the stakeholders for the remainder of the client's product.

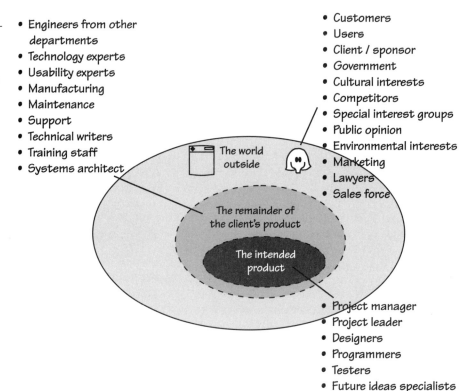

- Engineers from other departments
- Technology experts
- Usability experts
- Manufacturing
- Maintenance
- Support
- Technical writers
- Training staff
- Systems architect

The world outside

The remainder of the client's product

The intended product

- Customers
- Users
- Client / sponsor
- Government
- Cultural interests
- Competitors
- Special interest groups
- Public opinion
- Environmental interests
- Marketing
- Lawyers
- Sales force

- Project manager
- Project leader
- Designers
- Programmers
- Testers
- Future ideas specialists

Figure 3.9

Requirements discovery for a consumer product is concerned with invention. Many of the requirements are found by brainstorming and prototyping. The two important groups of stakeholders are those who have the ideas and can make them practical, and those who will affect the success of the product in the marketplace.

- Project manager
- Project leader
- Designers
- Programmers
- Testers
- Future ideas specialists
- Technology experts
- Usability experts
- Manufacturing
- Maintenance
- Support
- Technical writers
- Training staff
- Installation staff
- Package design

The world outside

The intended product

- Customers
- Users
- Client / sponsor
- Advertising
- Marketing
- Sales force
- Competitors
- Government
- Cultural interests
- Special interest groups
- Public opinion
- Environmental interests
- Lawyers

Stakeholder Map for Change to Existing System

Requirements for a change to an existing software system usually have a fuzzy boundary. If the existing system has been around for a while, or is large and complex, it can be difficult to understand the connections between the intended change and the existing software system. This is shown in Figure 3.10.

Of course, if you have accurate documentation for the existing software, that documentation becomes your source of stakeholder knowledge. Much more commonly, knowledge of the implemented requirements is scattered among a number of stakeholders having some knowledge of different aspects of the software. Regardless of whether the change is small or represents a major enhancement, you should still sketch a stakeholder map to ensure you identify appropriate sources of requirements.

Regardless of whether the change is small or large, you need to identify the appropriate sources of requirements.

Generic Stakeholder Map

The examples of stakeholder maps above illustrate how different rings in your project's sociology contain different stakeholders.

As mentioned previously, one of the authors, Suzanne, has been collaborating with Ian Alexander on the subject of stakeholders and project sociology. Figure 3.11 shows a generic stakeholder map you can use as a guide for finding stakeholders for your project. Ian coined the term *onion model* to describe how project sociology can be imagined, placing stakeholders in bands or rings radiating out from the product. We had many discussions about what to call the rings. The term "system" has many different meanings, but we use it here in the widest sense of the word.

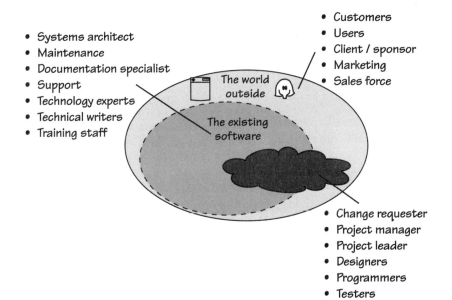

Figure 3.10

Defining requirements for an intended change depends on understanding the requirements that are already implemented.

Figure 3.11

This generic stake-holder map is a pattern for building the stakeholder map for your own project. Each of the rings in the model represents a grouping or cate-gorization of stake-holders. You make your own map by translating each of the generic roles into the specific roles that apply to your project.

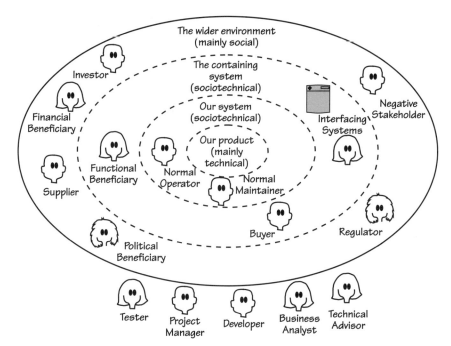

The development team is concerned with all the other stakeholders.

We call the innermost ring the *product.* This is whatever you are build-ing—a piece of software, a machine, a vacuum cleaner, a motor car—and in the case of a finished project, the product you have built. This product is not the same thing as the system that contains it. The *system,* the sec-ond ring, contains people who operate and maintain the product, along with support activities such as a help desk. *Normal operators* in the system ring operate the product to deliver results to *functional beneficiaries,* who reside in the next ring, the *containing system.*

Finally, the outer ring represents *the wider environment.* In this ring we find people—it is usually only people populating this ring—who derive some financial benefit from the product (e.g., owners or shareholders of the organization). You also find here negative influences on your project, hostile competitors, regulators, and people intent in invading or damag-ing your product. You usually cannot influence this wider environment, but you must know about it because it is the source of some of the re-quirements and influences on the product throughout its lifetime.

Note we have put the development team—project manager, analysts, developers—around the edge of the wider environment. We did this be-cause the development team is concerned with *all* the project sociology rings. The team needs to discover requirements from the wider environ-ment, the containing system, and the system (as defined above). Then they need to build a product using these requirements and thus satisfy the needs of all possible parties.

Interestingly, the development team does not remain part of the project sociology when the product is built and delivered. However, all other stakeholders maintain their stakeholding in the product. And they do so for the entire life of the product. In fact, changes in these stakeholders' worlds cause requests for enhancements to the product. Think of the project team as *project stakeholders* and all the others as *lifetime stakeholders*. In Chapter 4 you will see that your stakeholder map also serves as the starting point for your context diagram.

Each of the meta-roles on the generic stakeholder map represents a number of specific roles in your particular project. For example, one functional beneficiary can be your research scientists and another can be your accounts department. The downloadable stakeholder analysis template at www.volere.co.uk contains a checklist of roles.

The reason for making a big deal about finding stakeholders is because they are the sources of requirements. Missed stakeholders means missed requirements. For example, one of our clients was installing a new purchasing system. The analysts assumed purchasing throughout the organization occurred similarly. Thus, they specified a system in which purchase orders had to be raised at the initiation of the transaction, before any offer to buy could be made. But the training department routinely offered to buy training courses, advertised them, and then actually bought a course if enough people signed up. It was in no position to raise a purchase order until quite a few weeks after initiation of the transaction. Because the analysts had missed these stakeholders (the training department), the product did not work as needed for all users.

Keep in mind your team has only slight contact with many of the stakeholders, perhaps only for a few minutes in some cases. But however slight or serious the contact, you must identify all the stakeholders and then communicate to them they are part of your extended social envelope. This will be followed by a visit to them from your business analysts at some stage.

Think of the project team as project stakeholders *and all the others as* lifetime stakeholders.

RESOURCE NOTE
The stakeholder analysis template at volere.co.uk, produced in collaboration with Chris Rupp of the Sophist group, contains a checklist of roles to help you identify your stakeholders.

Missed stakeholders means missed requirements.

Decision Making

Every project needs many decisions, some of them quite small, all of them important. Even slightly wrong decisions can turn out to be calamitous in the long run. We have never seen better group decision making than when participants spend most of their time in close proximity, and conversation is uninhibited. So if you house your team in the same office space where they can talk to one another on a day-to-day basis, much of their decision making will be a natural progression of working together.

The necessity for a formal decision-making process increases in proportion to the degree of stakeholder fragmentation.

However, it is quite common for stakeholders' communication to be fragmented because they work in different geographical locations (sometimes rooms, sometimes buildings, sometimes different time zones), or undertake more than one project at a time, or are employed by another organization outside your project's influence. The greater the incidence of these situations, the more formality you need to introduce into your decision-making process.

An intriguing and effective example of a formalized decision-making process is the *Kgotla,* which is an ancient Botswanan custom woven into the lives of the people. Villages and traditional towns in Botswana are laid out around the Kgotla (pronounced *cot-la,* or courtyard), a fenced-off meeting area large enough for most of the village to gather and hear one another. They use it to make decisions of public importance (see Figure 3.12).

Suppose two of the people living in the village dispute the use of some common land. One villager wants to graze his cows on the land, the other wants to use it as a children's playground. If these two people cannot find some way to agree, a meeting is called by lighting a fire in the Kgotla. The villagers assemble to listen to the disputing parties describe their view of the problem and state their positions. The villagers discuss the problem and ask questions. Throughout these discussions the chief listens and observes. When the villagers have finished their discussions the chief sums up the situation, asks for any necessary clarification, and then decides what is to be done. The chief's decision is binding: the custom of the Kgotla dictates everybody abides by decisions made there.

Figure 3.12

The Kgotla, an ancient tradition in Botswana, has evolved into a way of involving the populace in consultations with the government. The contesting parties describe the problem and make their statements. Interested villagers discuss the problem while the chief listens. Then the chief makes his decision, to which all parties have agreed to abide.

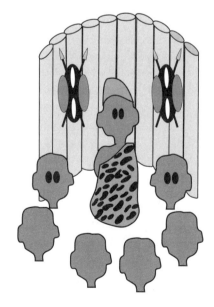

The ancient tradition of the Kgotla is still used in Botswana today; it has evolved into involving the populace in consultations with the government. The success of the Kgotla is not surprising considering it caters to two strong human needs: to be heard and to have a strong, listening leader. We can borrow ideas from this model to design a consultative decision-making structure for our own projects. Instead of the traditionally fenced Kgotla, we have the conference room. Instead of the chief, we have a project manager. Despite the change of scenery, the process is still valid.

RESOURCE NOTE
De Liefde, Willem. *African tribal leadership voor managers van dialoog tot besluit* (from dialog till decision). Kluwer-Deventer, The Netherlands, 2002. *This book should soon be available in English.*

Team Roles

Part of leading a team and creating a useful social envelope is to understand whether the mixture of people in the project team have the ingredients necessary to form an effective team. Meredith Belbin points out that there is a difference between *functional roles* and *team roles*.[3] Functional roles are assigned to a particular person and they usually equate to a job title like program manager, system architect, developer, and so on.

Team roles, on the other hand, define a range of useful behaviors that effectively contribute to the performance of a team. Belbin, after years of research and practical experimentation, identified the following roles whose existence maximizes the success of a team. As nobody is perfect, Belbin also identified traits that may *not* be possessed by a person having a particular team role but nevertheless do not detract from that person's performance. As these are commonly associated with the team role, Belbin refers to these as *allowable weaknesses*. Figure 3.13 summarizes Belbin's team roles and allowable weaknesses.

To get the most out of your team, Belbin suggest all team roles be represented by one or more team members. You have to look past members' job titles or functional roles. Also, think whether a person is eligible or suitable. Belbin points out people are *eligible* for a job if they are qualified, have the necessary experience, or perhaps have accumulated enough seniority. However, members are *suitable* if they have the attributes that match the requirements of the job.

It is unlikely any individual is strong in all team roles, indeed, it is not really necessary. Provided you accumulate all the roles in your team and have people with the appropriate team roles doing the correct work, there is no need to go looking for superstars who fill all the roles.

We should base our decisions on awareness rather than mechanical habit. That is, we act on a keen appreciation for the essential factors that make each situation unique instead of from conditioned response.

—*United States Marine Corps*

3. Belbin, R. Meredith. *Team Roles at Work*. Butterworth-Heinemann, 2001—*This is one of four books by Belbin on the subject of teams and team roles. It contains a clear explanation of team roles and how to use that knowledge to maximize the effectiveness of a team. For further information on team role assessment, contact CERT Consultancy and Training.*

Figure 3.13

This table is taken from Meredith Belbin's *Team Roles at Work.*

Role	Allowable Weaknesses
Plant	This person is creative and imaginative and solves difficult problems. Allowable weaknesses for people having this role are they ignore details and may be too preoccupied to communicate effectively.
Resource investigator	Extroverted, enthusiastic communicator. Resource investigators are good at developing contacts. The allowable weakness is they may be overoptimistic and tend to lose interest once the initial enthusiasm has passed.
Coordinator	Confident chairperson, promotes decision making. Delegates well. Can be seen as manipulative, which is an allowable weakness.
Shaper	Challenging, thrives on pressure. Has the drive to overcome obstacles. Allowable weakness may be that the shaper may provoke others or hurt their feelings.
Monitor evaluator	Strategic and discerning, judges accurately. Allowable weaknesses of lacking drive and overly critical.
Teamworker	Cooperative, perceptive, and diplomatic. Listens, builds, and calms the waters. Allowable weaknesses are that the teamworker may be indecisive and can be easily influenced.
Implementer	Disciplined, reliable, and efficient. Turns ideas into practical actions. Implementer allowable weaknesses are some inflexibility and slow to respond to new possibilities.
Completer	Painstaking, conscientious. Seeks out errors and omissions, delivers on time. Allowable weaknesses: Inclined to worry unduly and reluctant to delegate.
Specialist	Single-minded, self-starting. Provides knowledge and skills in rare supply. Allowable weaknesses: dwells on technicalities and overlooks the big picture.

Think of your team. Can you identify the attributes of your team members? Alternatively, if you are building a team, consider which people provide to you a mixture of all team roles.

As for team roles that make a good business analyst, we look to the *teamworker, implementer,* and *completer* roles as good candidates, with the

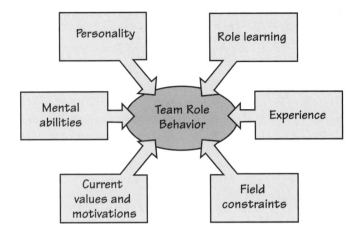

Factors that determine each team role behavior can help you understand an individual's behavior with respect to each of the team roles.

odd *plant* thrown in. However, do not take this too literally as each project creates its own demands in dealing with all the stakeholders.

Belbin also identified factors influencing team role behavior. Figure 3.14 shows his model. Recognizing these factors can help team members to understand one another. The figure requires some explanation.

The *personality* factor represents psychological behavior like extroversion and introversion and high and low anxiety. *Mental abilities* refer to high-level thought that can override personality to generate exceptional behavior. *Current values* represent a person's desire to cling to the *status quo*. *Field constraints* are the effects the working environment has on a person. A person's *experience* may conventionalize his behavior. *Role learning* represents people's ability to be versatile and to learn to play a needed role.

Team leaders use the model of team role behavior to look at factors that make one person fit into one or more of the team roles. Business analysts also use it to help understand the behavior of stakeholders and to frame questions accordingly. For example, when a business analyst has trouble finding what a requirer wants, it is not necessarily because the requirer is being difficult. It could be some combination of the requirer's team role behavior factors such as:

- They are introverted (*personality*).
- They do not understand what the business analyst is talking about (*mental ability*).
- The subject clashes with their ideas (*current values*).
- They cannot hear you clearly (*field constraints*).

Figure 3.15

The choir as a better metaphor for a development group.

- They do not know enough to answer you (*experience*).
- They do not know how to explain requirements (*role learning*).

We use this model as a checklist when we are having trouble communicating with one of our stakeholders. Just considering these reasons sometimes guides us to asking the right question or to realize we are perhaps talking to the wrong person.

Before leaving the concept of teams we should mention a metaphor for a team that we have found surprisingly useful over time. Tom De-Marco, one of our partners in the Atlantic Systems Guild, had the idea that project teams should be more like choirs than sports teams (see Figure 3.15). On a sports team every player tries to stand out, impress the coach, and get a higher salary. The choir member on the other hand is trying not to stand out, but to sing in harmony with other members of the choir.

On one of our Guild retreats, Tom arranged for all of us to take singing lessons. Verona Chard, a very gifted singer came and taught the group to sing harmony. It was enlightening—not to say embarrassing when we found an audience had accumulated outside the window—to find one can modify one's own behavior in order to be a better part of the whole. The choir metaphor for a team works particularly well when deadlines are tight. In "choir" teams members work closely together to ensure completion of the product as a whole with all parts working together smoothly. Contrast this to a "sports" team on which individual team members strive to excel but not necessarily to the benefit of the whole project.

Stakeholder Concerns

When asked their major concerns about stakeholders, project groups often inform us they are concerned about the difficulty of involving the right stakeholders in discovering and specifying the requirements. The problems we hear about most often and seem most serious are

- *Commitment*—People with authority (business and technical managers) do not commit enough time/budget for requirements.
- *Skills*—Stakeholders do not have the skills necessary to participate in the business of gathering requirements; they describe solutions, not requirements, and do not understand their work well enough to describe it.
- *Discovery*—We can't discover all the appropriate stakeholders, and subsequently miss requirements.
- *Maintaining involvement*—We can't keep the stakeholders interested and involved for the duration of the project.

During the period from November 2001 to March 2002, we ran a survey with groups from eight different countries. We asked the respondents to choose which of the stakeholder concerns was most important in their individual environment. The results are summarized in Figure 3.16.

Figure 3.16 This figure represents a survey on the most common concerns about stakeholders. The people surveyed were active business analysts and project managers engaged in the requirements activity.

Country	Commitment	Skills	Discovery	Maintaining Involvement	Other	Total
Germany, November 2001	18	40	14	3	7	82
Australia, November 2001	11	5	0	2		18
Australia, December 2001	10	14	5	4		33
Denmark, January 2002	37	39	4	1	7	88
UK, February 2002	14	6	4	1		25
Denmark, January 2002	4	7	5	1		17
Netherlands, March 2002	10	12	4	4	1	31
Australia, April 2002	13	3	16	8	2	42
Australia, April 2002		6	5	5		16
USA, April 2002	26	27	4	5	6	68
Italy, May 2002	3	4	3	4		14
Finland, May 2002	40	45	8	10	4	107
Total	186	208	72	48	27	541
Percentage of Total	34%	38%	13%	9%	5%	100%

Developing Skills

In the survey summarized in Figure 3.16, 38% of the respondents believe stakeholders are lacking in the skills and abilities needed to participate effectively in the requirements process.

Sometimes this perceived lack of skill is the result of how your business analysts communicate with the requirers. Our experience is requirers who have trouble communicating are usually poor at abstracting. To alleviate the problem, we suggest you use more prototypes and use them earlier in the requirements cycle.

Training is an obvious answer. We must report we are seeing more and more people from the business side participating in our requirements training, as word of the effectiveness of good requirements spreads. The most effective training sessions occur when participants are a combination of business analysts, requirers, and technical people—together they build a common language. Training implies you take a long-term view, but one you can profitably promote within your organization. Mentioning the high cost of rework and changing requirements due to bad input from the business side is a powerful argument. Similarly, sloppy work by your business analysts also results in the same high cost of rework.

Use more prototypes and use them earlier in the requirements cycle.

Getting Commitment

The other most common response to our survey is the 34% of respondents who point to lack of financial and time commitment on the part of business and technical managers. When extreme time pressure is exerted on projects, requirements are sometimes viewed as an unnecessary luxury. Unfortunately, the manager who insists requirements are too expensive always fails to see the cost of rework, missed opportunities, and abandoned projects is even more expensive.

The fact is specifying the requirements well is one of the best investments you can make in speeding up delivery of a working product. However, good requirements practice does not mean rigid phases, procedures, and documents. The opposite is true: Good requirements practices enable speeding up delivery with frequent incremental releases and delivering a product that precisely matches the requirers' needs.

It helps if you continually demonstrate to business people why their involvement is vital to the development of successful products. Each time one of your business analysts communicates with a stakeholder, have the analyst point out something he learned that will help ensure the delivered product is what the stakeholder needs. If possible, attach a stakeholder's name on new ideas as a way of showing the stakeholder's involvement is necessary.

Good requirements practice does not mean rigid phases, procedures and documents. The opposite is true—good requirements practices enable speeding up delivery with frequent incremental releases and delivering a product that precisely matches the requirers' needs.

Other concerns voiced in our survey come from 13% of respondents who had a problem in discovering stakeholders and 9% who had difficulty maintaining involvement. We examined one of these topics earlier in this chapter, and are going to look at the other in the next section. Finally, of the 5% giving the answer "other," the most common reason was lack of communication among stakeholders.

Involvement throughout the Project

Most of the stakeholders to whom you speak are not part of the core team; their real job is elsewhere, not talking to you. When you come over and talk to them you often represent an intrusion on their everyday work. It is a good idea to keep this in mind when you make demands on someone's time. And despite this, you have to get their attention and then keep it.

People don't want to talk about their requirements for a product if it will not be on their desk in the next 6–12 months. They know they will probably not be in the same job in a year's time, and even if they do plan on sticking around they know the nature of the business will have changed by then. Thus, you must plan to deliver a new release of a partial product every few months, even more frequently if the product lends itself to that.

People don't want to talk about their requirements for a product if it will not be on their desk in the next 6–12 months.

Additionally, you need to provide feedback on whatever they tell you. It is dispiriting for a requirer to spend hours with a business analyst then receive nothing in return. Initially, feedback should be in the nature of well-formed requirements statements. Later, prototypes provide the feedback. However, frequent releases are probably the best reinforcement you can offer to your requirers that they are contributing to something worthwhile.

The need for involvement also applies to changes. If some requirements change—and they will—it is vital you ensure all stakeholders connected to those requirements are consulted regarding the change. Your making changes without notification may cause the affected stakeholder to regard your team as arbitrary and possibly untrustworthy.

Consider uninvolved requirers may not want your product. Too often, we hear complaints from requirements teams to the effect their business users do not give them any time. Lack of business user time is understandably frustrating to the analysts, as analysts realize in order to build the right product they must spend time with these people. Why don't the requirers give up more of their time? Usually because they do not want the product. They see no advantage in having it and are thus un-

Uninvolved requirers may not want your product.

❝ *That's just the way it is nowadays," said Microsoft's Linda Stone, vice-president of corporate and industry initiatives. Despite her bureaucratic title, Stone is a creative thinker who has coined the term* continuous partial attention *to describe the way we cope with the barrage of communication coming at us. "It's not the same as multi-tasking," Stone says: "that's about trying to accomplish several things at once. With continuous partial attention, we're scanning incoming alerts for the one best thing to seize upon: 'How can I tune in, in a way that helps me sync up with the most interesting, or important, opportunity?' " She says: "It's crucial for CEOs to be intentional about breaking free from continuous partial attention in order to get their bearings. Some of today's business books suggest that speed is the answer to today's business challenges. Pausing to reflect, focus, think a problem through; and then taking steady steps forward in an intentional direction is really the key.* ❞

—Jill Hecht Maxwell,
Inc. Magazine,
January 1, 2002.

willing to spend the time needed for analysts to learn the work and make the right choices when it comes to new products.

The above points to a strong need for good stakeholder selection—ensuring the right people are involved in the first place and they all understand their stake in the intended product. You must have stakeholders whose judgment is respected by the rest of the team, as well as a group of stakeholders who give political legitimacy to the project. The project becomes devalued if the remainder of the organization thinks the wrong stakeholders are participating. We have found very few stakeholders want to remain attached to a project seen as a lame duck.

While we speak of involvement throughout the project, we do not mean continuous involvement. Except for the core team, most stakeholders are involved intermittently. That is, they might have several hours or days of talking about their requirements, then apart from feedback, not be called upon until, say, a sanity check is required on a prototype. Or their interest may be for one aspect of the product, say security and they do not expect to be contacted except for security issues. However, bear in mind they do expect to be contacted for *all* security issues.

Involvement is important: if little or no requirer involvement develops, requirements gathering becomes a meaningless exercise . . . one you do not have time for.

Continuous Partial Attention

Communication is changing. The thoroughness of communication is being replaced by sound bites. Our written language is being replaced by

I nd 2 cu 2day bc ic ur demo @IBM mtg.john is [:-(".

Instant messaging, text messaging, email, and cell phones have added to already-full channels to the degree actual communication may be taking a back seat to the medium of communication. Linda Stone of Microsoft described the increasing number of simultaneous demands made for our attention as leading to a phenomenon she calls *continuous partial attention*.

We have so many mediums of communication; each has an inbuilt status and priority, and each demands we attend to it first. Consider this (as shown in Figure 3.17): You arrive back at your desk and your email alert is telling you that you have new mail. However, a Post-it note is stuck dead center on your screen telling you your file has been corrupted. The boss has put a memo on your desk, and a coworker has given you a hand-written note that your spouse called and it is urgent that you get in touch. Your Instant Messaging window is full of messages from your

Figure 3.17

Continuous partial attention: We have so many ways of communicating, each vying for our attention, that we may be distorting the messages we send and receive.

team, and at that moment, just as your cell phone rings, your secretary lays your paper mail on your desk with a letter from your doctor on top. Which one gets your attention first?

The scenario may be exaggerated, but not much. We generally experience a continuous flow of interactions in which you can only partially concentrate on each. This means we are learning to think in sound bites, to look for short sharp answers to find a solution to this minute's problem, one that takes only a minute to implement because that is all the time we think we have.

The impression is actually false; we have a lot more time than we think. Ask yourself: How old is some of the software currently running at your organization? Five years? Ten years? More? How long is the software that you are building today expected to last? More than a few years? So why do minutes matter when you are building something that has to be both error free and functionally correct? However, a *perception* exists that minutes matter and we have to react to every signal and process our information in short sharp bursts.

If the perception exists, we must live with it and learn to communicate appropriately.

James Carville has had a very successful career as political consultant and campaign director. Carville says he has an attention disorder. He approached this seeming disability by teaching himself to communicate in short bursts. He learned to use sound bites as his principal means of getting his message across. Scott Adams, the creator of Dilbert shares the same affliction, and yet here is one of the prime communicators of the business world fitting amazing messages into a three-panel Dilbert strip.

As part of our project sociology we need to learn to communicate effectively in the face of intense competition for our message, with people who are paying us "continuous partial attention." What will get the attention of the intended receiver of your message? Before you go and talk to a colleague decide what you are trying to learn from the communication. Take an example or prototype of what you want to talk about to help the conversation focus on a relevant track. Develop the habit of providing a feedback loop, use sketches or diagrams to let the others see what you understand. Then they can tell you immediately where you are wrong.

Your social envelope should include a recognized method for your team to communicate. Rather than have to compete for attention, your team members can use one or two channels, and use distinctive subject headers—perhaps using intimate team words to make them stand out from the babble—to let other team members know the message concerns your project. They can thus break free of continuous partial attention and give sole attention to probably the most important aspect of the product you are building—its requirements.

Project Sociology Analysis

Identifying all the stakeholders makes it easier for your business analysts to start finding requirements. We show a suggested process for doing this in Figure 3.18.

As we discussed earlier in this chapter, you don't have to identify the roles, people, and knowledge types in any particular order. The *identify roles* activity uses checklists of potential stakeholders to determine which are relevant for this project. You look for job titles, responsibilities, or other organizations that might indicate a stakeholder. *Identify available people* is concerned with finding the specific people assigned to the project, along with other people mentioned as having an interest in the project. *Identify needed knowledge types* considers what you already know about the subject matter and the business purpose of the project. If you have domain knowledge from other previous or overlapping projects then that knowledge, together with your understanding of the scope and purpose, helps you identify the knowledge you need to investigate for this project.

Then it's a matter of putting it all together. *Assign names to needed requirements knowledge* produces a summary of who knows what. On our

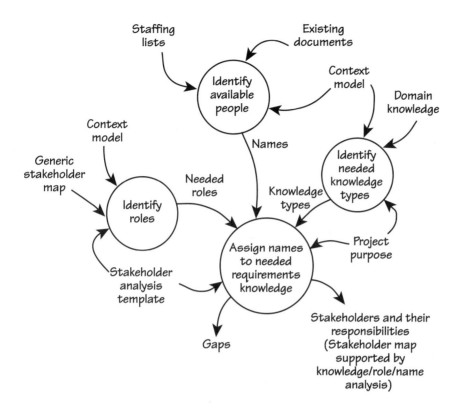

Figure 3.18

This diagram summarizes a project sociology analysis. Bear in mind this is not a rigid process. You can perform the analysis by either getting a group of people together in a workshop or performing the analysis over a period of time.

Volere requirements Web site, www.volere.co.uk, we maintain the Stakeholder Analysis Template. This is an Excel spreadsheet showing roles and knowledge types. We find it an excellent control mechanism to populate with names and job titles of your stakeholders, as well as to adjust roles and knowledge types to suit your project. This process also identifies gaps that occur when you have a needed knowledge type and no stakeholder to supply it.

The result of this sociology analysis is you and your business analysts have a complete knowledge of all the people you need to involve in your project. You should, of course, inform all of them they are indeed stakeholders, why they are stakeholders, why it is an advantage to them, and if possible how much of their time you need and when you need it. These people are your extended team. They are contributors to your project success.

What Do I Do Right Now?

Few projects fail for technical reasons. Most failures can be safely attributed to humans. The people who work on your project—and this includes all of your stakeholders—are crucial. All tools and techniques are of little help if you have the wrong people. Getting the right people involved is one of the better investments you can make.

In Chapter 1 we gave a list of project success indicators. These are factors that contribute to good projects, and their absence usually indicates a project in failure mode. We want to consider some of the indicators that involve people, and consider appropriate actions.

One of the project success indicators is *lack of creeping requirements*. Requirements creep is a bugbear of many projects, and it is caused largely by lack of involvement or lack of interest of appropriate stakeholders. When the right stakeholders are involved—that is, stakeholders with enough knowledge to ensure the right work context is chosen—requirements analysts can gather the requirements for the right product. No interminable stream of requirements occurs as users scramble to mould the product into something useful, and no late requirements materialize as people previously omitted from the requirements process try to get their ideas incorporated into the product.

We recommend that you relate the Knowledge-Role-Person model to your scope or context diagram. For each of the adjacent systems, consider the category of knowledge needed to understand it, the roles that it can provide or the person who knows the requirements for it. Consider the subject matter that falls within the scope and use Knowledge-Role-Person to identify the appropriate stakeholders. Also, inspect your requirements specification template. For each of the requirements types, go through the Knowledge-Role-Person routine to find the stakeholders relevant to that type of requirement.

Another project success indicator is *user or customer satisfaction*. That is, the people who use the product are happy with both its functionality and its qualitative aspects like usability, look and feel and so on. Another indicator is *correctly sized product:* Developers do not have to build any more product than needed for users to perform their work.

Both of the last two indicators are addressed by ensuring inclusion in your stakeholder group of people who actually do the work, as well as people who know what that work should be. The project sociology analysis we described above is intended to ensure you have the right people on your team.

One of the factors that we have found to be a significant contributor to effective product development is the project success indicator *good team morale*. We discussed the idea of the social envelope and how it forms a bond between the members of a group, specifically your team. While the social envelope is not something that can be mandated, the astute manager can nurture it. By providing suitable accommodation for your team, and encouraging the team to develop their own identity, jokes, language variations, eat together, and behave more as a family than an uninvolved group of people who just happen to work in the same building.

What's the Least I Can Get Away With?

Use a stakeholder checklist to identify the stakeholders. If you don't already have a checklist, download ours from www.volere.co.uk. Use the generic stakeholder map to help you find your stakeholders. Also, make sure that you include the stakeholders with a connection to the context diagram (see Chapter 4—Learning What People Need).

Tell each of them they are stakeholders, you require some of their time, and why you want it. It is helpful, but not always possible early on, to estimate how much of their time you think you need. Try and involve them by getting them interested in your product.

Now do a sanity check: Do you have enough stakeholders, and the right ones, for all the indicated requirements types? Refer to your specification template for these types. If you do not have your own specification template, you can download the Volere template from www.systemsguild.com and use it as a checklist.

Are your stakeholders showing interest? At this stage you might consider abandoning ship if you don't have the right people on board or if they show no interest in the project. It is almost universal: If requirers do not show interest, they do not want the product.

Last, give your team an identity. Make up a name, find them a war room for meetings, get some wearable entity such as T-shirts or caps printed, or create anything that makes your people feel that they are part of the same social envelope.

Additional References for Project Sociology

The following sources, in addition to those already referenced, have useful information on project sociology:

- De Liefde Willem. *African tribal leadership voor managers van dialoog tot besluit* (from dialog till decision). Kluwer-Deventer, the Netherlands, 2002—*This is a book on change management with a difference. The ancient wisdom of the Kgotla is applied to helping large organizations communicate and make effective changes.*
- DeMarco, Tom, and Tim Lister. *Peopleware: Productive Projects and Teams,* 2nd edition. Dorset House, 2000—*Practical and readable advice about finding the right people, making them happy, and making it possible for them to do good work.*

CHOCOLATE

When you are conceived, 50% of your DNA is inherited from your father, and 50% is inherited from your mother. (If we got all of our genes from one parent or the other then we would all be clones of that parent.) This half-and-half arrangement means your DNA is derived directly from two people (your parents) and indirectly from four people (your grandparents). If you go back another generation, eight people contributed to your genetic material, and that number doubles with each previous generation.

However, part of your genetic material, your *mitochondrial DNA,* is inherited only from your mother. She in turn got hers from her mother, and so on back through the generations. One aspect that differentiates mitochondrial DNA is it mutates only about once every 10,000 years. When the women came ashore at Plymouth Rock, each of them brought her mitochondrial DNA with her from the old world. That identical DNA is carried today by hundreds of thousands of Americans in a direct line of descent on the female side. Similarly, when native Americans arrived from Asia, the tribes brought their mitochondrial DNA with them that is still identifiable today. How do we know that they came from Asia? Because the mitochondrial DNA of most native Americans (and native South Americans for that matter) matches to people living today in north-central Asia.

This unbreaking chain of mitochondrial DNA gives us a link to female ancestors from the beginning of recorded history. If you fancy you are related to Catherine the Great, or Martha Washington, or Boadicea, you can prove it.

- Gottesdiener, Ellen. *Requirements by Collaboration.* Addison-Wesley, 2003—*Guides you in how to plan and conduct requirements workshops. Written by a skilled facilitator, this book contains practical tools you can apply immediately.*
- Highsmith, Jim. *Adaptive Software Development: A Collaborative Approach to Managing Complex Systems.* Dorset House, 1999—*A wealth of techniques, tools and approaches for helping people collaborate on personal, cultural, and structural levels. Adds discipline to iterative and rapid development methods.*
- Hoffman, Lynn. *Foundations of Family Therapy. A Conceptual Framework for Systems Change.* Basic Books, 1981—*Read this to understand how families work, or don't work, and how this knowledge can be applied to other social groups—in our case groups who work together to do projects.*
- Robertson, James and Suzanne. *Mastering the Requirements Process.* Addison-Wesley, London, 1999—*The chapter on Project Blastoff discusses how knowledge about the stakeholders is stored in compartments 2 and 3 of the Volere requirements template.*
- Senge, Peter. *The Fifth Discipline Handbook.* Doubleday, 1994—*Packed with examples and discussions on systems thinking and how to apply it.*
- United States Marine Corps. *Warfighting.* Currency Doubleday, 1994—*This is the Marine Corps' book on the strategy of managing confrontation. It contains sage advice that can be applied to any sort of project.*

Learning What People Need

The requirements activity is about studying the people who do the work, learning their work, and devising a product that will help with that work. This chapter looks at the first part: learning and understanding what lies behind what people are saying.

Building the Right Product

You are building a product to improve somebody's work. Whether it is software for internal use; software to sell to the marketplace; or a mass consumer product like a telephone, an in-car infotainment system, or a Web browser, you still have to think of the work your consumer is doing. This means you must connect with the people who do that work and understand what they do.

Without understanding their work you cannot improve it. It does not matter whether the work is being done by clerical workers, computers, a few guys pressing buttons and pulling levers, highly skilled scientists, or untrained members of the public. It is still work. It does not have to be paid work. For our purposes, somebody buying a cinema ticket online is working, as is the sports fan looking up the weekend's results. You, or at least your team, must come to an intimate understanding of the nature of your client's or customer's work and what it may become in the future. When you deliver your product it improves the work and at the same time subtly changes it.

> *For customer-centered design, the first task of a design team is to shift focus from the system that the team is chartered to build and redirect it to the work of the potential customers.*
>
> —Hugh Beyer and Karen Holtzblatt, *Contextual Design*

You understand the current work from having people performing the work—usually referred to as "users" or "hands-on users," although in this book we usually call them "requirers"—tell you about it. Although we refer to the activity as "requirements," it is a misnomer as it implies you are finding out what a future product is to do. However, before you can think about the new product you must understand the work soon to be changed or replaced.

There are some problems when you are trying to gather requirements based on the current work. Because internal users know a new product is in the offing, they tend to describe the product they already have or something very similar. External customers tend to ask for more and more refinements or improvements to their current product and rarely ask for something radically different. We are creatures who take a certain amount of comfort from familiar things, and when other people are involved, do not seek out the unknown.

A further complication is that instead of describing the work, requirers tend to tell you their solution to the problem. This premature implementation is understandable—we live in a technological world and tend to talk in terms of technology. For example, we say, "I get my email through the wireless connection to the Internet on my laptop" rather than describing the abstract work situation along the lines of "I communicate in text from most of my travel locations." The latter statement is rather ungainly, and most people from whom you get your information are not normally skilled at this kind of abstraction.

We often see projects launched in which a product has been determined before the work has been studied. "Let's do our inventory on the intranet" might be a brilliant solution, but as yet you have no way of knowing if it fits the work environment. Similarly, requirers describe a solution to the problem they have at the moment without considering the larger picture of how their particular work fits with the overall work of the organization.

Unfortunately, the hands-on users of your product cannot realistically be expected to know what they want. We are not denigrating your users: they are experts at what they do—accounting, science, retailing, whatever—but we do not expect them to excel at determining the best possible product to help them perform their work. That's your job.

So you, or at least your project team, are about to do a very human thing: Talk to people, understand what they do, understand the kind of people they are, and the kind of product they will find useful when you build it. Your team members have to be communicators and inventors. They must mediate between conflicting requirements (or requirers) and discern what people are thinking, when the people may not exactly be willing to spend time with your team.

If your product is to be sold to customers who are not part of your organization, the requirements problem subtly changes. You do not have direct access to your customers' work, but you have to improve it. You mainly *invent* this product and it is, of course, important to derive a useful product, one the customer uses and recommends to others. You must also derive a product with the right amount of usability, an attractive look and feel, appropriate security, and so on. And then you have to persuade your customer to pay for it.

Welcome to requirements elicitation.

Scope Is Always the Beginning

First, always determine the scope of the work to be studied. If scope is not clearly understood—and agreed upon by all parties—time will be wasted and the wrong product will emerge from the development effort. We have spoken of the need to understand the work before deciding the product to build. But before your team can begin to understand the work, they have to know how big it is. In other words, what are the boundaries of this work? Where does it start? Where does it end? What functionality is included, and what is specifically excluded?

The scoping activity establishes the part of the work covered by the requirements study. The process generally consists of interested parties coming to a consensus on what to include, what to exclude, and the connections between this work and other work. We strongly suggest you use a diagram to determine and then demonstrate the scope. Words alone are inadequate when it comes to expressing scope.

Consider the context model shown in Figure 4.1. It gives the initial impression of showing little more than connections between your scope and the outside world. Though mainly we intend to show these connections in the diagram, we will use the diagram to for much more than that.

First, consider data flow connections to adjacent systems. Each of these named arrows represents a packet of data. Normally you would define the data content of each flow to show its constituent data elements. Your definition must conform to that of the adjacent system project leaders or representatives. For example, note the flow in Figure 4.1 called *Boarding pass*. Rather than rely on various ideas of what a boarding pass is, or collect variable examples, you can define it as:

Boarding pass = Airline + Flight number + Destination + Cabin class
+ Passenger name + Departure date + Seat number
+ (Gate number) + (Boarding time) + Frequent flyer
number + Passport number + Passport country

If scope is not clearly understood—and agreed upon by all parties—time will be wasted and the wrong product will emerge from the development effort.

Figure 4.1

An example of a context model. It conceals the actual work inside the central bubble (this is intentional) and highlights the connections to adjacent systems. We will see how these connections are the real (and precise) definers of the scope of the work to be studied.

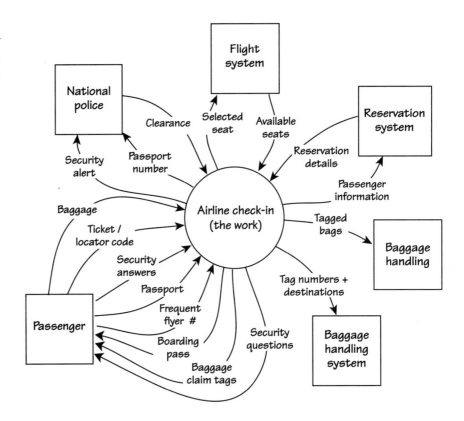

Note if you examine the boarding pass from your most recent flight, it may not agree with the above definition. However, the analyst has defined the boarding pass for *this* airline, so it does not have to match yours.

The output flows on the context model represent services, and thus the functionality provided by the work; the inputs are data needed to provide those services. Each flow of data on this model defines (more or less) the function that produced it. When a function is activated, it transforms some input data into output data. Sometimes the arrival of this data activates the function. The output data is the product of this function. Thus viewing the context model as a whole, you see from the output data the functionality included in the work.

As an example, the *Boarding pass* flow contains *Passport number* and *Passport country*. For these to be on the boarding pass, some functionality inside the work must exist to record passport information. An input flow must also exist to provide this information.

Similarly, data input to your piece of work represents the product of functionality existing in adjacent systems. By a thorough inspection of data flows in consultation with the project leaders of adjacent systems, you can agree precisely upon which processes or features reside in your piece of work and which are the responsibility of someone else.

Now the scope is set and you can use the context as raw material for estimating the size of the work area. We describe how to do this in Chapter 8—Measuring Requirements. An early measurement of the task size enables you to know whether the project is worth undertaking, as well as giving you a good indication of needed resources.

Keep in mind the scope described by this model is the scope of the work area you are going to study. The *product* you build may have a different scope, which happens when you (wisely) elect to study the human tasks your business people perform. The reason for studying business people tasks is to understand their work well enough not only to build the exact right product they require, but also to take every opportunity of providing the appropriate automation or improvement by other means.

Normally, the context model is the most frequently studied model on our consulting projects. We urge you not just to keep the context model in digital form inside your computer, but to print it on the largest sheet of paper available to you and to display it prominently. Many an argument, not to say catastrophe, has been averted by a quick reference to the context model. Make it an automatic deliverable on all your projects.

Chapter 8—Measuring Requirements has details of how to use the work context as the basis for function point estimation.

Chapter 3—Project Sociology shows how stakeholder analysis helps you define the most relevant work context.

Business Events—Your Secret Weapon

You have defined the work area by drawing a context diagram. The work area will always be too large and complex to study in its entirety, so partition the area into convenient pieces. Naturally, the pieces should reflect the nature and functionality of the work you are about to study. Which is why we suggest *business events* as a way of partitioning.

The idea of business events was originally proposed by Steve McMenamin and John Palmer in their seminal work, *Essential Systems Analysis*. They reasoned if partitioning was to avoid following the manner in which the current work happened to be implemented, then they had to start by looking outside the work and ignore internal boundaries. The work exists to provide some information or service or product for an external customer. To provide that information, the work needs to be sent information from external sources. If you glance back to the context model in Figure 4.1, you see flows of information originating in the external adjacent system and corresponding flows originated by the work. These flows are the direct result of business events.

Business events are things that happen in the world; they are important to the work because the work needs to respond to the business event

Business events are things that happen in the real world. The work always responds to the business events.

in some way. "Customer wants to buy a book," or "Employee gets a promotion," or "Policy holder decides to claim against a policy," or "User presses 'Play' on a DVD player" are business events. They are happenings important to the work.

Business events also occur when it is time for the work to carry out some periodic task.

Business events also occur when it is time for the work to carry out some periodic task. For example, these business events have names like "Time to produce monthly statements," or "30 days have elapsed since last invoice sent," or "Policy due to expire in one month."

Be careful not to confuse business events with interface events like "User resizes a window." The latter, while important, is of little use to you at requirements time.

Business events are scalable. On one hand you could have a business event called "Enemy launches nuclear missile attack" and on the other one called "Granny withdraws $5 from her checking account." Both are business events because they are triggered by happenings outside of the work.

Business events are identified by flows of information that enter and leave the work. Each time an input flow of data occurs, something must have happened in the adjacent system to produce the flow. *That "something" is the business event.* When Granny decided she wanted her $5 from the bank, that was the business event. The bank became aware the event has happened when Granny arrived at the teller's cage with her check. She could also have gone to an ATM—withdrawing money from an ATM is also a business event—but Granny is set in her ways and prefers to deal directly with the nice young man behind the counter.

The work's response to the business event is a business use case.

Once the bank receives the check, it responds. In this case the response is to verify the funds are available in the account, to deduct the withdrawal amount, and to hand Granny her cash. This response, illustrated in Figure 4.2, is the *business use case*. The response to "Enemy launches nuclear missile attack" is, of course, more complex, but follows the same patterns and rules.

Note the business use case has no processing connections to other business use cases. The only connection is by the stored data. This means the business use case is a self-contained amount of processing your analysts can study in isolation. Their communication point with analysts studying other business use cases is when some question exists about stored data.

The business use case is a self-contained amount of processing that your analysts can study in isolation.

The business use case that responds to each event is unique. That is, the total collection of processes and data are different from other business use cases. Some processes may exist that are duplicated by other business use cases, and there certainly will be data shared among cases, but the complete business use case is unique.

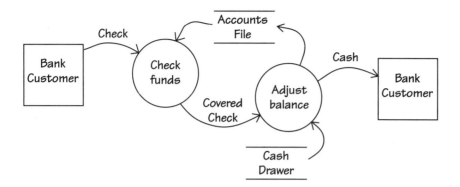

Figure 4.2

The response to the business event "Granny withdraws $5 from her checking account"—although it would be preferable to call this "Bank customer wants to cash a check." Note how the business event happens outside the work, and the work is notified by the triggering data flow. The arrival of this flow triggers the response to the event—this is the business use case—which is usually to reference stored data, carry out some process, and store some data.

We always try to find the "event owner" for each business event. The event owner is the person with the greatest interest in the business event and in the business use case that responds to the event. The event owner becomes the primary source of requirements and may be the person who adjudicates conflicting requirements for that event.

Business Events and Use Cases

The term *use case* is widely used, and widely means quite different things. A recent posting on a requirements mailing list pointed out there were, at the time, 40 published definitions of a use case, most of them quite different from one another.

Given the existence of this modern-day Tower of Babel (see Figure 4.3), let's not make matters worse by adding yet another definition. However, for purposes of this book, we need to differentiate between a happening relevant to the work being studied, how the work responds to the happening, and the part of the response we decide to make into a product. We refer to these three things as *business events, business use cases,* and *product use cases*.

Figure 4.4 illustrates the relationship between a business event, a business use case, and a product use case. The business event happens outside the work boundary. It can happen almost randomly, and it usually happens because someone or something wants the work to do something. The business use case is the work's response to the business event. The work's response is the processing and accessing of stored data, which represents the "something" the outside party wants the work to perform. At some stage, you determine how much of the business use case your product needs to perform. This part of the business use case is the product use case.

For the purposes of this book, we need to differentiate between a happening relevant to the work being studied, how the work responds to the happening, and the part of the response we decide to make into a product. We refer to these three things as **business events, business use cases** *and* **product use cases.**

Figure 4.3

Approximately forty published definitions exist for "use case;" people use the term for many different purposes so it has become nearly as meaningless as speaking to someone in the Tower of Babel. *Pieter Bruegel's painting "Turmbau zu Babel" supplied by Kunsthistorisches Museum, Wien oder KHM, Wien.*

It is important for your requirements analysts to understand the significance of the business event, the business use case, and the product use case.

The business event, as we have mentioned, is a happening outside the context of the work, usually a demand for some service provided by the work. Consider the significance of this external event. If the adjacent system (for that is where the event happens) is human, the requirements analyst must understand what the human is doing at the time of the event and what the human ultimately wants from your work. If it is an automated adjacent system, the precise nature of the reason for the event must become clear to your team. Only by understanding the true nature of the event and the intentions of the adjacent system can you find the most appropriate response to the event.

By understanding the true nature of the business event, and the intentions of the adjacent system, you find the most appropriate response to the event.

The response from the work is the business use case (see Figure 4.4). For the moment we concentrate on the response the work makes and leave for the moment the part of the response from the product. At this point requirements analysts can make a huge difference. By studying the true nature of the work, not just a quickly thought-up solution to a not-yet-understood problem, analysts can eventually specify a product with a longer-term beneficial effect. But if they start with just the product and have no idea how or why it is used, only by chance does the product provide maximum benefits.

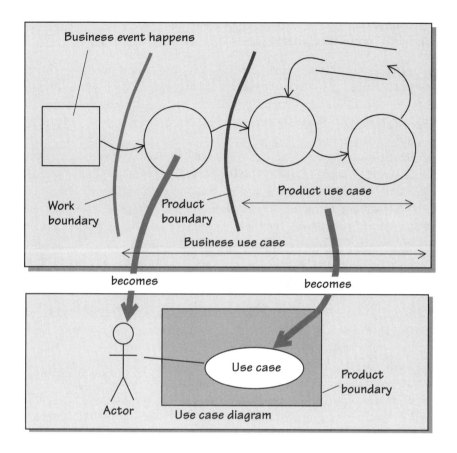

Figure 4.4

The work's response to a business event is a business use case. Once this response is well enough understood, you determine how much of the response is performed by the product: the product use case. The use case diagram shown in the lower part of the figure is the UML notation for a use case.

The analyst studies processing performed by the work in response to a business event, in addition to data stored and retrieved by that processing. When the analyst has sufficient understanding of the work, he decides, in consultation with various interested stakeholders exactly what part of the work is to be performed by the product. We refer to this activity as deciding the product boundary.

When the product boundary is decided, whatever is inside the product we call a product use case. For straightforward processes, normal practice is to chose a product boundary such that there is one product use case for each business use case. However, for technical or implementation reasons, you might choose a product boundary whereby there is more than one product use case. The designer and software architect decide the product use cases depending on the implementation environment and the product's constraints.

Now let's go back to the beginning of the business event.

The Real Origin of the Business Event Is outside Your Organization

The business event happens outside your work, and possibly outside your organization. The work you are studying provides services for some entity outside it. In context diagrams, these outside entities are represented by the adjacent system. The business event occurs when one of these adjacent systems wants a service from the work. To put it another way, the moment one of your customers decides to want something your work provides, that moment is the business event.

Because the business event happens outside your work area—your customers are outside, in fact they are outside your organization—it pays to consider what is occurring in the wider world when the external entity realizes it wants the service and makes its request.

As an example, Progressive insurance company has a fleet of Immediate Response Vehicles (IRVs). If you are insured with Progressive and have an auto accident, an IRV can come to the scene of the accident—sometimes the IRV even arrives before the police. The IRV driver, a trained insurance claim adjustor, assesses the damage to your car using a computer-based estimating program on a laptop computer.

The IRV driver can write a check for your repairs on the spot—you don't actually make a claim in the traditional sense of filling out a form. From that point, the customer can choose whether to have the car repaired. Progressive recognized *the real origin of the business event is the accident,* not filling out the claim, and decidedly not the insurance clerk who enters the claim into the company's computer system (see Figure 4.5).

The question is what was the person—this is probably your customer—doing at the moment the business event occurred. As another example, Amazon has hundreds of thousands of links on other people's

Figure 4.5

The Progressive Insurance *Immediate Response Vehicle.* Recognizing the true origin of the event is outside the organization, Progressive sends an IRV to the scene of the accident for on-the-spot assessing and paying of automobile accident claims. *Photograph copyright Progressive Casualty Insurance Company.*

sites throughout the Web. Amazon recognizes the true origin of a book-buying business event is when Web surfers decide they want to read a particular book. If you are browsing a site and it contains a book review, the business event is when you think the book looks interesting enough to read. Having a "Buy it from Amazon.com" link on the same page means Amazon captures the true actor at the point of origin. Incidentally, Amazon pays for these links: It runs an Associates' program in which a percentage of sales is paid to the Web site providing the click-through link.

What was happening at the moment the business event occurred?

Amazon is willing to pay a commission in order to capture a sale at the moment a reader wants a book. Amazon sells millions of books, many sales due to recognizing the buying decision is made in the reader's home or office, and readers are able to trigger the appropriate business use case then and there.

At what point does the business event of an airline check-in begin? Virgin Atlantic states that for its Upper Class passengers, check-in begins at the passenger's home. When you enter the Virgin-supplied limousine to ride to the airport, the driver registers your bags and radios ahead to the airport. When you arrive at the drive-through check-in, you are handed your boarding pass and baggage check receipts. (The papers are handed through the window; you don't get out of the car.) When you are dropped at the terminal, your only responsibility is to smile as you walk past the check-in queues and head for the lounge. (One of the authors hopes Virgin Atlantic thinks some more about the real beginnings of the business event and sends someone to his house to pack the suitcase.)

At what point does the business event of an airline check-in begin?

You may have someone in your office who counts stationery to see if more has to be ordered. This counting activity is actually the beginning of the business event. Some office-supply companies have shifted the event boundary and provide a service performing the counting for you. They don't actually come around and count your paper clips, but work out your average consumption and ensure you are kept supplied, but not oversupplied.

Your authors buy their groceries from a delivery service. The business event appears to originate when one of us picks up the phone to place an order. Conventional business analysis would have the actor for this use case being the sales clerk who answers the phone and keys the order into a computer. However, before we pick up the phone, we have walked around the house looking in cupboards to see what we need. We make a list before phoning it in. This counting activity could be viewed as the beginning of the business event, but it is even more preferable to consider the true origin is when we run out of something.

Our household will become a lifelong customer of any grocery delivery service that knows (not guesses) what we need and delivers it with no

What are your customers doing when the business event occurs? Can you do it for them?

action on our part. Such service is not far away. Soon—perhaps by the time you read this book—grocery items in supermarkets will carry radio frequency identifiers (RF/IDs). These identifiers enable you to scan shelves, cupboards, and whole warehouses to determine their contents. Indeed, supermarket checkout will become no more complex than wheeling your shopping cart past a scanner without stopping. The point here is not the technology, but the technology enabling you to get to the real origin of the business event.

What do you do with this perspective?

Examine any product use case in your current computer system. Now back away from the computer, back past the employee operating the computer, back past the message given to the employee, back into the outside world where real people—your customers—live. What are those people doing at when the business event occurs? Can you do it for them? Can you invent something to streamline or reduce the work they do before they contact your organization? Do you know what motivates your customers at the time of the business event, and can you insert something into their place of work or home to help them do it? If you can, you will have a very loyal customer.

Start with the context showing the work and not the product.

How do you perform such an investigation on your project? Start with the context diagram showing the work and not the product. Your analysts study the work or what happens before the computerized product is activated. By studying what happens in the work and by looking outside the work area, you come up with a better product. If you don't find a better product this month, your customers will ask for it next month. That, or they depart for another organization that puts in the little extra effort to determine the real work and the real origin of the business event.

What Do I Do with a Business Event?

Let's look at how you might approach an event once you have identified it. As we have said, the response to a business event is a business use case. The objective is to understand business use case well enough to be able to determine the appropriate product use case and specify its requirements.

Figure 4.6 illustrates the cycle for gathering the requirements for a business use case. The activities are not necessarily performed in any particular order, but some must be accomplished before you can start others. Implementation normally occurs fairly late in the cycle, but you can start with a prototype or a model, or almost anywhere else. It is simpler if we explain them in the order shown.

Partitioning the work into business use cases means your analysts can study each one independently, and we study them in this manner. We also assume you are selecting them from the list in some kind of priority

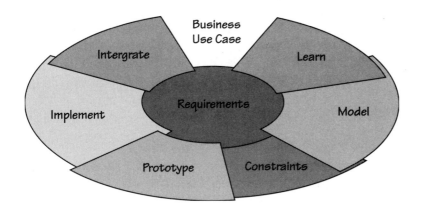

Figure 4.6

The requirements cycle for a business use case. Each of the activities overlaps the others, and they are not necessarily performed in the shown order. The requirements form the core of the cycle.

order. That being stated, the following represents the requirements cycle for a business use case.

Learn

Your analysts need to learn how the work functions for each business use case. For in-house IT projects, the analysts learn by apprenticing with or observing the intended users to discover how the work is currently performed. More on apprenticing later.

If your project aims to build a consumer product, what is the consumer doing with it? Let's take a radio, for example. Learning what a user does with a radio on the surface is easy: The user listens to the radio. However, there is more to it. What does your user listen to? Presumably a program he *wants* to listen to at the time. How was this program selected? Note the user *deciding to listen to the radio* is the business event. *Provide appropriate radio program* is the business use case. Either the listener knows the programs he wants and also knows the frequencies of various stations. Alternatively, he can scan the dial for a suitable program.

Don't think about the radio in this case, think about the listener. If the listener is a person of habit, the radio can "learn" what programs are listened to at what times. No reason exists why the radio cannot then turn itself on to the customary programs at their start times. If the user scans looking for something to listen to, he must know what kind of program he wants—classical music, jazz, talk, news, and so forth. Again, why can't the radio accept the listener's preferred program types and find all of the stations that are currently broadcasting them?

Don't think about the radio, think about the listener.

This is learning, not what the product does now, but what the external agent for the business event is doing. From that you learn the appropriate response your product must make. We find techniques such as event workshops and brainstorming are most effective in determining the best future response to a business event. We have more on this later.

Model

Modeling is another technique for learning more about the business use case (see Figure 4.7). Analysts may build models to help them understand current and future business use cases, to try out ideas on the requirers, and to determine the feasibility of possible approaches. Many models are available to business analysts. For example, UML 2 provides an activity diagram, or you can use data flow models or IStar models or any of the other bewildering array of models that are available. Analysts also use class models, state models, sequence diagrams, and a variety of home-grown diagrams to represent the work.

We mentioned this earlier, but it bears repeating: Models can in some cases serve as functional requirements. If the analysts build a model that correctly demonstrates the required functionality, there may be no reason to transcribe that model into written requirements. It depends on the audience for the requirements. The caveat for doing this is the model must demonstrate correct functionality, be supported by a data dictionary, and describe all functionality in atomic detail.

Figure 4.7

Modeling the processes is a way of understanding and demonstrating the work.

Constraints

Constraints are restrictions that exist, either in the current environment, or as restrictions on what can be designed for the future. Constraints are things like deadline, budget, hardware that must be used, software that must be used, interfaces that cannot be changed. If you have a valid constraint (not just somebody's solution in disguise), it is not negotiable. However you solve the problem, you must adhere to this constraint.

Analysts learn the constraints as they learn the work and build models of the work's response to an event. Knowledge of business use cases together with constraints and goals are the basis for making decisions about product use cases and hence boundaries of the product. Constraints are recorded in the requirements specification along with the functional and nonfunctional requirements.

Knowledge of business use cases together with constraints and goals are the basis for making decisions about product use cases and hence boundaries of the product.

Prototype

By this stage, assuming that you have performed some or all activities in more or less the order described, you determine the product to carry out the requirements. This is usually accomplished by deciding how much of the known functionality needs to be incorporated in your product, and how much remains to be performed by humans or other products.

We cannot give you a formula for determining the product. The exact product depends on the available (or affordable) technology; competitors' products; resources, time, and money available to build it; ongoing operating cost; the client's intentions; hands-on user capabilities; and accommodation of many other factors. However, we *can* say that a prototype focusing on a key business use case is an effective vehicle for involving your client in determining the product boundary and discovering the precise requirements.

Prototypes at this stage demonstrate your intentions for the product. You are stating to your stakeholders: "This is what we envision the product to be. This is the functionality that we intend to include, and these are some of the nonfunctional properties we think are appropriate for the product." The idea is to get agreement and demonstrate the probable outcome of the project. In some cases you reveal new requirements, clarify requirements already discovered, or remove requirements that turn out to be irrelevant or have little benefit.

Prototypes can be in any form—sketches on whiteboards, software prototypes, scenarios, or any of the items we discuss in Chapter 6—Requirements Simulations.

You will find even when you build a prototype, it is still necessary to write requirements—the prototype is not a satisfactory recorder of reasons behind design decisions. Additionally, the prototype might be interpreted by product builders in a number of ways that do not necessarily to reflect actual requirements.

Implement

Implementation is building the product. You cannot complete implementation until you know the product's requirements. Note the intention is to implement one product use case at a time, thus providing feedback to the requirers and justifying the investment to gather the remainder of the requirements.

Integrate

Whatever you have implemented has to be integrated into the working product, and it goes without saying testing is continuous.

As you implement and integrate each business use case, you learn from it. In the cycle, what were the most valuable activities? What were the least valuable? What major problems were encountered? Thus with each cycle you learn to establish the requirements for this project. Apply this learning and move on to the next business use case.

Learning the Work

You are learning about work, so the ideal place to learn it is where the work happens. Your team must be prepared to spend a lot of time in the users' work environment. Here we look at some of the way to learn about the work and discover the requirements.

Apprenticing

> *Craftsmen, like users, are not natural teachers, and teaching is not their primary job.*
>
> —Hugh Beyer and Karen Holtzblatt, *Contextual Design*

This is based on the time tested idea of learning work by doing it: The apprentice learns the work from a master craftsman. In our case, the business analyst is apprenticed to the user and comes to understand the work by spending time under the user's supervision, actually doing the work. Such activity is often preferable to asking a list of questions, because sometimes—especially if unfamiliar with the domain—it is very difficult to know what questions to ask. By becoming an apprentice the analyst learns enough about the work to do it.

Apprenticing is particularly effective when tasks being performed by a hands-on user are well known to him, perhaps too well known. We all tend to become less conscious of what we are doing when it becomes familiar—for example, do you think about how to manipulate the car when you are driving? By having the business analyst sit with the user and observe and do the work, unconscious requirements are more likely to come to light (see Figure 4.8).

Figure 4.8

The analyst is apprenticed to the hands-on user and learns the work by watching, asking questions and finally doing it himself.

Add to this the advantage users do not have to take time away from their work, which is often seen as a nuisance. In any event, a user is far more likely to be better at explaining the work while doing it.

Event Workshops

Workshops are intensive sessions involving requirers and analysts. The objective is to find the desired response to each business event. The analysts demonstrate understanding of the business use case using whatever artifacts—scenarios, models, prototypes, and so on—the requirers can best relate to.

When the business use case is well-enough understood, the next step for workshop participants is to determine the product boundary and thus the product use case. This boundary is determined by considering the work to be done along with goals and constraints. The objective is to come up with the most effective product to help with the work. Scenarios are useful to demonstrate how the proposed product is to be used in the workplace. The scenario demonstrates the actions taken by the product and the actions taken by its user. When the product's actions are known, analysts write the functional and nonfunctional requirements for them.

We recommend your team use event workshops when requirers are unsure of the details of the business use case, and when they can spend time away from their work. Workshops are effective when an element of invention is needed to come up with the best response to an event. We

Workshops are effective when an element of invention is needed.

usually create better products by using the energy and ideas that come from analysts and requirers working together in the same room.

Brainstorming

Although we are talking about eliciting requirements from the stakeholders, every requirements project has some room for invention. We talk about this more in the next chapter. Brainstorming is an effective way of inventing, and works because a group of people is more likely to come up with great ideas than a solitary requirements analyst working alone. Brainstorming works because each brainstormer gets seeds of ideas from the others that then individually trigger better ideas (see Figure 4.9).

A brainstorming session is fairly simple to set up: A like-minded group from your team starts with the objective for the session. This objective should be well defined enough to head the brainstorm session in the right direction, and open-ended enough to not preclude reasonable possibilities. So instead of "The objective is to come up with ideas to put MP3 music on wireless phones," try "Let's explore options for portable phones, including MP3."

Number your ideas. It shows how well you are doing.

During the session—which should last about an hour—record and number all ideas on whiteboards, flipchart paper taped to the wall, or if needs be write on the walls. Computer screens are too small for participants to see all the ideas generated. Keep in mind each participant is using ideas already generated to build on and trigger his or her own better ideas. Number your ideas so participants can refer to them easily and to give everyone a sense of how well they are doing. If, for example, after 30 minutes you have only 5 ideas on the wall, abandon the session, it is

Figure 4.9

Brainstorming uses the human ability to inspire one another to produce better ideas. A brainstorm produces as many ideas as possible, before weeding out the unworkable and impractical.

going nowhere. On the other hand, if participants see those 30 minutes have produced 30 or more ideas and some of them are quite promising, they are motivated to come up with more.

After the generation session, evaluate the ideas and discard the truly unworkable or unsuitable ones. As it is likely you will have more ideas than you can comfortably fit into your schedule, prioritize them using the same techniques we discuss in Chapter 9—Managing the Requirements.

Do not expect your team to be effective if they walk into a brainstorm cold. To be productive they must do their homework beforehand. Ask them to look at examples of similar products, or search the Web, or talk to people who know something about the intended product. The more participants know before the brainstorm, the more familiar they are with the problem, the more creative their ideas can be.

Interviewing

Interviewing is the most widely used requirements trawling technique. We do not spend a lot of time on it here because most people working today as business analysts or requirements engineers already have fairly sound interviewing skills.

Interviewing is best when you have the opportunity to talk to a stakeholder about a bounded area of subject matter. To get maximum benefit from the interview, have a well-formed intention of the information you're seeking. We suggest you:

1. Define the purpose and boundary of your interview so that you can keep it on track.
2. Have a fixed time limit.
3. Talk to the people who have hands-on experience with the subject.
4. Use models and sketches to feedback and improve your understanding.
5. Listen, listen, listen to your interviewee.
6. Illustrate the relevance of the interview by highlighting something significant you have learned.
7. Thank the interviewee for giving you the time.

Interviewing can be very effective but is often misused. Misuse stems from the expectation people know what they want, and if we ask them they will be able to explain it. Not so. When we say "listen, listen, listen" we really mean "Listen to what is being said, and try and understand *why* it is being said." Even if the people you are talking to do not explain themselves initially, most people given enough time and gentle prodding, will reveal their motives and aspirations.

Listen to what is being said, and try and understand why it is being said.

The Essence of the Work

One of the most disappointing aspects of our consulting work is to see solutions developed before the real problem is understood. We think we know why. People do not have a suitable language to talk about their business problem. For example, suppose that you are talking to a hotel booking clerk about his work. He tells you,

> When a customer calls and asks for a hotel room, he gives me the dates and the price range that he wants to pay. I use our internal Web site that shows me all available choices. Before I read any of them I look in the binder here that has late specials, memos about special customers to see if there are any overriding instructions from the boss. Then I go through the list with the customer starting at the Web site's first choice. When we agree on one, I book it through our parent company's Web service. That automatically links to the hotel I have selected . . .

This description is about *how* he does his work at the moment—the implementation he uses. It is probably not what you would see in a few years time when technology has changed. Nor is it what you would have seen a few years ago when technology was different. And yet, the actual business being carried out by her organization, booking hotel rooms, has not changed fundamentally over the years. If you disregard the technology and physical artifacts the clerk uses, you begin to see the underlying business reason. We call this underlying reason the *essence*.

To find the real business, look past the physical artifacts and see its underlying reason.

For example, suppose you need to know the cheapest price for a component used in a device your company manufactures. You can look in all the catalogs on the bookshelf and find each price, keeping track and going back to the cheapest; you can search Web sites and do something similar; you can access a Web site that gives competitive prices for this component; you can write a Web crawler that searched every online database to find the best price.

Regardless of how you do it, the essence of the problem seems to be to find the cheapest price. But is it deeper than that? Why do you need the cheapest price? Is the essence really to *buy* at the cheapest price? Knowing a price and buying at that price are different things. For example, you can ask suppliers to bid on supplying the component. This can often result in you being able to buy the component at a cheaper, nonpublished price. Or perhaps the essence is to *have* the component at the cheapest price. Perhaps your company can make the component itself and by saving transportation charges, get the component at the cheapest possible price.

The point of this is essence. The essence is the underlying business, and not any of its implementations. The essence is the work, the trade, the commerce, the policy, the business rules of the organization. The essence exists regardless of how the work is done, or what technology is used.

The essence is the soul of the work.

We stress this because you are trying to learn the true work, not the first guess about the technology that *might* be appropriate for that work. When you talk to people, they usually tell you their solution to the work situation, and not the situation itself. The essence lies beneath the solution. You can think of it as the soul of the work.

We can make abstractions from what is said to reveal the essence. We live in a technological world in which it is fairly natural for people to talk in technological terms. For example, a stakeholder might say that he sends an email. This is how at some time in the past he has chosen to implement "a fairly immediate communication." There are other ways of making this kind of communication, so you should consider email as a solution, and abstract its underlying essence.

Why make this abstraction? Because the implementation may be concealing the real business need. If the need is to reach many employees with the same message, then email, though convenient to the sender, may fail its purpose. Many corporate employees today get about 100 emails a day. How do you ensure yours is read? And does the solution conceal the fundamental purpose? Is it appropriate to email an announcement of a restructuring? Probably not as an email almost certainly serves to add to the uncertainty surrounding most corporate restructures.

People can only tell you about the technology they know. Usually this is based on the technological experience of the teller, and is not as up to date as it should be. If you listen to proposed solutions, and not the essence, you risk reimplementing whatever the current system happens to be. The essence, when you find it, is independent of any technology that can be used. McMenamin and Palmer describe this as *perfect technology*.

By seeing the essence your analysts see the real work and not a perceived solution to the problem.

They ask you to imagine the system if it were implemented using a technology that was failsafe (no backups), infinitely fast (no batching), had infinite memory (no Web searches), and was free and occupied no real estate. We guess it would also have a telepathic interface. They offer this idea to suggest if you have perfect technology, all you implement are essential processes, and nothing to do with implementation technology.

Figure 4.10 shows two implementations of the same essence. The top example is a firewall. Firewalls act, as the illustration shows, by blocking traffic from the Internet. To allow someone from the outside to connect to your computer, you have to punch a hole in the firewall. The bottom illustration shows the filtering approach. Here all incoming traffic is inspected for suspicious behavior, and if any is found the filter blocks that and any future intrusions of that kind. While these two styles of protection go about their business in different ways, the essence of either is they protect your computer from intruders on the Internet.

Figure 4.10

Two ways of protecting your computer from the Internet. While the technology of the two is quite different, their essence is the same.

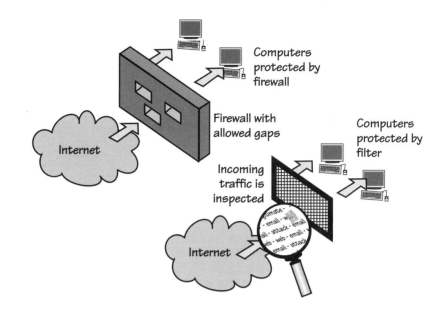

Simply asking "Why?" often reveals the essence.

The implication of essence for your analysts is that they need to look beyond any requirement that suggests an implementation. Simply asking "Why?" often reveals the essence. On our requirements Snow Cards we make a space for the answer to the question. Figure 4.11 shows components of a requirement. Note *Rationale,* the justification of the requirement. The analyst uses the rationale to find the reasoning behind the request, which is often the essence of the requirement.

Feedback Using Requirements

An atomic requirement is perhaps the most precise and powerful device a business analyst can use to communicate with requirers. By atomic requirement we mean the requirement must be written to build a communication bridge. Snow cards, shown in Figure 4.11, are a low-tech but highly immediate technique to record requirements. If your project is large, you will naturally use some kind of automated requirements tool. Most of our clients configure their tool to look somewhat like the original snow card. Let's demonstrate three of the attributes we record when gathering requirements. These are *Description, Rationale,* and *Fit Criterion.*

The *Description* is whatever the requirer says he wants or needs. Suppose your analyst is working on the requirements for a home financial management product and your requirer asks for a product "that allows him to write provisional checks." That's the *Description.* We suggest you record whatever the requirer says, then consider the next part of the

| Requirement #: 110 | Requirement Type: 11 | Event/use case #: 6, 7, 8, 9, 10 |

Description: **The product shall be easy to use.**

Rationale: **We want our customers to switch to using the product in preference to calling us on the phone.**

Source: **Phillip Marlowe, Operations**

Fit Criterion: **Within three months, 60% of order-tracking inquiries will be done using the Web product.**

Customer Satisfaction: **3**   Customer Dissatisfaction: **5**

Dependencies: **None**   Conflicts: **None**

Supporting Materials:

History: **Raised by AG. 04/06/21**

Volere
Copyright © Atlantic Systems Guild

Figure 4.11

The Volere Snow Card. These are printed on 5 by 8 inch cards and we use them as a temporary requirements-capture device. We use it here to illustrate the components of a requirement, particularly the description, rationale, and fit criterion. Note how the requirement starts as a vague statement, and is formed into a testable requirement that reflects the requirer's true need.

requirement. *Rationale* is a justification of the requirement. To find it, ask "Why?"

"Why do you want to write provisional checks?"

"Well, sometimes I do not have enough money in the account and don't want to write checks that will overdraw the account."

Note what is happening here: The original statement "The product shall write provisional checks" is really the requirer's *assumed solution to the problem*. By asking for a rationale, the analyst discovers a slightly or significantly different requirement that has not been explicitly stated so far. The description and rationale have led to an understanding that the requirer does not want the product to pay a bill when insufficient money is in the account. Which leads to the *Fit Criterion*.

The *Fit Criterion* makes the requirement testable such that any solution to the requirement can be categorized as either it fits the requirement or it does not fit the requirement. In this case, the fit criterion seems to be the product shall not write a check that reduces the balance to less than a predetermined amount (it is probable that the requirer does not want the balance to go all the way to zero).

A requirement that is not testable is not a requirement.

If you look more intently at this example, it may be that the requirer's original request is not only a solution, but also is the *wrong* solution. Perhaps the real need here is for the product to categorize all the requirer's bills in order of due date and write enough checks to reduce the account balance such that it always remains above a predetermined level.

Notice when you ask enough questions to write the fit criterion, you raise other requirements questions such as:

- What does the requirer mean by due date?
- Is the predetermined level always the same, or can it vary depending on the number of days before payday?
- Is due date the only criterion for prioritization?

Any of these could be critical requirements. It would be a pity to miss them.

We have structured the requirement so if the business analyst uses *Description, Rationale,* and *Fit Criterion,* it makes it practically impossible not to discover the true need. But this act of discovery needs the cooperation of the requirer. The requirer not only participates, he also receives feedback—reinforcement really—that the analyst is working hard trying to understand and eventually deliver a product that will be beneficial to the requirer. We can think of no better inducement for requirers to participate in the requirements process.

Feedback Using Models

Prototypes and models play an interesting part in the elicitation of requirements: They are an unambiguous demonstration of some part of the work, or some part of the product.

As an example, we have discussed the context model as a way of demonstrating the scope of the work. We arrive at the model by negotiating and reaching a consensus with appropriate stakeholders. At all stages of the negotiation, stakeholders can see exactly what functionality is included and what is specifically excluded. Thus, the context diagram unambiguously demonstrates the boundary of the work. This kind of feedback about the scope of the requirements investigation enables your team and the other stakeholders to trap misunderstandings early.

66 A picture reveals overall pattern and structure by showing each part in relationship to the whole. 99

—Hugh Beyer and Karen Holtzblatt, *Contextual Design*

Similarly, when we use other kinds of models—data flow, entity-relationship, class models, state models, and so on—stakeholders always appreciate what we are showing them. Little need for imagination (and possible misunderstanding) exists on their part. They can see what we are telling them, and thus participate more fully in the requirements process.

Diagrammatic models are part of the feedback story. Prototypes are another. In Chapter 6 we discuss use of simulations. By using a variety of techniques, you bring your ideas, and those of your stakeholders, to life and create an early feedback loop. We have found being able to show simulations to requirers accelerates the job of requirements discovery.

Choosing the Appropriate Technique

The trawling techniques we use must continue to keep pace with our ambition in terms of size, complexity, fragmentation, and level of human involvement in the products we build. With the growth in the number of techniques available comes the question, "Which technique is the best one in a given set of circumstances?" No simple answer exists to this question because the choice of technique is driven by characteristics of the knowledge source, and in most cases that means the characteristics of individual people. This situation leads to the necessity of using techniques in combination. To aid these choices, think of the strength of a technique in terms of its ability to discover *conscious, unconscious,* and *undreamed of* requirements.

The requirer is well aware of conscious requirements. These may be new requirements or things uppermost in his mind. Unconscious requirements on the other hand are things so common, so routine, or so longstanding the requirer forgets they are needed. Undreamed of requirements are things the requirer has no idea that he could have and consequently does not ask for them.

When you interview someone they are most likely to tell you about their conscious requirements. Apprenticing is likely to uncover unconscious requirements, because the requirements analyst observes requirements the stakeholder does not mention—they are simply too familiar. Brainstorming is very good for undreamed of requirements because it helps to free people from preconceived ideas and encourages them to dream.

The sociological profiles of projects drive the need for discovering new trawling techniques. Technological advances encourage organizations to become more ambitious, which results in projects involving more people in more locations. Which in turn leads to the need for trawling techniques to deal with these specific situations.

For instance, if your project involves stakeholders from a wide variety of different organizations you have an increasing need for helping very different people to talk to each other. Rather than start from scratch, we have discovered we can draw inspiration from several other disciplines. For example, the field of family therapy provides useful ideas for dealing with conflicts and helping people to converge.

The sociological profiles of projects drive the need for discovering new trawling techniques.

If your sources of requirements are scattered, a combination of surveys, systems archaeology, and use case workshops for the event owners often works in this situation.

Figure 4.12 summarizes various trawling techniques along with indications of what we have experienced as their relative strengths. Note we have not discussed all the techniques mentioned in Figure 4.12. If you

Figure 4.12 This table groups trawling techniques according to their applicability to activities of Strategy and Planning, Capture and Generation, or Analysis. Each technique is graded according to its relative strengths in discovering conscious, unconscious, and undreamed of requirements: 1 = limited effectiveness, 2 = effective, 3 = very effective

Trawling Technique	Strengths	Conscious	Unconscious	Undreamed
Strategy and Planning				
Business Events	Partitions a system according to functional business happenings	3	2	1
Family Therapy	Uses knowledge of family behavior to understand stakeholder groups	1	3	1
Soft Systems	Uses systems thinking to understand a problem	2	2	2
System Viewpoints	Takes a number of different points of view in parallel	2	2	2
Capture and Generation				
Apprenticing	Spend time observing the expert and learning the questions to ask	2	3	1
Brainstorming	Facilitate creativity and invention	1	1	3
Interviewing	Good for one-to-one communication, works best when interviewer has prepared for guiding the interview	3	2	1
Mind Mapping	Use nonprocedural technique for gathering information then discovering useful connections	2	2	3
Scenarios	Help people relate to the problem from their own point of view and stimulates ideas	2	2	2
Low-Fi Prototypes	Stimulate imagination through a combination of informal sketches and artifacts that quickly stimulate imagination	2	3	3
Hi-Fi Prototypes	Formally (usually automated) demonstrate an interface or product feature that uncovers assumptions	3	2	1
Systems Archaeology	Review existing documents to arrive at a structured understanding of a domain	1	3	1
Help Desk Review	Observe what is happening every day to better define scope of the investigation	2	3	1

Figure 4.12 (*cont.*)

Trawling Technique	Strengths	Conscious	Unconscious	Undreamed
Event Workshop	Start with a group of people studying a business event, then derive the business use case, constraints, and the product use case leading to atomic requirements	3	2	2
Surveys/ Questionnaires	Gather input from a large number of people; success depends on the design of the survey	2	1	1
Video	View the video as many times as necessary to extract requirements	2	3	1
Analysis				
Principle of Essence	Focus on the fundamental problem independent of solutions	1	2	2
Neurolinguistic Programming	Helps in getting from the general to the specific; identifies linguistic patterns that can cause loss of meaning	1	3	1
Reusing Requirements	Prevent duplication of effort	2	2	1

want more information please refer to our previous book *Mastering the Requirements Process,* Suzanne Robertson's article "Requirements Trawling: Techniques for Discovering Requirements,"[1] or one of the books identified in the Resources section at the end this chapter.

The Importance of Culture

Culture is what people value. So it is safe to say people are reluctant to depart from their cultural norms. You must understand your target audience's culture to ensure your product does not deviate from it, nor should your product introduce elements foreign to the culture.

Culture is sometimes quite subtle. Tim Lister, one of our partners at the Atlantic Systems Guild, was involved in a system for Wall Street traders. These guys participate in the "Masters of the Universe" world of buying and selling stocks on the New York Stock exchange. Tim heard one of them say "Traders don't type." They considered typing to be suitable

1. Robertson, Suzanne. "Requirements Trawling: Techniques for Discovering Requirements," *International Journal of Human-Computer Studies,* Volume 55 number 4. Academic Press.

Figure 4.13

Culture dictates a certain way of doing business. If your product is to succeed, it must work correctly and take account of cultural mores of your target audience.

only for back-office staff, foreign to the culture of a floor trader. If the development team had delivered a product with a keyboard, the traders would have refused to use it. This potentially show-stopping requirement is purely cultural.

Culture is often invisible, rarely written down, and not always recognized by people who are behaving in conformance with it. For example, your authors are very fond of Burgundy wine. In our early trips to the winemakers' cellars we noticed they seemed slightly reluctant to sell us their wine. However, after repeated visits, the situation improved (from our point of view) and we were able to buy more of their product. In some cases, we were able to purchase wines to which we had not previously been given access.

This slightly strange behavior was later explained to us as part of French culture (see Figure 4.13). One has to become a *fidèle client* (true customer) before a merchant is truly happy to deal with you. Yet very few French people with whom we deal will actually come out and say they behave this way.

Your requirers have a work culture. They may be quiet, orderly people who dislike noise and any apparent disarray. On the other hand, we have worked with groups who are gregarious and like a certain amount of activity noises to be part of their work environment. Ask yourself this: Do you have a sound that plays when a new email arrives? Does the computer belonging to the guy next to you play a tune when email arrives? Does this drive you crazy? Or do you consider it part of the workday environment? These are questions of culture.

Culture is often invisible, rarely written down, and not always recognized by people who are behaving in conformance with it.

When we compiled the Volere Requirements Specification Template, we included a category of requirements called "Cultural and Political." This category prompts the business analysts to ask questions about the intended users' feelings about work and what they value. Just as we change our opinions to conform to groups to which we wish to belong (don't ask yourself if you have ever changed your opinion to fit with a group, you are not aware that you are doing it) we also adopt cultural artifacts of groups to which we wish to belong.

These cultural artifacts—colors, images, styles, music, and so on—become requirements. Or at least the business analysts have to recognize the cultural requirement so designers can find appropriate images or whatever. Analysts must also recognize cultural taboos and ensure the product does not contravene them.

Spelling and the words we use are cultural. There are well known, and often joked about, differences between how Americans use the English language, and how other countries use it. While generally these are harmless and amusing—to "knock someone up" in the UK means calling at his front door—there are some that could cause confusion or inconvenience. We know of one American who was sent around the world when he asked his Asian client for a "round-trip ticket." In the world outside the U.S., when you go to a destination and back it's called a "return ticket."

We can sum up cultural considerations by stating if you plan to deploy your product outside your own country—such as a Web product—a cultural advisor should be one of your stakeholders.

Incremental Delivery of the Product

We have already mentioned the importance of feedback in the requirements elicitation process. We want to amplify that here by mentioning the value to business analysts of being able to demonstrate results of the requirements process. If they show the time spent gathering requirements is not wasted, but rather results in a product completely relevant to the requirer, the analysts are far more likely to get wholesale cooperation for the remainder of the project.

You create positive dynamics if you deliver a product incrementally, as well as deliver parts of the product with the highest business value first. The requirers in this case must determine the parts of the product most useful to them. In most cases these are recognizable business events. We suggest you prioritize your list of business events in conjunction with the requirers to arrive at the optimum delivery plan for the product.

Another aid to elicitation is when you deliver an early partial product; you get confirmation your scope is correct and that you and your requirers are indeed working on the correct product.

The Big Picture

Even though it consumes your daily life like almost nothing else, your project is only one part of the whole picture. Your organization is building a network of systems to be deployed throughout the entire organization. Keep in mind your sources of requirements are localized. Their business problem is of paramount importance to them, but you need to look further afield. You have to see how your product connects to the rest of the organization. Otherwise you end up with a patchwork of products, each solving a local problem and working only difficultly with other products. The danger here is overlapping the functionality of other products, of duplicating data unnecessarily, and not making best use of development resources.

See Chapter 10—Requirements Meta-Management for more on how to manage the dependencies between projects.

Although we cover the big picture in Chapter 10, we mention it here, as you may sometimes find it necessary to remind your analysts they need to liaise with other projects to ensure that inputs and outputs match exactly those of the adjoining projects.

Requirements Elicitation

There are several points about the elicitation of requirements we would like to leave you with.

First, requirements are free if you pay for them. Numerous studies and surveys have conclusively shown the effort put into gathering of correct requirements is more than compensated by the rework avoided as a result. Free does not mean you don't have to put the work into discovering requirements. And it does not mean doing requirements work is cheap, it's not. But when you look at the entire cost of development, effort you expend on requirements is always paid back with interest.

Requirements are free if you pay for them.

How much does it cost? We usually advise our clients to expect to spend one-third to one-half their development budget on requirements, analysis, and design. This half-budget figure is not scientifically measured: It comes from our observation of projects that deliver the right product on time and within budget. That sounds like a lot of money, but many traditional projects waste *more* than half their final expenditure on debugging. (Debugging is correcting defects introduced by skimping on requirements, analysis, and design and coding so that the project can arrive at the debugging stage earlier.) We do not mean half the project time elapses before anything besides requirements is started. If you have short release cycles, then requirements, analysis, and design should take up about half the expenditure for each cycle.

Next, requirements come from people. Your business analysts have to sit down with your stakeholders and discover the requirements. The process cannot be automated; it entails figuring out what people truly need—they cannot be relied upon to know this—so it takes time.

Finally, because you are writing requirements in nontechnical albeit precise language, you can focus the involvement of the appropriate stakeholders in parts of the specification directly relevant to them. Your project team gets more accurate answers because stakeholders understand the requirements rather than having to wait until the product is built and then saying, "Hmmm, what I really meant was. . . ."

What Do I Do Right Now?

Eliciting requirements is about finding the real needs for the product. This alone makes the activity worthwhile. But let's revisit project success indicators from Chapter 1 and consider the effect of good elicitation techniques.

PSIs relevant to this section read like everybody's wish list for their next project. However, consider how they can be met by better elicitation of the real requirements. The first indicators are

- No excessive schedule pressure
- On-budget delivery
- Lack of creeping requirements
- Control of changes

You meet these by establishing the scope of the project using a context model or some similar and compatible model. We stress here the context model demonstrates through its boundary data flows the precise functionality contained therein. It is also suitable for counting function points as an accurate measurement of the amount of effort needed for requirements analysis. By fully using this model, you are able to predict and monitor effort, as well as monitor and regulate changes for the project.

Another PSI is *good-quality code*. It has been the experience of our clients that by knowing exactly what is needed, your programmers write the code once and do not have to constantly change it.

Additional PSIs are as follows:

- User or customer satisfaction.
- Correctly sized product.
- No nasty surprises.
- The product conforms to product goals or company vision.

These are addressed by finding the right requirements. Simple to say and obviously much harder to do. However, we have outlined some techniques in this chapter that make it easier for your analysts to get the right requirements. Also consider that business events partition the work into convenient study units, allowing for incremental delivery.

- No misunderstood requirements.
- Testing is effective.

Analysts use a fit criterion to determine the precise requirement. You negotiate the criterion with the requirer so both parties reach an exact understanding of what it really needed. The fit criterion is a quantification of the requirement such that it is readily testable. Your quality assurance people should consult with the analysts on how to write effective fit criteria, and naturally, the quality assurance people are stakeholders in all your projects.

Another PSI is *adequate documentation*. The requirements themselves are the best documentation. The requirement, as we have suggested it here, carries with it the reasoning behind the need. We have found over the years, adequate documentation is most valuable when requirements are changed or when the inevitable version 2 of the product needs building.

No litigation is the last of the PSIs. This sadly is becoming a major risk of product development, especially contracted software development. In all litigation we have seen or on which we have been consulted, lack of an adequate requirements specification has been common. If you are building your product for a second party, it is crucial to correctly record its requirements, which includes a way for you to demonstrate the delivered product exactly matches (fits) the client's needs.

What's the Least I Can Get Away With?

Taking shortcuts is risky here, but since you asked we suggest the following:

- Set the scope of your study using a context model. We know of no better method than a context model to negotiate the scope of the project with the stakeholders, to communicate the scope to your team, and to ensure all requirements are relevant and within scope.
- Partition the context using business events. The response to each business event—the business use case—is a self-contained unit of work, and is a convenient amount of work for your analysts to study.
- Use event workshops with selected stakeholders as a way of eliciting the business use case for each event. Many project leaders use the completion of analysis for each event to keep track of the project. Simply ticking off each business use case as it is completed is not as precise as it could be, but is a reasonable substitute for accurate project measuring.
- We cannot state the importance of *essence* too strongly. By discovering the real requirements, and not some proposed solution, you have a far better chance of building a product that has relevance and a long life.
- Provide feedback to your stakeholders. Keep them in the loop and keep them informed of the requirements you have gathered. They are the source of your requirements; they should be aware of progress and the state of the requirements.

CHOCOLATE

Many years ago when we first visited Thailand we fell in love with the spicy, fresh taste of the cuisine. We decided we wanted to learn how to cook it and searched for books that would teach us the secrets of how to create these wonderful tastes. When we asked our Thai friend why so few books existed about the cuisine she was astonished. She told us Thai people do not write their recipes down, they learn to cook by watching and doing, and she invited us to come and work with her in her kitchen. What followed was a most enjoyable revelation of new (to us) ingredients like wing beans, birds-eye chilies, and lemon grass. And most important, the specific Thai preparation and cooking techniques.

Since then, many books have been written about Thai cooking. The most notable one is *Thai Food* by David Thompson. His studies in Thai kitchens led him to the understanding that Thai cooking reached its best in the last decades of the nineteenth century, and was the cooking of the Thai Royal Court which includes the most complex and ambitious of Thai dishes. His intention—carried out very successfully—was to describe this cuisine in English before modern influences change it so that dishes are lost or altered. Here is one of the least complex recipes from his book.

4 long green or Japanese eggplants	large pinch of roasted chili powder
2 tablespoons mint leaves	2 tablespoons lime juice
3 red shallots, sliced	1 tablespoon fish sauce
2 tablespoons chopped spring (green) onion	half teaspoon ground dried prawns

Grill the eggplant until charred and soft. Place in a bowl, cover until cool, and then peel. Add all the other ingredients except the prawns to the bowl with the eggplants and combine. The salad should taste smoky, hot, and equally sour and salty. Arrange on a plate and sprinkle with the ground dried prawns.

Additional Resources for Learning What People Need

The following sources, in addition to those already referenced, have useful information on learning what people need.

- Alexander, Ian, and Richard Stevens. *Writing Better Requirements.* Addison-Wesley, 2002—*Understandable and practical advice on how to write clear and simple requirements. Includes helpful hints on how to involve stakeholders in negotiating requirements.*
- Beyer, Hugh, and Karen Holtzblatt. *Contextual Design—Defining Customer-centered Systems.* Morgan Kaufmann, 1998—*Highly recommended, discusses how analysts work with users to learn the work. Wonderful insights in each chapter.*
- Checkland, Peter. *Systems Thinking, Systems Practice.* John Wiley & Sons, 1981—*Systems-thinking models to identify useful viewpoints and to guide the development of systems.*
- Gause, Donald, and Gerald Weinberg. *Exploring Requirements: Quality before Design.* Dorset House, 1989—*Very readable book packed with examples of how to discover the relevant requirements.*
- Gottesdiener, Ellen. *Requirements by Collaboration—Workshops for Defining Needs.* Addison-Wesley, 2002—*Contains lots of ideas, tools and techniques for planning and running workshops to discover requirements.*
- Hoffman, Lynn. *Foundations of Family Therapy.* Basic Books, U.S.A., 1981—*Explains the principles behind family therapy, many of which can be used to help stakeholders communicate with one another.*
- Jackson, Michael. *Problem Frames—Analyzing and structuring software development problems.* Addison-Wesley, 2001—*Jackson talks here about looking at the problem instead of leaping into the solution. He defines the problem using problem frames to give you a clearer view of it.*
- Maiden, Neil, and Gordon Rugg. "ACRE: selecting methods for requirements acquisition." *Software Engineering Journal.* May 1996—*The ACRE framework identifies a set of trawling techniques and discusses their application.*
- McMenamin, Steve, and John Palmer. *Essential Systems Analysis.* Yourdon Press, 1984—*Their idea of business events remains the most useful for partitioning work areas. This is because business events are based on the work itself and how it relates to its surroundings. The business event response is the relevant use case.*
- Robertson, Suzanne and James. *Mastering the Requirements Process.* Addison-Wesley, 1999.
- Wiegers, Karl. *Software Requirements.* Microsoft Press, 1999—*Contains helpful advice on how to find and hear the voice of the customer.*

Inventing Requirements

The requirements activity is traditionally seen as specifying the product the stakeholders say they want. However, some of our most useful products are things that nobody asked for: the mobile telephone, the World Wide Web, the personal computer, and many others. Once they were invented we wonder how we got along without them. Your task is to deliver a product your customers will use. By inventing part of it and helping others to be inventive, you are more likely to deliver a product that becomes an essential part of your customer's work.

Traditionally, the task of the business analyst is talking to the stakeholders, finding out how they work, determining what they need, asking what they want, specifying a requirements document, and getting the designers and developers to build it. While the traditional approach is still needed, something is missing: It doesn't necessarily *improve* anything. To make things better, when you understand the true nature of the business, we suggest adding a step to the requirements activity: "Invent something better." This chapter describes how you can increase the value of your product by inventing something better.

It doesn't matter what your project is. It may be to build another order-entry system, or payroll, or the eighteenth incarnation of the management information system. Regardless of how mundane or run-of-the-mill

> *Our job is to give the client, on time and on cost, not what he wants, but what he never dreamed he wanted; and when he gets it, he recognizes it as something he wanted all the time.*
>
> —Dewys Lasdon, *designer*

Figure 5.1

The mobile phone is an example of an invention—something that nobody asked for until they saw one. Once you have one, you wonder how you ever got along without it.

your project is, if you want to move it into the 21st century, you must add the title "inventor" to the skill set of your team (see Figure 5.1). Let us explain why, and suggest how you and your team can become inventors.

Look at your computer and its interface. That interface is an invention. Whatever interface you are looking at is a descendant of the graphical user interface (GUI) developed for the Star system at Xerox PARC. But at the time the team was developing the Star, nobody was asking for it; people seemed quite content with the command line interfaces of the day. Yet this unrequested invention, or a derivative, is now implemented on practically every personal computer in the world.

We have been making telephone calls (nobody asked for the telephone before Alexander Graham Bell invented it) for quite a few decades. Yet we cannot recall people saying "Gee, I really wish I had a telephone that I could carry around in my pocket." Why? Because until the mobile phone was invented people did not know they could have it. So naturally they did not ask for it. What about that cool PDA you bought recently? Before you knew they existed did you ask for one? But now that you have these things, do you think you could get along without them?

And what about all the other highly visible things that nobody asked for?

- Gutenberg's printing press is a prime example of something that everybody uses but nobody asked for.
- MP3s: Most of us were happy to play music from our collection using a CD player until we were told we could download or upload music from the Web, rip our CDs, and play them on our computers or iPods.
- Spreadsheets: when VisiCalc first appeared, accountants rushed out and bought an Apple II just so they could run spreadsheets. Why hadn't they asked their internal IT department for a spreadsheet?
- World Wide Web: How many people would have thought of asking for a GUI into the Internet so we could read our newspapers online,

buy books, look at photos of other people's children, or read all the technical information you can consume?

- Digital photography: One of the authors (James) has been a photographer, shooting film for most of his life. He never thought to ask for a camera that would bypass the paper stage.
- PDF: We can send a printed page to anyone and they get exactly what we send. We used to do this by sending a printed page. We never complained when we sent the paper version in lieu of sending an email where precious formatting could be lost.
- When Diners' Club introduced the credit card in 1950, not many people had asked for it. But how many plastic cards are in your possession now?
- The computer mouse was invented in 1963. This predated GUIs, so nobody then was asking for it.
- And let us not forget the computer itself. Admittedly it was invented to meet a need, but the early predictions were that never more than 100 would be made in the whole world. John von Neumann and company never imagined that high school students would do their homework on one, nor that five-year-olds would play games on a computer. For our purposes, we can call the computer an invention.

All these products, and countless others that make a difference, came about by invention, not by people asking for them. Invention then can make your next product one your customers use with new enthusiasm. Not because it has everything they asked for, but because it has something they didn't.

Your customers ask for constant improvements. And they keep asking until they jump ship for a new technology. Some of our readers are old enough to remember vinyl records. (For younger readers, music used to be recorded onto 12-inch-diameter flat discs made from black vinyl. These were rotated on a turntable, and a diamond-tipped stylus picked up the music by vibrating in the grooves on the disc. Ask your father about it.) Recorded music enthusiasts constantly clamored for better and better turntables, and kept on clamoring right up until Philips invented compact discs. At that point enthusiasts abandoned their turntables and vinyl and started buying CDs.

In his book, *The Innovator's Dilemma*, author Clayton Christensen gives examples of companies that were leaders in their field, but eventually went out of business when some "disruptive" technology came along. It was not that they did not know about the new technology, rather they were unable to resist the siren call of their customers to keep improving the current range of products. In turn, customers abandoned them when capabilities of the new technologies surpassed those of the old.

> *"Our most beloved products were developed by hunch, guesswork, and fanaticism, by creators who were eccentric— or even stark raving mad."*
>
> —Jack Mingo, *How the Cadillac Got Its Fins*

❝ The customer is a rear-view mirror, not a guide to the future. ❞

—George Colony, Forrester Research

We must avoid becoming victims of our customers. Our task is not to accommodate their never-ending flow of requests to perfect the current order-entry process, but to invent a brand new way of processing orders, one that gives your client a great competitive advantage. The task is not to provide every button and pull-down menu your hands-on user asks of you, but to invent some completely new way of doing things, one that will thrill and amaze him. Once he sees it, he wonders how he got along without it.

Infrastructure

Information technology (IT) provides the infrastructure for every organization. From now on, every advance your organization makes is dependent on IT. The IT department is not only responsible for keeping the infrastructure working well, but also must frequently make significant improvement to that infrastructure. The "technology" part of IT means just that: making use of innovative technologies, making innovative use of technology, inventing new technologies, and inventing better ways of working.

❝ You can't shrink your way to greatness. ❞

—Arthur Martinex, chairman and CEO Sears-Roebuck

This quote from the then Sears CEO about not shrinking your way to greatness is particularly appropriate. In these days of cost cutting and downsizing and trimming every possible piece of organizational fat, we tend to lose sight of the goal. While having a slim, agile organization is commendable, it does not guarantee you stay in business. To stay and prevail in business, you need to invent new products or services, or new ways to deliver your product or service.

The term "inventing" does not mean a random moment of inspiration. We are not talking about the lonely inventor shouting "Eureka!" from the bathtub. Some strong guides exist concerning what you should be inventing and how you might go about inventing something better for your client. If you think inventing is too strong a word, try "design or discover a better way to," then consider the following areas for invention. At least one of the headings below represents an area in which you can make an inventive difference to your organization.

Service

Think of the product that your company sells to its customers. How different is that product from the one offered by your competitors? Is it unique? Is it so different no consumer would consider an alternative? Or is it, as almost all products on offer today, only marginally different from those of its competitors? In which case, providing a better service may well be the way to differentiate your organization and product from your competitors.

For example, how many banks are there with a branch close to you? Likely more than one. They all offer much the same in the way of products—various account types, competitive interest rates, ATMs, and so on—so it is probably the level of service that makes you choose one bank rather than another. Most of us leave a bank if another bank offers a noticeably better level of service. Your customers are looking at your organization the same way you look at your retail bank.

The requirement is to invent a better service.

If your service is worthwhile, it must provide value for your customers' work. Federal Express provided the service they branded with the slogan "When it absolutely, positively has to be there tomorrow." FedEx reasoned people would pay for a reliable delivery service. It knew people place a high value on getting their documents to another part of the country by the next morning. So FedEx started asking people to pay $21 for a service that had formerly cost about 21 cents. Today this service delivers 3.3 million packages each business day (see Figure 5.2).

Any service your organization provides must of course relate to what your customers will value if you give it to them. In the UK, unlike continental Europe, we drive on the left hand side of the road. Hertz offers *Le Swap* to UK customers who want to take a car to continental Europe. You rent a right-hand-drive car in England, drive it to Folkestone and put it on *Le Shuttle* train that goes through the tunnel to France; the price of the *Le Shuttle* ticket is included in the rental. Hertz books the train and gets the ticket for you. At the French end of the tunnel, Hertz gives you a French car with left-hand drive. On the way back, you reverse the process.

Figure 5.2

Federal Express started asking people to pay $21 to get a letter to the other side of the country the next day. Standard delivery had previously cost 21 cents. FedEx could ask $21 because it was providing a service for "When it absolutely, positively has to be there tomorrow." Today, enough people value that service to make Federal Express the second largest airline (number of airplanes) in the United States.

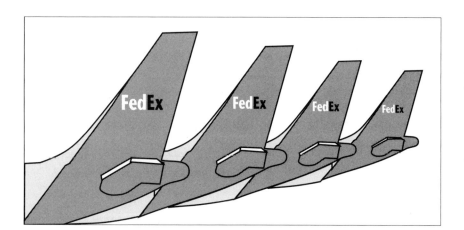

*The most visible
part of your
organization is
your information
systems.*

Hertz realized *Le Swap* is a service people would value. So they invented a better way of renting a car. Of course, having invented this better way—we like to think of it as a better service—the next task of the requirements team is to find requirements that come about because of the invention.

The most visible part of your organization is your information systems. By visible we mean what your customers see when they come in contact with your organization. For example, when customers log on to your Web site they are seeing an information system. When someone makes a telephone call to a customer representative, it is obvious the rep is manipulating an information system—you can sometimes hear the keyboard, or the rep says things to indicate he is looking at a screen. In this way the information system is visible to the customer.

Now ask, what kind of service does the information system provide? One that is easy, innovative, informative, and provides the occasional pleasant surprise to the customer? Does your customer leave your Web site or support desk thinking your organization provides a better service than the other fellows? Do your customers feel the service they just received is superior to that provided by your competitors?

Maybe you feel you cannot invent a way to improve on the service you already provide. In which case, can you invent some extra service? Wells Fargo bank understood its customers were wealthy enough to have a bank account and thus probably traveled. Wells Fargo began offering travel services to its customers, and picked up a lot of business that would otherwise have gone to travel agents. This is simply an invention based on the idea of providing an extra service.

Ideas

Sometimes products are little more than an idea. Nobody asked for them, but when they were built, customers wanted them. Post-it notes are possibly the ultimate idea. Art Fry, the inventor, knew of the repositionable adhesive that had already been invented by 3M. This adhesive seemed destined for the scrap heap of inventions when Fry came across it. He had become annoyed at how his scrap paper bookmarks kept falling out of his church choir hymnal. His idea—and this *was* one of those "Eureka, I've got it" moments—was the repositionable adhesive would make a wonderfully reliable bookmark. Post-it notes soon followed (see Figure 5.3), and when they were demonstrated to random people they became a sales success. Keep in mind the wonderful simplicity of this idea—you have never seen instructions on how to use Post-it notes.

*Some products are
little more than
an idea. That is,
the product is so
simple that it is
little more than
the idea.*

We call these things "ideas" as the product is so simple; almost nothing is there except the idea. eBay is another such idea. Meg Whitman had

Figure 5.3

The ubiquitous Post-it notes are an invention. Nobody asked for them, but once invented, how do we live without them?

the very simple inspiration of putting auctions on the Internet. After a faltering start in which the first few items submitted for auction were a used computer disk drive and a broken toy light saber, eBay went on to register 10 million users in its first 5 years. Not bad for an idea. Napster took less than one year to get to one million users, and estimates of music downloads run into the billions. Admittedly the product is free, but look at the idea: peer-to-peer networking by strangers whose only thing in common is an appetite for music. Can you use the idea of peer-to-peer networking in your organization? How about replacing the central mail servers and using peer-to-peer email? There are hundreds of application areas that will eventually use peer-to-peer. Invent yours now.

Ideas are free, and somewhere there is an idea that would be of tremendous value to your organization—an idea for a better service, an idea for a new product, a new way of presenting an existing service or selling your products. And while the idea itself is not exactly a requirement, requirements come from the idea. But first, you must have the idea . . . and hear it. When a member on your team has an idea, how do you learn about it? Does your organization have a way of hearing its own ideas? Can you listen harder and not miss out on the next Post-it idea?

Ideas are free.

Speed

Speed is a requirement. Whatever your product or service, your customers want it faster. We live in the era where attention spans are short, we get news in sound bites, and everything is flashing before us. We have become used to instant communication, next-day delivery, and living in the fast lanes. If your customer thinks you take too long to deliver whatever you are selling him, he gets impatient and goes elsewhere.

For example, the time needed to get a mortgage is now down to 15 minutes, and you can get it 24/7. You can bank 365 days a year, you can order goods at any hour and expect them to be on your doorstep the next morning. We expect to be able to open a bank account, or find competitive rates, and insure our cars in less than 10 minutes.

Why is speed important here? Because it captures the customer at the time of the customer's buying decision.

We have grown used to buying books on the Internet and having them delivered the next day. But the next day is too far away. Why should we wait for the deliveryman? If we have paid for the book, why can't we download the first few chapters and start reading? Now! Much of the software that runs on our computers is downloaded from the vendor's Web site. We do not have to wait for the CD: The software, including the user manual and anything else we need is running in a matter of minutes, not days.

Why is speed important here? Because it captures the customer at the time of the buying decision. By having the software on the customer's machine, paid for and registered in a few minutes, the vendor is far more likely to make a sale than if the buying process is laborious and slow. Particularly if it involves several "cooling-off" waiting periods.

Two views of speed are important here.

- How long should it take for your customer to order your service or product?
- How long should it take you to deliver it?

Generally speaking, the more expensive the product, the longer it takes. We don't expect to be able to order a hydroelectric dam during a commercial break on television. Similarly, we would not expect a Boeing 747 to be delivered tomorrow. For less expensive products however, no good reason exists for you not to be able to order them within a few minutes and have them delivered the next day, if not straightaway. Look at Amazon's 1-Click ordering. This reduces the time needed to buy a book to a few seconds. Why can't your product be bought like that?

When a customer does buy something, can you deliver part or all of it immediately?

As a general rule, your customers should be able to order your product or service online or over the telephone in a time measured in minutes. Consider the selling price of your product, and ask if the ordering time exceeds one minute for each $100 or €100 of price. If it does, then you probably need to invent a way of making your customer's buying experience faster. And when a customer does buy something, can you deliver part or all of it immediately? If not you may need to invent a better way to deliver it.

Can you perhaps speed up the buying process by performing part of it before the customer even asks for it? Again, look at Amazon's recommendations. It is trying to reduce the buying time by anticipating what its customers might want. My bank's ATM makes me answer the same questions every time I access it, despite the fact I always get the same amount of cash: The ATM never displays a message "Hello, Mr. Robertson. The usual?" My bartender can do this, why can't my bank?

It is safe to say in these fast times that if you do not do whatever you do quickly, you risk losing your customers to the guy who does.

Information

We live in a world of information. We swim daily in oceans of facts and factoids, and despite the huge amount of information each of us consumes daily, we continue to have an insatiable appetite for the stuff. So do your customers. Today's consumers are far better informed than they were a generation ago when people were accustomed to being kept in the dark. If a bank was slow to tell them how much interest they had earned for the year, customers accepted it: "Well, that's banks for you." No longer. If any organization refuses to provide information it can look forward to a departing customer.

Your customers already have lots of information, and they expect more of it. Your systems must give customers access to your company's information. The customer is king, and expects to be treated royally when it comes to information (see Figure 5.4). As an example of good information, the Web site of Progressive Insurance provides car insurance rates for all known insurers. They perform this service regardless of whether or not a competitor's rates are higher. Consider how the consumer shopping for insurance reacts to the openness of this kind of information.

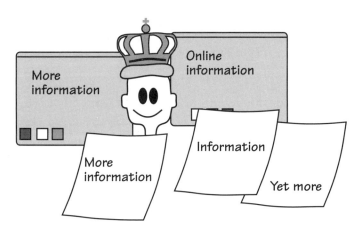

Figure 5.4

The customer is king and expects to be treated royally when it comes to information.

The requirement is to open the corporate information kimono by inventing some way of getting more information to customers and potential customers.

Visit Charles Schwab's site or any other online brokerage site. Look at the amount of information you can get, and a lot of it is free. Today investors can get information that was until a few years ago considered arcane and privileged to stockbrokers only. Schwab online is a huge hit. He took his brokerage business online and gave customers what they wanted—lots of information—and he lets them get on with it.

Federal Express has launched its InSight service. This allows anybody to get proactive delivery and delay information. The reasoning is if people can get information on incoming FedEx shipments, regardless of whether they know who sent them or when, then consignees will ask their suppliers to use Federal Express as their carrier. So here we have a service being sold on the back of information.

How much information does your customer get? What is it your organization knows, or could know, that your customers would also like to know? You need to open the corporate information kimono by inventing some way of getting more information to the outside world.

Technology Generates Requirements

Some technological advances generate their own requirements. If a new technology comes along and enables the organization to do something useful that previously it could not do, then naturally the organization will want to do it. Now a requirement exists—in fact many requirements exist—for the work to take advantage of the technology.

For example, at the time of writing, phone companies are pushing telephones with built-in cameras and the ability to send a photograph to another similarly equipped mobile phone. We realize by the time you read this, these phones will be old hat (or possibly extinct) but at the moment they represent a new technology. If this technology could possibly be used by your organization, what does your organization do about it? Can it set in motion a project to devise how to use this technology (send photos of houses to prospective buyers as soon as a suitable house comes on the market, transmit photos of cars to buyers in the market, transmit graphic information to your customer), or does your organization wait for your competitor to invent a way of using a new technology?

Any new technology is potentially a source of requirements.

Consider any piece of new technology. What can you do with it? Does the technology open a new business opportunity? Can you build a new system on the back of it? This may sound heretical as it reverses the traditional order of requirements. Here we are suggesting that you start with a solution and find a problem to fit it. However, if the problem you discover is well worth solving, who cares that you did the requirements backwards?

Any new technology is potentially a source of requirements. Does your organization have a process in place to learn about potentially useful technologies? Does it wait until the technology has become mainstream and then act? People often tell us they do not have time to do requirements because they will miss their window of opportunity. Try thinking about it differently: If you pay more attention to new technologies coming down the pike and think about their potential earlier, you create your own window of opportunity in the first place.

Choices Are Requirements

Consumers today are better informed than ever before. Thanks to almost universal access to the Internet and the startling growth of information, people feel informed and in a better position to make their own decisions. For example, you can find a flight that suits you and book your own travel online, find and reserve a hotel room from the many on offer, buy books from huge selections, find and listen to an almost unlimited selection of music, and find and choose almost anything else. Choices . . . so many choices, Web sites exist to summarize the choices available.

Dell, Gateway and other companies encourage customers to configure their own computers (and place their own orders). The customers have choices—processor, hard disk, Ethernet, wireless, graphics processor, memory, and so on—when it comes to their own machine. These choices are provided to the potential customer, and a company gains a competitive advantage by providing better choices than the other fellow.

You gain a competitive advantage by providing better choices than the other fellow.

What does this mean to you? It means you have a requirement to provide choice. You need to provide more information and more choices in the services and products that you offer.

Your customers want to decide how to use your resources. They want to be able to customize how they deal with your organization. There are always many ways for services to be performed or delivered, and multiple ways for your hands-on users to do their work. People no longer tolerate being told how they must deal with a company. They want to decide how they do things and what they get; thus your requirement is to provide whatever resources or information they need to make their decisions.

Self-Service

Self-service is an extension of the service you provide to your customers. Customers sometimes like to solve their own problems, and sometimes they like to do without the personal touch, especially if it means bypassing a wait on the telephone to speak someone. People seem happy to go online and manage their bank accounts themselves or to log on to their airline's frequent-flyer account rather than have the airline send a statement. The popularity of Amazon points to the willingness of readers to buy books and music online. Supermarket customers using the self-service checkouts report they prefer doing it themselves to standing in line waiting for the clerk.

If customers are doing the work themselves, they are far less likely to complain about the service.

Federal Express, DHL, and UPS spent millions on systems to facilitate self-service. Visit any of these company's Web sites and look at the options for self-service they provide. You can do an amazing amount of the shipping work yourself. While the shipper probably won't give you a discount because you have done the work, giving your customers this ability encourages loyalty. And if customers are doing the work themselves, they are far less likely to complain about the service (see Figure 5.5).

We are seeing the rise of cut-rate airlines. Self-service makes a major contribution to their cheaper fares. One of the more notable players in Europe is easyJet. This airline is coming close to a complete self-service airline. If you want to fly easyJet you must go online and book the flight yourself. No seat assignments, you find your own seat. No tickets, just bring yourself. Most easyJet passengers bring food and drink on board, as cabin service is not included in the fare. easyJet still handles your luggage and flies the plane, but as much as possible, or acceptable, is done by the passengers themselves. And the airline is very popular with the growing number of passengers who fly with it.

Most of the customer-service issues in your organization relate to your customers' accounts. This means things like changing their profiles, reviewing invoices, checking payments, opening and closing accounts, checking balances, monitoring deliveries, and so on. All of these are ripe for self-service.

Figure 5.5

United Parcel Service spent millions to enable their customers to book and track their own shipments. People seem quite happy to do a lot of the work themselves.

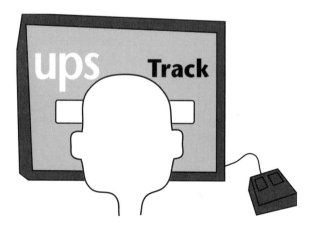

Note that this is not so much of an invention, as you directing your analysts to look closely at your customer data and find new ways to enable customers to service their own accounts.

Retailing is increasingly becoming a self-service activity. You can buy cars and houses online. Real estate Web sites can give you the virtual tour of an apartment—you do it yourself without having to listen to a fast-talking sales representative. Your customers should be able to learn about your company's products and services, and order them, all without the need for a human representative. You are trying to invent a better way of showing off your wares and innovations and make your product look better than your competitor's. If your customers can get all the information they need themselves, they are likely to lean toward your product.

Retail is a self-service activity.

Self-service is more than putting your catalog on line, it's enabling your customers to inspect all aspects of your products or services. Think of this as an electronic "squeezing the avocado." You must make it possible for your customers to find all the information they want for themselves. Then, if they can order it easily and quickly, they're your customers and not someone else's.

One of your authors (James) was recently buying lights online. I was searching for some difficult-to-get spotlights for mains voltage halogen bulbs. I found a company, and its Web site let me interact to the extent I could see all options, dimensions, and specifications. As a result, I had complete confidence I was buying exactly what I wanted.

I had to go elsewhere to buy the light bulbs—the spotlight company did not sell them. I found many companies selling light bulbs online—I chose the one that showed me clear photographs of what I wanted, explained the difference between GU10 and GZ10 bases (I really needed to know that), gave me confidence I knew all I had to about PAR 16 halogen lamps, and even told me the difference between dichroic and non-dichroic lamps. (You can write and ask me if you need to know about that last one.)

You can get online healthcare or, if you will pardon the oxymoron, use an online personal trainer. It is hard to imagine a product or service that cannot be sold on a self-service basis. The requirement is to invent a way of self-serving your product before your competitor does.

The requirement is to invent a way of self-serving your product before your competitor does.

Direct Manipulation Is a Requirement

People want to manipulate the resources of companies with which they do business. Amazon.com gives you a forum to write and post your own book reviews. You may write anything you like about a book. Why does Amazon allow people to post a negative review that might turn away a

Why does Amazon allow people to post a negative review that might turn away a potential customer for a book?

potential customer for a book? Because Amazon knows that by encouraging the truth and letting its customers play with the crown jewels—the Amazon Web site—its customers will feel they belong there, and keep coming back for more.

Most computer hardware and software companies enable customer postings on their support notice boards, even when a posting may not be all that complimentary to the vendor. Why? Because those postings are answered by people who participate in or moderate the boards, and the disgruntled customer will likely get an answer to his problem and turn into a happy customer. This is direct manipulation: The customer is using corporate resources to perform his own technical support.

❝ *Give [your customers] the perception of control and ownership . . . over you.* ❞

—Tom Peters, *The Circle of Innovation*

Ask yourself: Do your customers participate in your business? Do you give them access to all the information they can use? Do you provide them with a mechanism that enables them to do much of the work themselves? An honest answer will tell you if you can profit by inventing something to enable direct manipulation, as well as what to invent.

Good Design Is a Requirement

❝ *The most memorable and persistent brand message a company can send is a well-designed product—second only to a poorly designed one.* ❞

—Craig Sampson, *IDEO Chicago*

Most products must be well designed. Some products are beautifully designed, and these are always a joy to use. Their good design is a constant reminder of the wisdom of the buying choice. We use Apple's iPod to play music in our seminars (among other places). Our students always admire it. Although the iPod has superb performance, it is almost as if the design is its most important requirement (see Figure 5.6).

Boots, a very successful pharmacy chain in the UK, runs stores where design permeates every product. The stores are well designed. The products stand out from others because they are superbly designed. Yes, even the Boots own brand of athlete's foot cream is designed to be attractive to the customer.

❝ *At Sony, we assume all products of our competitors will have basically the same technology, price, performance and features. Design is the only thing that differentiates one product from another in the marketplace.* ❞

—Norio Ohga, *chairman and CEO, Sony*

Design is a constant reminder to your customers, or potential customers, of your product. The design of the Volkswagen Beetle is a constant advertisement for the car. The design of the new Mini entices people to buy them. Visit Apple's site www.apple.com to see how design is making it profitable in spite of competing in a marketplace dominated by Microsoft.

How does your organization include design in its requirements process? What are you doing at the moment that can be better designed? If your project is a Web site and you are not using a trained, talented web designer, you are missing one vital requirement. Any report can be designed to be more readable and more useable. Any screen can be improved by good design. While good design is not exactly an invention, it is a serious requirement.

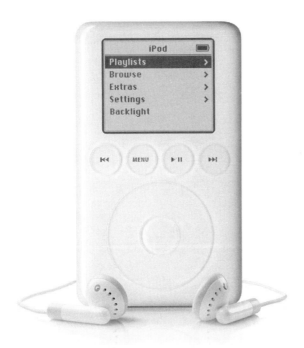

Figure 5.6

Apple's iPod. This is, at the time of writing, the best designed and best selling MP3 player. Its good design—both ergonomically and aesthetically—is the main reason for its success. Photo used with permission of Apple Computer, Inc.

Brainstorming and Prototyping

We have given you some directions to prompt your inventions. So how do you go about the actual inventing? You can do several things: Mainly, brainstorming and prototyping (see Figure 5.7). If you think you use brainstorming at the moment, ask yourself how often do you brainstorm? If less than twice a month, you really are not brainstorming. How many prototypes do you build for your typical product? If in the low single digits, you are not really prototyping.

In the previous chapter we discussed the brainstorming technique. In any event, most readers are familiar with the idea of gathering a few willing people and making use of the group effect to have each member come up with as many ideas as possible. But we would like to present you with some other ideas to augment what you already know.

First, play leads to invention and creativity. Bright ideas do not come from regimented people. Can you imagine Albert Einstein's boss saying "Albert, I want you to come up with a theory on relativity and have it on my desk by Monday morning? Oh, by the way, make sure that you stick to our ISO 9001 certification." The best ideas come when people are happy, playing, and playful.

And unafraid. Trial and error is an important part of invention. Unless you have incredible geniuses working for you, they are never going to

> *What is to be sought in designs for the display of information is the clear portrayal of complexity. Not the complication of the simple; rather the task of the designer is to give visual access to the subtle and the difficult—that is, the revelation of the complex.*
>
> —Edward Tufte, *The Visual Display of Quantitative Information*

Figure 5.7

This is the tablecloth your authors used when we were brainstorming. It belonged to the Crocodile Café in Pasadena, California, and we thank them for it. We were planning one of the creativity workshops Suzanne and our colleague Neil Maiden ran for Eurocontrol in Paris. We scribbled and drew as we brainstormed the plan for a successful workshop.

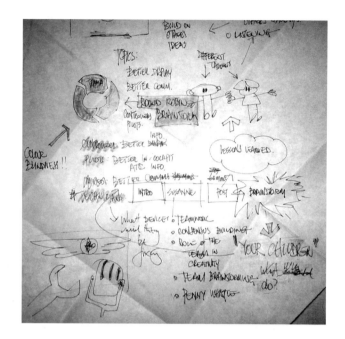

come up with the great idea straight out of the box. Every great idea goes through several iterations of experimentation and refinement. If people are afraid they will be mocked or even punished for poor-sounding ideas, they will never have better ones.

Peter Gordon is one of the hot, young chefs making a name in the London restaurant scene. Peter is a fusion chef—one who uses the flavors of one cuisine (in this case Thai) to cook dishes from another cuisine (in this case Italian). Peter teaches his apprentices this imaginative way of cooking by asking them to "Imagine if olive trees grew in Thailand." The apprentice has to think out of the box and come up with dishes he thinks would be the result of olives growing in Thailand, or any other combination that Peter sets him. The basic idea here is using disparate ideas to provoke new thoughts. By bringing together ideas from different sources, he provokes his students' creativity.

You can do the same thing with your project team. Challenge them to dream up ways of using technology not normally associated with your business. For example, a technology of self-printing "paper" using electronic ink is emerging. The ink pixels are arranged to form text by applying voltage through a thin-film transistor panel. The paper is reprintable at will, either directly or by wireless. How could your project use this? The MIT Media Lab is experimenting with wearable displays in eyeglasses. How could you use this for an inventory control system? How can you use a 3D display on a computer screen for an accounting prod-

66 Fail faster to succeed sooner.99

—David Kelley, *IDEO Product Development*

66 The best way of having a good idea is to have lots of ideas. 99

—Linus Pauling

uct? The idea is to set seemingly impossible situations, and then sit back and wait for the pleasant surprises.

Suppose your team is working on a system to register patients into a hospital. Ask your team to imagine the registering system their children would build. And then ask then to imagine the product their grandchildren would build. Any kind of future technology can be assumed whether it is practical or acceptable by today's standards or not. For example, you might imagine that patients arrive at the hospital with the identity, medical history, and doctor preferences recorded on a microprocessor implanted in their bodies. Anything you imagine is treated as an acceptable idea. Then you ask yourself and your team how much of what we have just imagined can we build? Could one of the crazy ideas we generated be made to work in some way?

Brainstorming is not intended to produce workable ideas right away. You must expect 95% of brainstorming time produces unworkable ideas. This is intentional. The whole point of brainstorming is to let imagination run wild and come up with ideas—any ideas, good and bad—in order to get the gems that otherwise would not see the light of day. Make sure that your project team knows this. And unless you are a very sympathetic boss and are well trusted by your team, stay away from their brainstorms. Remember the old saying about the cat being away? Let your people play. It is their ideas you want not their timesheets.

Let your people play. It is their ideas you want, not their timesheets.

Scope Creep and Invention

Scope creep is a well-known phenomenon in requirements projects. The modest project bloats into something large, and the ambitious project becomes so huge it collapses under its own weight. Throughout this chapter we have been advocating that some features of your next product are pure invention, which suggests the invention process may cause severe scope creep. Though the potential exists, it does not need to cause your project to bloat to an uncontrollable size.

Let's attack the problem with the notion you do not have to implement every requirement. Although they are called "requirements," you should not infer all of them are needed. At least not right away. Because you may not implement every one of them, the requirement should carry an indication of how important it is. In Chapter 2—Requirements Value we suggested you use a satisfaction and dissatisfaction rating to show customer value and enable you to prioritize the requirements.

The requirements you invent are also rated for customer value. Naturally, if they end up with a low rating—you have invented something the customer does not want—discard them. But if your invented requirements end up with a high customer value, they displace others of lower priority.

The invention process occurs at the same time your analysts are studying the business area and trawling for requirements. It is quite possible they invent something that replaces some existing functionality instead of adding to it. And just as every requirement does not have to be implemented right away, some of your inventions will turn out to be the subject of future projects.

What Do I Do Right Now?

We have looked at the idea of inventing the requirements. This is not to say you ignore the current work of the business. Nor do you ignore whatever the business people are requesting. Instead, we suggest you enhance what they say with useful innovations. For example, inventing a better service—remember that it will almost certainly depend on IT—is such an enhancement. Providing better information is something IT is in the best position to do.

Consider which PSIs (listed in Chapter 1) are affected by the practice of inventing requirements:

- The product adds value.
- Good team morale.
- User or customer satisfaction.

If any of these PSIs are key to your project, here are some ways you can improve them by being more inventive.

First, if you invent something you will certainly be delivering a product that adds value to the organization. It is difficult to see how a rewrite of the employee benefits system adds value. It is easy to see inventing a new method for doing employee benefits—putting it on an internal Web site or on employees' handheld devices or their mobile phones—does add value. If you are going to expend precious resources, make sure you build something that contributes to your organization's success.

Team building and morale is another PSI to which inventing contributes. Practically everyone we have met in the systems development world (after 25 years of consulting and training, we have met thousands) is motivated by his or her work. People like their work and want to do it well. The greatest motivator of all is to give them work that is interesting. Provided they feel they are adequately rewarded for their work, systems developers prefer to do more interesting work than to get paid a little more for something routine.

We are not suggesting you can use interesting work to keep employees' salaries low. Rather, if you want happy and motivated teams, abandon the 17th rewrite of the inventory control system and give employees not only an innovative project but also the freedom to make their own inventions.

Customer delight with the delivered product is probably the most obvious success indicator. Apart from delivering required functionality, we know no better way to delight our customers than to deliver something they did not expect and they find useful. It's easy to tell if you succeed with this one: Your customers use your product and say "Thank you."

What's the Least I Can Get Away With?

The following points give you a minimal effective inventive process:

- Introduce brainstorming as part of your requirements process.
- Give your team the topics we have covered in this chapter—service, speed, information, technology, choice, self-service, direct manipulation, design—and suggest they use them to seed their sessions: "This time we will invent a better service, tomorrow it's direct manipulation."
- Tell the team that you want them to invent a better product, one that will *thrill* your customer.
- You must budget a time for invention.
- Keep in mind that you are making a preemptive strike on your customers. By giving them a better, more innovative product today, you forestall their requests for enhancements tomorrow.

Resources for Inventing Requirements

The following sources, in addition to those already referenced, have useful information on invention relating to the requirements activity:

- Christensen, Clayton. *The Innovator's Dilemma—When New Technologies Cause Great Firms to Fail*. Harvard Business School Press, 1997—*Clayton makes a solid case for not following your customers' every demand, as companies that do so are usually left behind when a new, "disruptive" technology comes along.*
- Gershenfeld, Neil. *When Things Start to Think*. Henry Holt & Co., 1999—*Inspirational ways of looking at the future and predicting ways that emerging new technologies may change tomorrow's world.*
- Kelley, Tom. *The Art of Innovation—Lessons in Innovation from IDEO, America's Leading Design Firm*. Doubleday, 2001—*Insights into how the IDEO company uses brainstorming and prototyping as their design methodology.*

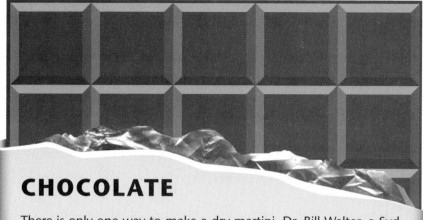

CHOCOLATE

There is only one way to make a dry martini. Dr. Bill Walter, a Sydney surgeon, introduced your authors to it, and we are grateful. The first rule is to keep your gin in the freezer. Provided that it is a reasonable strength gin, it will come to no harm. The all-time taste test gives the nod to Plymouth gin.

Half-fill your cocktail shaker (or better still a glass pitcher that you keep in the refrigerator or freezer) with ice and pour in a small amount of dry vermouth. Most reasonable dry vermouths are satisfactory, but if you want your martini to be the best then use Noilly Prat. Swirl the vermouth in the ice and empty almost all of the vermouth out. We know that it is a crime to waste good liquor, but you can't live your life as a complete innocent. For each person pour in four ounces of the gin, straight from the freezer. Shake it and strain into a frozen martini glass. There is only one type of martini glass. It is the triangular shaped one. Twist a thin strip of lemon peel over the drink to release the oils from the skin, and then drop it in. Sit down, look your loved one in the eye, and sip slowly.

• Levine, Rick, et al. *The Cluetrain Manifesto—The End of Business as Usual*. Pearson Education, 2000—*It used to be possible to impose hierarchical control on an organization. But now the Internet makes it possible for anyone to communicate with anyone else. This book discusses how this freedom to communicate encourages openness and creativity.*

• Norman, Donald. *The Design of Everyday Things*. Doubleday, 1988—*Full of examples of why everyday objects should be well designed and why consumers should not blame themselves for bad design.*

• Peters, Tom. *The Circle of Innovation*. Knopf, 1997—*A handbook of innovative ideas designed to help you develop your creativity muscles.*

- Schrage, Michael. *Serious Play—How the World's Best Companies Simulate to Innovate*. Harvard Business School Press, 2000—*How today's innovative companies use prototyping, models, and simulation to create valuable new ideas.*
- Tufte, Edward R. *The Visual Display of Quantitative Information.* Graphics Press, 1983; *Envisioning Information*. Graphics Press, Connecticut 1990; *Visual Explanations*. Graphics Press, 1997—*Tufte's inspiring trilogy of advice and examples of how to come up with the most effective visualization for each particular situation.*

MIT Media Labs are coming up with some very innovative products. Some of these can be harnessed to provide useful and practical products. You can find a list of current projects at www.media.mit.edu.

Fast Company is a magazine that always runs articles on state-of-the-art business practices and technology. Slightly breathless at times, but always challenging.

Wired. This magazine takes a little getting used to but is worth the effort. They present technology and business in a fresh and challenging way.

Requirements Simulations

Simulations—these include prototypes, scenarios, stories, and any other way of bringing a product to life—are an aid to discovering requirements. Simulation techniques motivate people to be playful, to use their imaginations, to think past the obvious, and to discover requirements that are otherwise missed until after the product is implemented.

Why Simulations?

You cannot realistically expect your stakeholders to know all their requirements. They know their work, they know what they do, they may know what they want to do, but they are rarely in a position to know or imagine all the requirements for a product that help them to do their work.

Requirements are an abstract statement of capabilities and properties of a future product. Even if it were possible for someone to imagine all the required functionality, it is doubtful they could remember all of it while you calmly write it down. It beggars belief to think someone could know all the nonfunctional requirements without having some kind of physical artifact to prompt them and provide inspiration for experimentation.

A simulation, when used for requirements gathering, means expressing requirements in some physical manifestation. For example, a simulation is a prototype, a scenario, a screen sketch, a three-dimensional model, or some other visible and touchable thing that pretends to be the product. Your final product does not have to be completely faithful to

> *Prototyping is problem solving. It's a culture and a language.*
>
> —Tom Kelley

Figure 6.1

Simulations are used to visually portray the requirements and to prompt the requirers for whatever else they need.

the simulation, but a simulation helps you to arrive at the requirements for the final product. You are using a simulation to prompt your stakeholders to tell you their requirements (see Figure 6.1).

Keep in mind a simulation expresses the work, or what the requirer needs or wants to do. The simulation is not the requirements, but a make-believe implementation of the requirements. For example, if you build a software prototype, naturally it shows various windows and buttons on screen. The requirement is not that the user has a screen but that the product supplies the user with certain data. Note the difference, it's important. The implication is when you have some kind of simulation another step exists for deriving the requirements from the simulation. Later we go into more detail on why and how.

Why use simulations?

66 *Players, not users.* 99

—J.C. Hertz, *Joystick Nation*

It comes back to what we are trying to do: to get the requirements from the requirer's head as quickly as possible. Instead of asking requirers to do something impossible, such as telling us all their requirements, you invite them to "play" the requirements. People are good at playing: It comes easily to us. We start playing when we are very young and never really lose the ability to pretend.

We also know how to separate reality from representations. When you go to the movies and see an actor getting shot, you know it is theater. No matter how realistic the portrayal on screen, you never imagine you will be attending his funeral tomorrow, no matter how realistic the portrayal on screen. You know you are looking at a *representation* of reality and for the sake of enjoying the movie you suspend your disbelief. Similarly, when you show a sketch on a whiteboard of a proposed Web site, your client does not believe it possible to click on the link you have drawn. But the client is amenable to pretending it is possible. By playing with the simulation, the client can see the possibilities and make better suggestions than without it.

We are all used to this kind of thing. By now you have seen several hundred thousand television advertisements. Many of these are simulations; they show the product being used or suggest what you can do with it. This kind of simulation is intended to trigger a buying response. In your case, when you show your client a simulation, you would like him to either buy into the product as is or (more likely) suggest improvements. In either case, your client now can approximate how this product works, or what functionality it has.

> *People are good at playing: it comes easily to us. We start playing when we are very young and never really lose the ability to pretend.*

Why Bother?

Why not just implement the product and see if the customer likes it? The answer lies in the difference between the solution and the problem. If we start with a solution, it is very difficult to tell if it is solving the real problem. Several barriers exist: A requirer usually tells you a perceived fix to his immediate problem. However, you cannot know by listening whether the requirer has considered other parts of the organization, whether the solution is really the best available, or whether the solution is suitable if another person replaces him in the job. Similarly, the requirer's perceived solution is limited by his technological knowledge and experience. Also, consider that it is far cheaper to throw away prototypes than it is to change installed product.

Instead of rushing into the first solution suggested, the savvy requirements analyst knows that understanding the real problem is the basis for finding the most effective solution. The purpose of requirements simulations is to discover the underlying business situation, the real work, and from those simulations derive a solution both technologically aware and satisfying to the entire organization.

> *A requirer usually tells you the perceived fix to his immediate problem.*

Serious Play

The term "serious play" was coined by Michael Schrage to mean play to achieve some valuable outcome. He argued we need to play if we want to think past obvious boundaries and build competitive, innovative

RESOURCE NOTE
Schrage, Michael.
Serious Play: How the World's Best Companies Simulate to Innovate. Harvard Business School Press, 2000

The best innovations come from organizations in which the work ethic is relaxed.

Chapter 5—Inventing Requirements is devoted to the subject of how invention is a vital part of the process of discovering requirements.

❝❝*Good companies embrace a culture of mini-failures.*❞❞

—Tom Kelley

The simulation acts as the conversation space.

products and services. Today, we have so much "stuff" nobody needs anything anymore. You have your computer, your software, your telephone, your car, your gadgets, and a lot more besides. Apart from something breaking, what can persuade you to buy more stuff?

Innovation can persuade you. You buy new products, new software, or new services if they are innovative products offering you a genuine differentiation from your previous version, or if they contain some genuinely new product or service previously unavailable.

What does it take to persuade your customers to buy your products or services? What convinces your clients you should build their new software or provide their new service? Again the answer is innovation. Whatever your product or service, you must make it into a new and improved experience. To imagine this experience, pretend you are having that experience. This pretense in a good cause is serious play.

An organization's ability to innovate is commensurate with its ability to play. You cannot get much innovation out of a rigid, and rigidly controlled, work process. We have never seen a formal process description having a step called "Invent something here"—it would not work. The best innovations come from organizations in which the "work ethic" is relaxed, people can play, experiment, try things out, build many prototypes without constantly being asked, "When will it work?" and "Are you doing this according to the established process?"

Organizations must be willing to experiment without fear of failure. The people in your organization must be able to try things to see what happens and not be ridiculed if their experiment does not work the first time. James Dyson, inventor of the bag-less vacuum cleaner, took 5 years and 5,127 prototypes to bring his invention to fruition. Clearly, he did not regard a less-than-perfect prototype as a failure. Similarly Michael Dell, founder of Dell Computer, talks of the absence of punishment if some business venture does not work out. Instead of blaming the person who tried something new, managers review the failed attempt to see what they can learn and to determine if they can change it a little to get the intended result. The point is the original innovator does not suffer because an idea did not work out the first time it was tried.

Playing, or serious play, is working with simulations, playing at using them to do work, suggesting better functionality and features, and being unafraid to make suggestions. Simulation becomes the focus of the play. That is, in playing with the simulation, people play with one another. The simulation acts as the conversation space. The result of this serious play is that your team is able to innovate, and through innovation, improve the final product.

Prototyping

Requirements prototypes are a way of finding out if your ideas of the requirements match those of the requirer.

A prototype is some physical artifact—a software mockup, a whiteboard sketch, or a quickly crafted three-dimensional model of an appliance—you use to tell your story back to the requirer. The prototype says, "This is what the product might do, or how you might work in the future." The prototype contains enough implementation ideas to bring the requirements into the requirer's world. It is not intended to be a design but rather a *reflection of the requirements*.

Prototypes carry more information than words. The solid object, the screen snapshot, the mock-up report are heavier in information than a written description or verbal instructions. The prototype, above all, is a language used for communication between your business analysts and requirers. Think of the prototype as a visible language, far less ambiguous than English and far more illustrative, demonstrative, and erudite than most of us can manage. If you have William Shakespeare or Mark Twain on your team, they would have the words to adequately describe a suggested product. But while Will and Mark can weave their images with words, your requirers are hardly likely to have F. Scott Fitzgerald and Virginia Woolf on their side to adequately describe what they want. The reality is people can tell you what they want if they can see it and not just imagine it.

By letting your stakeholders "see" the product, you get the wrong ideas out of the way early in the process. The intention is to avoid writing a requirements specification, building the product, then have the requirers say "Well, we know we said that was what we wanted, but now that we see it, we realize that is not what we need." Early failures are not really failures—they help the requirements analyst to understand. They also help requirers understand whether what they are requesting is what they truly need. Failing often means you have the requirers' attention and they are participating in the requirements process. If you are not failing, they will not be talking to you.

Learning from Prototypes

Let's look at an example of how we learn from prototypes. Figure 6.2 shows a whiteboard prototype of the checkout area of a hypothetical book-selling Web site. You build this prototype early in the development cycle to discover if you understand the basic functionality of the checkout process. Then you test the prototype with potential hands-on users, test it often and make changes to it.

> *66 . . . prototypes can be more articulate than people . . . 99*
> —Fred Brooks, *The Mythical Man-Month*

> *66 Instead of introducing a new language, a prototype builds on users' own experiences using computers. A prototype enables them to interact with the proposed system as they would with any system and respond in a language that is immediately relevant to them. 99*
> —Hugh Beyer and Karen Holtzblatt, *Contextual Design*

> **People can tell you what they want if they can see it and not just imagine it.**

> *66 Fail often to succeed sooner. 99*
> —saying at the design firm IDEO

Figure 6.2

This low-fidelity (lo-fi) prototype drawn on a whiteboard shows the checkout page of an online bookseller. Build this kind of prototype early in the development process and let the business analysts use it to learn the more important requirements.

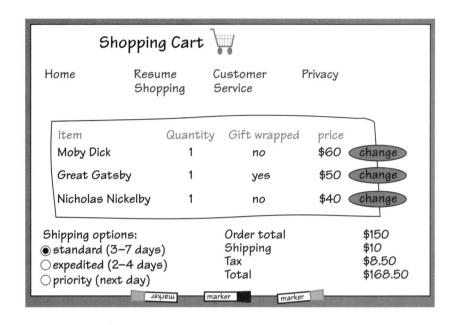

What do you learn?

- Concepts and purpose—Does the prototype match the original business purpose you determined for this product? Does it match the concepts and metaphors the requirers apply to this kind of work?
- Content—Is the content of the prototype suitable to do the work for which this product is intended? Have you understood all the necessary data, provided the right information for requirers to make decisions, and shown all needed actions, warnings, and information to be offered to the user and so on? Does it have extra information users don't need or that would annoy them?
- Functionality—Does your prototype demonstrate the needed functionality for the intended hands-on user to successfully complete his tasks?

Keep in mind this is a prototype, and not intended to be right the first time. In fact, be very suspicious if a prototype is pronounced correct on its first viewing. Play with your prototypes . . . a lot. With each iteration you discover missing functionality, aspects of the product to which no one had yet given any thought, or functionality you included but your customers don't want. The more you iterate, the better you understand the requirements.

If you are building a consumer product, you are most likely working with three-dimensional simulation models—the physical attributes of

66 *The more frequently you get usability data and iterate your design, the better the usability of the end result . . . the number of times* you *test different designs is the most important element in a Web project.* 99

—Jacob Nielsen

the product are often a major factor in its appeal to the buying public. However, the physical appearance of the product is not all there is to it. We also use scenarios and sketches to work out the ideal sequence of operating actions. For example, we used a combination of physical simulations and scenarios to help a manufacturer produce a better interface for its mobile phone. By playing through the scenarios, the development team discovered how their original ideas for menus had some procedural flaws and they were paying too much attention to features few users wanted.

For tailored software development, we always urge the building of an early prototype. This ensures builders and client are on the same wavelength and the shared experience of the prototype means closer relations for the future.

We have observed many in-house software development projects ignore prototypes. Our inquiries have revealed the requirements team feels the product is just not exciting enough to build a prototype. This often happens when the team assumes the product will use the standard Windows (or whatever) interface. So long as all the required data shows, all is well. However, when we have persuaded the team to put together a few rough prototypes and try them out with the requirers, the team always finds several breakthrough ideas that improve the product and the its acceptance by the requirers.

Involving Customers in Your Prototyping

The prototype is a shared communication medium. Its purpose is to stimulate ideas from many different stakeholders: marketers, engineers, analysts, developers, and of course the customer. Whether this product is to be bought by external customers or bought *into* by business users within the organization, you should share the development of the prototype with them.

66 Creative organizations generate lots of prototypes. More rigid companies generate fewer, more elaborate and more expensive prototypes. 99

—Michael Schrage,
Serious Play

The computer-aided design product I-deas was originally developed by SDRC, now owned by EDS. SDRC had the policy of inviting their key customers along as soon as they could show some working (sometimes barely working) product to them. Key customers wanted to participate because they got the features they wanted, and SDRC got a lot of free help and input from people who made buying decisions about the product.

Microsoft sent out approximately 400,000 beta-version copies of Windows 95 to potential customers and others in the marketplace. The amount of debugging at customer sites was phenomenal. Michael Schrage estimates Microsoft was the beneficiary of $1 billion worth of effort before Windows 95 was released, and the product was far better

Not one successful piece of software has been launched without customer input.

because of this debugging and improving effort. Amazingly, Microsoft received all this effort virtually free.

When do your customers see your prototypes? The earlier in the development cycle they see them the more requirements and features input you get. Early prototypes are naturally less fully formed, but they can help to prevent you making expensive mistakes building products nobody wants. If you are building software for in-house consumption, showing early prototypes to the intended users is extremely beneficial for discovering what people need before you build the product.

"Never Go to a Meeting without a Prototype"

The above comes from Dennis Boyle, studio head of the IDEO product design company, and is illustrated in Figure 6.3. Boyle advocates prototyping as part of the iterative process. He likes to make lots of prototypes early in the development process ". . . to make his mistakes—and discoveries—as soon as possible."

Our partner Steve McMenamin speaks of prototypes as "requirements bait." Steve has observed, when showing a prototype to his requirers, they always responded with a laundry list of other things they wanted. So prototypes seem to help people find their voices. When they have seen a prototype, all sorts of people weigh in with their own opinions and ideas.

Figure 6.3

"Never go to a meeting without a prototype."

There are few rules about prototyping, but there *are* some.

- Generate lots of prototypes—Your team learns something each time they build a new prototype. And there is no reason to assume the most recent prototype you built taught you all there is to know.
- The purpose of the prototype is to help your team invent something—It is not intended, at this stage, to design something. Keep the team aware of the need to discover what the prototype must do and away from the diversion of designing cool icons, buttons, and screen artifacts.
- Build prototypes quickly—The prototype loses its effectiveness if the team invests too much ego, then defends the prototype in the face of user criticism.
- Prototype early in the life cycle—To get the mistakes, miscommunications, misunderstandings, and miscarriages out of the way as early as possible. Later stages of the requirements should be about refinement, not correction.

Prototyping sums up why you are concerned with requirements in the first place—to find out all you can as early as you can. Once you have understood the users' work, and know what you have to build, you can concentrate on finding the best solution.

So far we have looked at the idea of inventing and understanding by building prototypes. But prototypes and requirements are different animals. So let's look at using the former to find the latter.

Extracting the Requirements from a Prototype

The prototype is a physical medium; it represents actions and information using real, touchable, and visible artifacts. Which means the prototype is not the requirement, but the *appearance* of the requirement (see Figure 6.4). Thus, it represents an imagined version of what the requirer wants; a representation, *not* the real thing.

Because the prototype is a representation, something that has to be done before you start construction of the product is to translate the requirements from the prototype. The prototype hints at why some facet may be desirable but does not say why. It demonstrates functionality without being testable and illustrates nonfunctional properties without providing any measurement for them. The prototype is not built to last. For that you need an industrial-strength version. And to build that, your building team needs measurable, testable requirements.

Converting the prototype to its foundation requirements is not so difficult, and is easier if we consider any product has functional and

> 66 *Once several people have seen an interesting prototype, others hear about it and the researcher gets requests to show off his work.* 99
>
> —Michael Schrage,
> *Serious Play*

The prototype pretends to be the requirements, but it is not the requirements.

Figure 6.4

The prototype is a physical representation of the requirements, but not the requirements themselves. You must translate what the prototype shows into testable requirements.

nonfunctional requirements. Functional requirements are what the product must do. Start with any aspect of the prototype and ask, "What is it doing?" or "What is the hands-on user doing with it?" Whatever the prototype must do, those actions are functional requirements. Along similar lines you ask, "Why is the prototype like that?" or "What qualities is it displaying?" These properties, things the product has to have, such as usability, security, maintainability, and so on, are its nonfunctional requirements.

Consider an example. Figure 6.5 shows a prototype of a music player for a personal computer. Interested stakeholders would have sketched this prototype on a whiteboard to show some of the product's functionality, as well as to discover what would make a good music management product.

Functional Requirements

Functional requirements are signified by verbs.

Functional requirements describe the actions the product takes—doing arithmetic, producing output, checking input, and so on—or, to put it more simply, verbs. The product shall *verify,* the product shall *calculate,* the product shall *inform,* and so forth. Obviously, requirements analysts must write all the product's functional requirements to ensure develop-

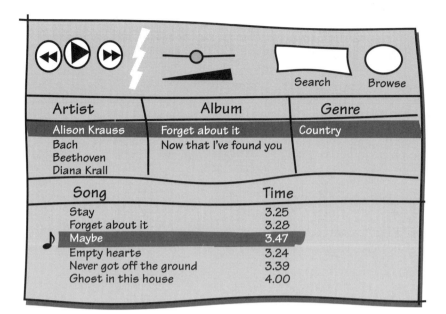

Figure 6.5

An example of a lo-fi prototype for a personal computer music library and player. The task is to accurately undertand the requirements this prototype displays.

ers, designers, builders, and programmers develop the correct functionality for the product.

So what functional requirements do you get from the prototype shown in Figure 6.5? From this prototype you learn the product shall store and play individual pieces of music (let's call them songs). The songs might be attached to an album. At this stage the requirements analysts must determine if the order of songs in the album is fixed or can be changed, and if a song can be moved from one album to another. Each song must have a title, be attached to an artist, have a genre (possibly more than one genre), and have a duration. The product must communicate these properties to the user.

The product shall play the music when requested, but it is not clear from the prototype if, when the user selects one song to play, the remainder of the album is also played. Neither is it clear whether the user can select an artist and play all of that artist's songs. Such requirements would also have to be considered for classical music where a "song" would be one movement of the composition.

. . . though the prototype is an excellent aid to finding requirements, it is not sufficient for specifying them.

The prototype also suggests the user is able to search for an individual piece of music: The requirement for this search is indicated by the search window. What is not indicated is whether the user can search for an album or an artist or a genre. The existence of the search window in the prototype helps generate these questions. Also, does the search apply only to the selected source or to all possible sources?

The point is though the prototype is an excellent aid to finding the requirements, it is not sufficient for specifying them. Only when you start asking the detailed requirements questions do you discover the complete functionality.

Nonfunctional Requirements

Nonfunctional requirements are properties or qualities the product must have to facilitate its functionality. The product we are discussing here has functional requirements to store music and search for it. The connected nonfunctional or qualitative requirements specify how much music it must store, how secure it must be, how easy to search, and so on. Legal requirements come under the heading of nonfunctional requirements, covering such issues as the legality of storing a particular piece of music on the computer.

We have identified eight main categories of nonfunctional requirements, and most of these have subcategories. Let's look at some of them.

Look and feel requirements are first. This requirement type covers the appearance and image of the product. As this product is aimed at a younger audience, appearance and image are very important. The prototype in Figure 6.5 shows a flash at the top. This suggests the prototype designer wants a polished metal appearance. Keeping in mind the difference between a requirement and its implementation, you write the requirements to state the product is to have a modern appearance; probably it also shall be consistent with other company products. Another look and feel requirement might exist where words like "cool" and "user friendly" are used. You also want your user to be able to change the look and feel almost at will. These requirements are not yet testable—they are not yet complete. Your requirements writer must add a fit criterion to provide an objective measurement for these vague adjectives.

Usability requirements cover ease of use and ease of learning. The prototype in Figure 6.5 shows highlighting for the selected artist, album, and song. The usability requirement here is that users be easily aware of the songs they have selected. The prototype implies users should also be able to play a song, or songs, without training. Personalization is part of usability, and you expect your team to gather requirements about changing the way the product presents information, that it can operate in different languages, adapt to different encoding protocols, and so on. Not all of these are necessarily apparent from the prototype, but your team uses the prototype to prompt questions about these kinds of requirements.

Performance requirements cover such things as speed and capacity. Here the analytical team uses the prototype to prompt such questions as how many songs must the product hold, how fast can you download, and so on.

RESOURCE NOTE
Robertson, Suzanne and James. *Mastering the Requirements Process.* This provides a complete description of deriving fit criteria for all requirements.

There are more nonfunctional requirements types, but rather than work through all of them here, we suggest you download a copy of the Volere Requirements Specification Template from www.volere.co.uk for a complete description of all the nonfunctional requirements.

Nonfunctional requirements are properties or qualities the product must have. Although the commonly used term "nonfunctional" suggests these are less important, usually these nonfunctional requirements determine whether a product is liked and used. Naturally the functionality has to be correct. Once the required functionality exists, nonfunctional requirements become most visible to the user—usability, look and feel, performance, security—and thus largely determine the experience of using the product. They often become what potential consumers use to make their buying decisions.

Although the commonly used term "nonfunctional requirement" suggests these are less important, usually the nonfunctional requirements determine whether a product is liked and used.

Using Informal Narrative

Narrative is a kind of simulation. We use narrative to describe situations and in so doing convey a second or deeper meaning. For example, when your mother or father read stories to you when you were small, they were doing it for several reasons. The immediately apparent one was to get you to go to sleep. Another reason was to entertain you, and depending on the choice of the story, its narrative would hopefully convey a lesson (see Figure 6.6).

It is no trivial matter for a human to understand his needs thoroughly, and be able to articulate them as requirements. However, most of us are fairly good at narrative. If you can get your requirers to use narrative to

We use narrative to describe situations and in so doing convey a second or deeper meaning.

Figure 6.6

The stories parents read their children often contain some message or lesson they want the children to learn. This is typically our first learning experience, and it is carried on in later life.

describe their work situation or what they would like to do in future, you have the foundation of their requirements.

Narration and stories are how we make sense of things. When you are telling someone how you gathered requirements on your last project, or the crazy thing someone asked for, or the cool way you can have a new song automatically downloaded to your telephone each day, you are telling a story. Without the story all we have is data. The story connects the data and helps you to understand it.

Encourage stakeholders to tell you about their work, what they do and what they hope to do, and use their stories to derive their requirements. This is the nub of it. If people just talk to you, their narrative reveals how they want their product to work. If you can get good enough narrative, you can get good enough requirements.

For example:

> *A fact may be the smallest unit of information, but a story is the smallest unit of meaning.*
>
> —Kieran Egan

- People can tell you what they do, how they work, how they would like to work. Instead of trying to give you facts, they tell you how all the pieces fit together. Suppose a telephone salesman tells you he looks up a lead in the telephone book before dialing. That's simply a fact and you assume the salesman wants to know the telephone number. But he continues the story and tells you he sees how the prospect is listed—a lone initial before the name probably means a single female, JP & GT means a married couple, and so on. So now you know why he uses the phone book. Then his narrative continues with how he uses that information to vary the timing of his call and his sales pitch.
- Narrative reveals how people perceive situations, and how they might deal with them. All of these are grist for your requirements mill. You do not need requirers to tell you the features they want. In fact, you probably don't want them to. Instead, you need them to tell you stories of how they want to work or what they think might happen.
- Narrative strings happenings together to give meaning to a situation. The order of happenings in the story counts for a lot. The order establishes the relationship between the stages of the narrative. When this stakeholder is finished telling you his story, you have established how the parts fit together, and why the current sequence of happenings exists.

Getting Requirements from Narrative

Have your requirers narrate stories about their work situations: how they do their work, exceptions that occur, how people might use the intended product, how the product affects people, and so on. More important,

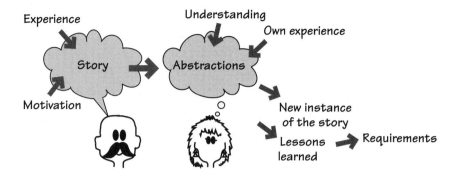

Figure 6.7

The requirer is telling his story to the business analyst. The story is made up of the requirer's own experience, either experiences from the past or experiences he would like to have in the future. This is colored by his motivation—what does he want? He colors the story to make what he wants seem more attractive. The business analyst then makes various abstractions from the requirer's story and eventually derives requirements for a product that will make the story a reality.

gather stories of what they do now and what they might do with the intended product.

Figure 6.7 shows a requirer narrating his experience to the business analyst. The analyst makes abstractions from the story to filter out perceptions and prejudices about the requirer. For example, is the requirer making his job out to be more important than it is? Is he hiding something? Is he trying to change the job to what he would like it to be?

The business analyst must attach his own meanings to the story—his own experience is different from the requirer's. He also needs to abstract so he can look past the artifacts and implementation the requirer employs. He probably creates new instances of the story so he can try out different versions to see if they fit with his constraints and the rest of the product. He would also create new instances of the story to filter out his perceptions of the requirer. These and the lessons he learns from the requirer's story lead to requirements.

Let's look at an example of useful narrative, and from it derive some of the requirements.

The Bookshop

"I went out to buy a book yesterday. I like going into bookshops. When I come through the door I take a few moments to stand there and soak up the atmosphere of the place. I mean, if this bookshop does not feel like the kind of place I want to be, then I leave. But I like most bookshops. There's something stimulating about those tables near the front with the books on display, the new releases, the staff suggestions, the specials . . . I always look to see if one of my favorite authors has written something new, or if there is anything so different I have to have a closer look at it. When I am done with the stuff near the entrance—I assume there are more people like me as the bookstores always put their new, notable, and special books right inside the front door—I move on to the sections that interest me.

Figure 6.8

Narrative reveals many of the functional and nonfunctional requirements.

"I like those stores where they have clear signs that hang above the shelves and tell me where the computing section is, where the photography books are, where the fiction, and so on, can be found. When I look at these signs I decide which one I will head for first. If I am in the mood for some classic literature, then I want to bypass the latest celebrity diet book.

"When I find a book that looks interesting, I pick it up and read the synopsis, the reviews, and whatever else it tells me about the book. I also like to open at random pages and read a few paragraphs to see if I like the author's style.

"I am an enthusiastic book buyer, and usually end up carrying a pile of books around the store. Then I realize I cannot possibly buy all of them and usually have to hand several back to the people at the customer service desk. They don't appear to mind having to put the books back, but that could be their good training . . . or their good manners.

"Then I check out of the store. I pay by credit card, and the assistant has to get authorization. I also have customer loyalty or discount cards at some stores, and I show the assistant my card. I always take one of the free bookmarks they have at the checkout counter. I like to use a bookmark and like the idea of having a different one for each book.

"When it's all done, my books are packaged and I go on my way. If the experience has been pleasant, I will return. I guess I am like most people and end up buying more books than I can possibly read."

Deriving the Bookshop Requirements

The narrative is a book buyer talking about his preferences, and how he likes the experience of going to a bookshop. Let us say you are leading a project to build an online bookstore, and your client is targeting customers who usually go to bricks and mortar bookshops. We can say for sake of argument this narrator is typical of your intended customers.

The narrator likes bookshops. Note the part about getting the feel for the place. This suggests some important look and feel requirements. Don't try to design the site at the moment, but capture the requirement for a "welcoming appearance with a bookshop feel to it." Note also the narrator likes the "new releases" and "staff suggestions" selections near the front door. Apparently he is amenable to recommendations. This makes a strong argument for a requirement that the initial page of your bookselling site includes some suggested books and new releases.

Requirements gathering is often a marketing activity. Ask yourself, what can we do for this customer? What convenience functions can we provide? What parts of his narrative identify areas where we can do something to make the customer's life easier? For example, can you provide a well-thought-out categorization of books and an easy way to find them? Can you use his past purchases and buying habits to categorize books so he will more readily find something to buy? At this stage you do not know enough to know what he considers "book category" to be, but you do know categories exist and they are important to his book-buying activity.

Requirements gathering is a marketing activity.

Often, narrators do not say what they really need, nor can you expect them to. You might have to invent something here. For example, what does he want when he says, ". . . usually [I] end up carrying a pile of books around the store. Then I realize I cannot possibly buy all of them and usually have to hand several back to the people at the customer service desk"? Does this mean he wants a virtual shopping cart? Or does he want some kind of wish list or list of tagged books where he can later find these books? Should you keep track of the books looked at or tagged, but not bought, as indications of the book buyer's interests?

Your goal is for the narrator to buy as many books as he can manage, and have a pleasant experience doing so. "I like going into bookshops," "I am an enthusiastic book buyer," and ". . . [I] end up buying more books than I can possibly read," all indicate the online bookstore must give the buyer similar sensations to what he gets in a real bookstore. Furthermore, to tempt him to switch, you need to invent some sensations he cannot find in a real bookstore.

Keep in mind when you are using narrative, separate the physical artifacts used in the story from their essence. For example, when your storyteller talks about books on the tables, what does this really mean? Consider: At a bricks and mortar bookshop when you see the books stacked on the tables, which books attract you attention first? We are willing to bet the books in the tallest piles (assuming all the books in the one pile are the same title) get your attention first. What does the tall pile

When using narrative, separate the physical artifacts used in the story from essence.

say? It says the bookseller thinks this is going to be a popular title and has stocked up in anticipation of heavy sales. So a potential buyer perceives the stack contains a popular book that could appeal to him also. Thus the actual requirement is for a representation of popularity, and not photographs of tables or tall piles of books.

Getting People to Talk to You

People talk to you if you give them something to talk about. For example you can ask them:

- How do you process [your main service] when everything works as it should?
- How would [your main service] be if no constraints existed?
- What is the worst thing that can happen?
- What pleases you most of all?
- What if the third thing you do doesn't work? (There is no magic about the third thing. We just want to trigger something other than the obvious first thing.)
- What about the customer (for the product you sell) from hell?
- How about the boss from hell?
- What is the environment from hell?
- What is your dream scenario? In other words, tell me about a product, or parts of a product, that would make life incredibly easy for you.
- Can you tell me about things that happened to you in the past?
- What makes you smile?
- What do you think about the products your grandchildren will use?

The last one opens all sorts of doors. You are asking your stakeholder to ignore all current technological constraints and imagine a future world and the kind of products that might be in use. It will probably be obvious to you, and possibly not to your narrator, what at first seems far-fetched is entirely possible or soon will be.

. . . what at first seems far-fetched is entirely possible or soon will be.

There are other ways of prompting. Susanne Kandrup at one time was director of talent development for Lego, the Danish (now worldwide) toy manufacturer. It was Susanne's job to help employees free their imaginations to discover their potential, skills, and ambitions. In a workshop—one of a series we ran with Professor Neil Maiden—for air traffic controllers, Susanne demonstrated how to use physical artifacts to free the imagination and tell creative stories.

She had a bag filled with a variety of objects—such as an empty perfume bottle, a toy frog, a train ticket, a pair of spectacles, a brightly colored marble, a paperclip. Each group was asked to dip into the bag and take one object. Then the groups were asked to use the object to trigger a story about the worst possible air-traffic situation they could imagine. The group that selected the toy frog imagined airports were inundated by a plague of frogs making it impossible for planes to take off and land. It was silly, playful, and a lot of fun. It was also very productive. The frogs were quickly replaced by other hazards—storms, ice, birds, grasshoppers—to which most of the frog scenario applied. The point here is everyday objects can trigger the imagination and take the narrator away from the obvious. By using this idea with the air traffic controllers, we discovered many requirements that otherwise would never have seen the light of day.

Use Cases from the Narrative

There is a lack of clarity surrounding the definitions of use cases, mainly because different people use them for different purposes. Alistair Cockburn's definition has more clarity than most: "A use case captures a contract among the stakeholders of a system about its behavior. The use case describes the system's behavior under various conditions as the system responds to a request from one of the stakeholders." As Cockburn points out, in order to be able to write consistent use cases, you need to define precisely what you mean by the system under discussion.

From the point of view of requirements, you need to know whether you are talking about a business use case that affects the work area under study or a product use case internal to the product you intend to build.

When you start working with requirements, the business use case provides the work view of them. Here you are trying to understand the wider business problem. When you understand enough, you can identify the boundaries of the product use case—and then specify the requirements that will be carried out by the product you intend to build. To make the discovery and definition of business use cases more precise, we define a specific business event as the driver for the business use case. *Traveler wants to buy ticket, bank customer wants to withdraw money, pilot wants to change course* are examples of business events that lead to business use cases. This makes it possible to break the work into easy stages or units of functionality we can study discretely.

Let's go back to the narrative about visiting the bookstore and look for business events in the story. The first is when the buyer enters the bookshop. Although the buyer does not do very much in this stage, he seems to want some kind of reaction to his appearance—the display of suggested books and an indication of where he might go next. The next business event happens when he wants to look at a particular type of book. Another business event happens when he finds a book and wants

Refer to Chapter 4—Learning What People Need for more on business events and use cases.

RESOURCE NOTE
Cockburn, Alistair. *Writing Effective Use Cases.* Addison-Wesley, 2001.

to browse inside it. Selecting the book to add to the pile he carries around the store would be another event, and then checking out is yet another business event identified by this narrative.

The reason to look for business events is to identify influences or stimuli that exist outside our work. It does not matter for the moment how the work is currently organized, or what technology or procedures are in place. The important thing is the outside world sees our work as a provider, or potential provider, of services. A request for a service is a business event. To be more precise, the moment the outside entity realizes they want the service is the business event.

When we know the existence of a business event, we can think about how our work should respond to that event. Whatever the work does in response to a business event is a business use case. Note the business use case starts outside our work, and sometimes it starts outside our organization. It is certainly outside our computer. The inference to be drawn is the business use case may involve some human activity.

For each business use case determine how much of it you want your product to do. In some cases you can elect to have the product do all of the response, in some cases you include some human activity in the business use case. Whatever your choice, the part of the response you elect to include inside the product is a product use case. You write requirements for product use cases. That is, requirements are what the product must do, or the properties it must have.

So once you have identified product use cases, the easiest way to arrive at requirements is to write scenarios.

Product Scenarios

Product scenarios are a step-by-step narrative of a product use case.

Narrative is unbounded. The narrator can talk about anything within reason, and the narration can range over many areas of the work you are studying. Product scenarios on the other hand are bounded. That is, they are a step-by-step narrative of one product use case and assume the existence (without detailed design) of a product.

Consider the scenario shown on Figure 6.9. It was written for a car navigation interaction where the navigation feature is part of the car's infotainment system. It breaks the product use case down into a limited number of steps, with the intention of confirming with the stakeholders the proposed behavior will in fact do the correct work of the use case.

The scenario tells one instance of the story of a driver selecting a destination and getting directions from the on-board infotainment system. You can write other scenarios to illustrate other cases of this story. For example, if the key belonged to a teenage member of the family, the driver must enter a destination before the car starts. The car starts if the

1. Laura inserts her key in the ignition.

2. The product recognizes Laura's presence and adjusts the car's seat position and mirrors to suit.

3. The product asks, "Do you need directions?" and communicates direction options: [no/home/previous/street address/landmark]

4. Laura chooses a destination.

5. The products communicates that it is getting directions based on Laura's previous road usage preferences.

6. The product selects Laura's preferred radio station or MP3 playlist used when driving to similar destinations.

7. The product checks for traffic and weather problems along the chosen route, selecting an alternative if conditions warrant.

8. The product communicates driving directions.

Figure 6.9

This scenario shows the normal case for the product. The business analyst writes the scenario to confirm his understanding of the requirements and that the appropriate product has been invented to fit the needs.

destination is on a parent-approved list. Additionally, the car's position is monitored along the way to ensure the driver does indeed drive to that destination. If the driver has a provisional license, the car does not exceed a preset speed limit.

You can use scenarios to try out ideas. In the previous chapter we discussed the idea that your project team invent some of the requirements. Here we are suggesting you use scenarios to demonstrate ideas to interested stakeholders. The scenario is written using any available technology and requirements the requirements analyst has invented. The scenario is then used to seek approval from the business people, marketing, and other interested stakeholders.

Scenarios are used to demonstrate your ideas to interested stakeholders.

Note the example scenario assumes the existence of some kind of product—it is almost always employed to demonstrate the interaction between the hands-on user and a product. Which means a danger exists of committing too early to what the product will do and what the hands-on user will do. However, if you are prepared to iterate often, it becomes less of a problem: Your analysts feel freer to experiment with different product scenarios. By trying different automation boundaries—in effect different products—the analysts usually discover alternatives that provide a better product than the original.

The step-by-step approach of the scenario also helps with experimentation. The requirer can see each step, examine it, consider the consequences, and try to imagine a better alternative. For example, let's use the example shown in Figure 6.9. Step 2 reads:

> 2. The product recognizes Laura's presence and adjusts the car's seat position and mirrors to suit.

What do you get from this? The recognition is important because many of the car's functions are tuned to this recognition. What if someone else is using Laura's key? Should the car also check this is not a teenaged son using his mom's key so he can drive to the pool hall (a destination forbidden by his parents)? Does this indicate the key itself must have properties to defeat using another's key? Should there be a default or guest key so Laura can let the garage guy who is a good foot taller than Laura, drive the car? And naturally there must be another scenario where different drivers adjust their preferences.

Scenarios are also used for exceptions. The usual way of working is to write the scenario for the normal case, or "happy case"—this is where you assume everything follows a predictable, normal path—and then write a new scenario to tell the story for each thing that can go wrong. And within each exception or alternative path several variations are possible. Thus some redundancy may exist in the scenarios: You have to work through each of them with your requirers to know you understand all the situations and that your product is responding correctly to each of them.

Personalization makes it easier to invent stories and determine the correct behavior of the product.

Last, we find it useful to include the names of people in our scenarios. We have found people respond well to the different personas we create as we write our scenarios. In the scenario shown in Figure 6.9, Laura can be the wife in the family. If we wanted to illustrate the product's actions when a teenager is driving the car, we can invent Brad, and give him a personality. This personalization makes it easier to invent stories and determine the correct behavior of the product.

The Essence

Throughout this chapter we have discussed using some kind of simulation to help gather requirements. And throughout the chapter we have given examples in which the simulation makes use of what appear to be real products. Our intention is not to suggest you simply conjure up a product and forget the real requirements. Instead, we encourage you to use these pretend realities to help find the most suitable product for the stakeholders.

Every time we talk, we invoke physical things. Every time we build a prototype, we design a physical appearance. But these physical artifacts are simply *the medium for conveying the requirements*. They are not the requirements themselves.

In Chapter 4—Learning What People Need we discussed the difference between the physical incarnation of some object and its essence. The essence is the underlying reason for the object's existence. A car is there to provide personalized transport, a report is there to provide information, and an MP3 player is there to provide music. In all of these cases we have to separate the essence from the implementation in order to ensure we are not solving the wrong problem and we have in fact found the best possible implementation for that essence.

When your team is using any kind of simulation, it is vital they keep in mind they are using the simulation to find the requirements—not to design a cool solution before they fully understand the business problem to be solved. Which implies they constantly abstract away from the displayed technological solution to ensure they understand its underlying essence. It also means they must impress on the stakeholders they are gathering requirements, not designing. There must be no commitment to deliver exactly the same interface, and the final product may look substantially different from the prototype on display.

The requirements analysts must constantly abstract away from the displayed technological solution to ensure they understand its underlying essence.

Naturally, when building simulations, clever people generate good ideas about potential solutions. We do not advocate you ignore these ideas and run the risk of losing them. Instead, develop the skill of being able to separate requirements from solutions and keep the solutions until you are ready to make a decision. We created Section 27 of the Volere requirements template to record potential solutions. Whenever there is an idea for a way to solve the problem, enter it in here so you can refer to all the ideas when you understand the requirements well enough to be able to design the product.

What Do I Do Right Now?

Requirements simulations contribute to a number of the project success indicators detailed in Chapter 1.

- Lack of creeping user requirements
- Good quality code/solutions
- User/Customer satisfaction
- Correctly sized product

- Product adds value
- No misunderstood requirements

To build the right product, your business analysts have to get thoughts from the heads of the requirers and translate them into well-formed, testable requirements. If any ambiguity or omissions exist in the requirements, the product will be flawed, possibly fatally so.

The requirers and stakeholders on the other hand are often not all that interested in spending time with your business analysts. These people have their own work to do and describing their needs is not what they are paid to do, nor is it part of their skill set. So your analysts have to make it as attractive as possible for the requirers to participate in the requirements process.

Playing is attractive if it appears to be yielding results. You need to develop a team culture in which it is okay to play, it is okay to make a few missteps along the way, and it is okay to iterate. You must get the message across that a discarded prototype is not a waste. Your team will have learned something from it. It also means you have to make the stakeholders aware that playing with the aim of finding the right requirements is not frivolous. After all, your stakeholders have a strong interest in you developing the right product.

66 Humanity has advanced, when it has advanced, not because it has been sober, responsible, and cautious, but because it has been playful, rebellious, and immature.99

—Tom Robbins

Simulations may be more hard work than fun but they are enticing. They are also productive: We discussed the idea of eliciting a narration from the business people, then having the analysts interpret it to determine the underlying requirements. Though it takes a lot of insight for anyone to know his or her requirements, most of us can tell a reasonable story.

The task is to come up with the most innovative and functional product possible within the constraints. While stories are an aid to finding known requirements, you need something more to invent great products. Try prototypes. Prototypes are used by every other industry as an aid to invention. Every bridge you drive across, the car you drive, and the radio you listen to while driving was prototyped. Engineers of those products used prototypes to prove the products would work and were wanted. Software prototypes have exactly the same use.

Even though the requirements aids we discussed in this chapter—stories, scenarios, prototypes—are all physical media involving real world devices, finding the requirements still entails refining the essence from the physical. The essence represents a view of the product that does not involve any technology. By gaining this "clean slate" view of the requirements, your designers are in a position to select the best possible design and your team is in a position to avoid coming up with a solution to the wrong problem.

What's the Least I Can Get Away With?

You want to ensure you build the right product. This is the fastest way of finishing the project, and also the cheapest. The least you can do is:

- Build an early prototype of the "mother lode" product use cases. These are the ones closest to the prime reason for building the product.
- Build a prototype as soon as you have a reasonable grasp of the scope of the product and how it breaks down to its use cases.
- Arrive at a consensus with the key stakeholders that the prototype represents the kind of product they have in mind.
- Elicit requirements using scenarios. Write the normal case scenario first before delving into exception scenarios.
- Uncover the essence of the work being discussed.
- Derive the requirements from the scenarios.
- Write down the requirements; don't trust the scenario or prototype to accurately convey requirements.

Resources for Requirements Simulations

The following sources, in addition to those already referenced, have useful information on requirements simulations.

- Alexander, Ian, and Neil Maiden. *Scenarios, Stories, Use Cases—through the System Development Life-Cycle*, John Wiley, 2004—*Guidance and advice on how to apply scenarios to projects throughout the life cycle. This advice comes from the combined expertise of top researchers and industrial consultants in the field. The book considers the full range of types of scenario, including storyboards, user stories, and sketchy and fully detailed use cases.*
- Beyer, Hugh and Karen Holtzblatt. *Contextual Design*, Morgan Kaufmann, 1998—*Focuses on how to design systems that fit into the way people do their work. Lots of hints and models for iterating between requirements and solutions.*
- Christensen, Clayton et al, editors. *Harvard Business Review on Innovation*. Harvard Business School Press, 2001.
- Cockburn, Alistair. *Writing Effective Use Cases*. Addison-Wesley, 2001—*Practical guidance on defining and writing use cases. Contains plenty of useful examples. Works well as a tutorial and a day-to-day reference guide.*
- Gershenfeld, Neil. *When Things Start to Think*. Henry Holt & Company, 1999—*Inspirational ways of looking at the future and predicting ways that emerging new technologies might change tomorrow's world.*

CHOCOLATE

All good stories have a structure. The symphony has a defined structure, as has the sonnet and the haiku. The movie structure is, generally speaking, three acts.

The first act establishes the normalcy of the situation and introduces us to the main characters. Very early there is some incident that sets out the reason for the story, and gives us an insight into the protagonist who is leading a comfortable but not necessarily fulfilling life: Ugarte (Peter Lorre) disrupts Rick by giving him the letters of transit; Thelma's husband is such a jerk she can't bring herself to tell him she's going away for the weekend.

The second act starts with an incident that disrupts normalcy. This usually happens a little before the half-hour mark: Ilsa walks into Rick's nightclub; Maximus the general finds his wife and son murdered by Commodus; Peter Parker is bitten by the radioactive spider. Sometimes the incident is when one of the protagonists makes a wrong choice: Louise shoots Harlan; the captain of the *Titanic* decides to keep full speed despite the threat of icebergs; Ash opens the airlock to let Kane back on the ship after Kane was attacked by the Alien. The disruption turns the story in another direction. Now the second act develops the plot, the protagonist is set on his or her journey, and things are decidedly not normal. Act II takes up half and often more of the movie.

Act III begins with another incident or twist that eventually leads to the resolution. This comes at a time when things seem as if they cannot get worse. The incident sets the protagonist out in a different direction, and along the way he realizes qualities he possesses but previously ignored. Movies, unlike life, end with a resolution, and it has to link back to the beginning: Ilsa and Victor escape with the letters of transit; Peter Parker forsakes Mary Jane despite being in love with her; Rose drops the diamond into the sea where it goes to join the *Titanic,* which is where the movie started.

With thanks to Susan Rogers, Director of MA in Feature Film, Royal Holloway University of London, for introducing us to the three-act concept.

- Kelley, Tom. *The Art of Innovation—Lessons in Creativity from IDEO, America's Leading Design Firm.* Doubleday, 2001—*Insights into how the IDEO company uses brainstorming and prototyping as their design methodology.*
- McMenamin, Steve, and John Palmer. *Essential Systems Analysis.* Yourdon Press, New York, 1984—*This classic examines how to look past the implementation and arrive at the essence of a system. Techniques to help business analysts separate a solution from a requirement.*
- Poundstone, William. *How Would You Move Mount Fuji? Microsoft's Cult of the Puzzle—How the World's Smartest Company Selects the Most Creative Thinkers.* Little Brown & Company, 2003.
- Schank, Roger. *Tell Me a Story.* Northwestern University Press, 1998—*Schank explains how humans communicate with one another by telling stories. He investigates how people use stories and narratives and also how intelligence applies to both the telling and the listening.*
- Schrage, Michael. *Serious Play: How the World's Best Companies Simulate to Innovate.* Harvard Business School Press, 2000—*How today's innovative companies use prototyping, models, and simulation to create valuable new ideas.*

Requirements for Existing Systems

 *Not all projects are for completely new pieces of work—
in fact the majority are to enhance some existing
product. In this chapter we tackle the problem of
managing requirements for new development that must
integrate with existing systems.*

At some level of abstraction, all systems are existing systems. Even a
brand new product you are inventing has some connection to existing
parts of the world. After all, any product is an abstraction of a collection
of partly existing ideas. When built, the product must fit with and influence systems—people, software, hardware, procedures, physical conditions—that already exist.

When Jeff Hawkins invented the first Palm handheld it was perceived
as a new system for managing a calendar and contacts. But consider how
many existing systems with which the Palm connects. A few that spring
to mind are the calendar, our system for measuring time, technology of
batteries, LCD technology, the size of human fingers, the diaries people
have on their computers, manual diary systems, human systems of language, and so on. If we look at it this way, the project to build the Palm
was really making changes to a much larger system.

So what makes us view one project as a change and another as something new, and what impact does it have on requirements? When we talk
about requirements for existing systems in the world of software engineering we usually mean changes or additions to some existing body
of code that is already in production. We hasten to point out changes to

*At some level of
abstraction all
systems are
existing systems.*

163

existing code are difficult to manage unless one communicates consistently.

Years ago, both authors worked as maintenance programmers on a huge suite of programs for managing investments. The first version of the system had been implemented seven years earlier. Our work consisted of investigating new requirements and implementing them in the existing software. Some of the requirements existed because customers asked for something new, some were due to legislative changes, and many were not really new requirements but *fixes*. In those days we did not have any formal process for describing and communicating requirements. We simply interpreted the requirement on our own, then made changes to existing code; we wrote new code and did what we thought was needed to produce the desired result. This approach, although the only one available to us at the time, made it difficult to manage the work in the maintenance department. All the work was fragmented as we did not have an overall understanding of the system—so for every change, we spent time rediscovering knowledge that had often been investigated by someone else.

Given the advances in software and requirements engineering, things should be different today. But quite commonly people tell us they cannot use engineering principles because they are making changes to existing software systems. Which inevitably leads to repetition of effort and out of control spending on changes to systems. To overcome this problem, a project manager needs to be able to take a holistic systems-oriented view of the world and use this to make and communicate plans and progress.

A Systems-Oriented View of the World

When you need to solve a problem in your everyday life, you try to consider the problem from the point of view of all the parts of the world that might affect it. Suppose you are planning to shop for food: You consider what you want to buy, who will be eating the food, the shops you should visit, the transport to use, the weather forecast, and so on. In short, you consider all systems that may be affected by your plan to shop for food. So in the present context what do we mean by the word "system"?

In the software industry we often use the word system to mean some collection of program code, and often it refers to a computer. But many other types of systems exist. For a start, consider political systems, biological systems, mechanical systems, business systems, and social systems. Peter Checkland introduced his soft systems theory as a basis for understanding how any system—and this includes a new requirement—fits with other systems in our world. Checkland classified systems into a number of different classes.

The software system you change, regardless of how small the change, can affect many other systems that exist in the wider world.

- *Natural Systems*—Phenomena such as gravity and other laws of the universe
- *Designed Physical Systems*—Man-made constructions such as buildings, planes, rockets, paintings, screwdrivers, and software
- *Designed Abstract Systems*—Ordered conscious products of the human mind, for example, physics, philosophy, astronomy, and mathematics
- *Human Activity Systems*—A person using a screwdriver, a game of tennis, a political meeting, a bank clerk using an automated interface to look up a balance
- *Transcendental Systems*—Systems beyond provable knowledge: religion, spirituality

The software system you change, regardless of how small the change, can affect many other systems that exist in the wider world. If you change a calculation, do you know how the results of that calculation are used by all the human activity systems within your organization? Are the results of the calculation used by any other software system in your organization? How about systems outside your organization—does anyone use the results of the calculation to make decisions? Are the results of the calculation used as input to building other systems? Systems thinking implies your awareness that every system is some combination of social and technical systems and possibly other types of systems. This awareness enables you to realize the enormous potential even a small change has for unexpected results.

However, if you apply systems-thinking principles before you make a change to an existing system you can avoid unwanted side effects and also discover more effective ways of achieving the real goal of making the change.

66 Business and other human endeavors are also systems. They too are bound by invisible fabrics of interrelated actions, which often take years to fully play out their effects on each other. Since we are part of that lacework ourselves, it's doubly hard to see the whole pattern of change. 99

—Peter Senge,
The Fifth Discipline

A Systemic Approach

It is helpful to think of every new requirement, no matter how small, as a miniature project in its own right. You do the same amount of thinking as for a new project but, depending on the size of the requirement, you may do it in half an hour. Figure 7.1 is a model of the thinking process one needs to go through to analyze a change and decide whether and how to implement it. Let's go through the process.

Figure 7.1

The five steps shown are used to analyze requirements for changes to an existing system.

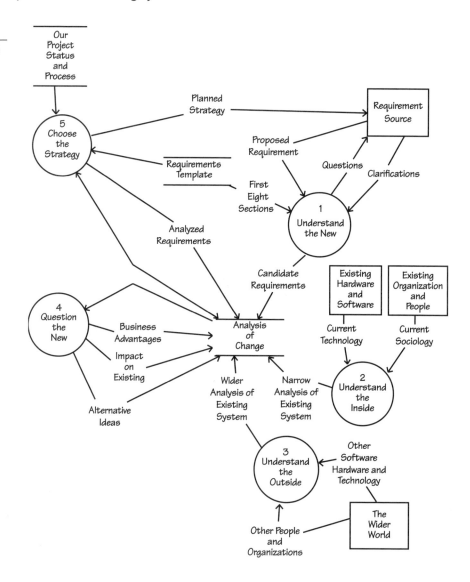

1. Understand the New

This process is triggered by the appearance of a *Proposed Requirement*. Proposed requirements can be thought of as falling into one of the following categories:

- Another requirement to be included within your current project
- An additional requirement that affects the scope of your current project

- A change to an installed system, including changes to the system already installed by the current project

Let's look at these in a little more detail.

Part of Current Project, or Scope Creep?

If you discover the requirement while the product is still undergoing development, use the work you have already performed to help you determine whether the requirement should be included in or excluded from your current project. Some questions to help you decide.

- Is the new requirement within your declared scope of investigation? Use the context diagram to determine if the requirement introduces new interfaces on the work scope or changes the content of declared interfaces. If so, the requirement is not legitimately part of your project.
- Is the new requirement within the declared scope of the product you intend to build? Your ability to answer this question depends on how far you have progressed with the project and whether you have made any decisions about product scope.
- Does the new requirement contribute to the goals of the project— the stated purpose of the product? By asking this question you identify requirements that, even though they are additional, may be requirements with a higher priority than other changes.

The answer to these questions provides the basis for assessing whether the proposed requirement is part of your project, a change to your project, or can be safely considered outside your project. If you decide to include it in the product, then you have to change the work scope, product scope, and project plan. If you decide to defer the requirement to another version, then put it in the waiting room along with your notes so the work you have done can be used later on.

New Requirements during Maintenance

A number of reasons exist for proposed requirements to arrive after a product has been implemented.

1. Something new occurs in the scope of work and users need the product to include new or changed rules.
2. An outside body (the government or some other authority) introduces new rules that necessitate a change to the product.
3. New technology makes it possible for the product to implement requirements more effectively.

4. You discover one or more requirements missed by the original requirements gathering activity.
5. The team misinterprets a requirement and the product does not reflect what the requirer wants.
6. The technology cannot satisfy the requirements.

The first three reasons are requirements that didn't exist when we were building the product. You can think of these requirements as enhancements. These requirements arrive because there is some unpredictable change in the world. The better we are able to respond to these sorts of requirements the more competitive (even if we are producing product for internal use) our service. This is maintenance with real business value.

Good requirements practices preclude zero-value maintenance.

The last three reasons reflect flaws in the original requirements and development process. These are not new requirements; these are faults in the product. For whatever reason we did not ask the right questions or we made the wrong assumptions. Or we did not communicate the requirements with enough precision, so someone somewhere along the line assumed another meaning. Alternatively, we assumed the available technology could provide a solution to fit the requirements. This is maintenance that has costs without benefits. Good requirements practices preclude zero-value maintenance.

If you know how much you are spending on repair work due to requirements defects, then you can estimate the benefits you can realize from improved requirements practices. In *Quality Software Management— Volume 4,* Jerry Weinberg tells about a New York financial company that discovered it cost it $2,000 for every requirements defect discovered after the requirements stage was finished. When they did a pilot project using an improved requirement process they reduced the number of faults from 12/KLOC to 3/KLOC—a reduction of 75%. They then used their new requirements process on a 120KLOC project, and estimated they would prevent 1,080 faults. The result was a total projected savings of $120 \times \$2000$, or $2.16 million.

There are some questions to help you quantify the potential benefits from improved requirements practices.

- How much of your maintenance cost is spent on fault repair (defects as identified in points 4, 5, and 6 above)?
- What is the average repair cost per fault?
- How many faults do you have per function point or per KLOC?
- How much can you save if you reduce the faults by 75%, or even by 50%?

If you don't have these figures you owe it to yourself to look for them and identify improvements you can make . . . and to monitor the actual progress you do make. These are some of the benefits you can realize by improving your requirements process.

Exposing the Requirement

When you are working on understanding a new requirement, use Sections 1–8 on the Volere Requirements Specification Template (see Appendix B) as a checklist for the questions to ask. The questioning does not have to be in great detail, it can take only 10 minutes. The point is to ask the questions represented by the following categories:

1. The Purpose of the Product
2. Client, Customer, and Other Stakeholders
3. Users of the Product
4. Mandated Constraints
5. Naming Conventions and Definitions
6. Relevant Facts and Assumptions
7. The Scope of the Work
8. The Scope of the Product

Use the first eight sections of the Volere requirements template to prompt the questions to help you understand a new requirement.

When we tell each other what we want, we usually talk in terms of a solution: I want a thin plastic ticket, the telephone screen should be backlit, I need an 'okay' button on this window, I need a controller to divert this signal, please print the urgent notices on pink paper. These are solutions, and they may be wrong solutions.

Requirers tend to state their requirements, not so much in an abstract form, but in the form of how they think the requirement should be implemented. Naturally their implementation ideas can only be as up-to-date as their experience and technological knowledge. This solution-oriented thinking is a perfectly normal human way of communicating and most of the time we don't even realize we are doing so. But if you are going to make a change to a larger system you need to understand the real problem rather than one potential solution.

Following is an actual conversation between an architect and the owner of a house about to be renovated:

"I want a 70-cm-wide oven."

"Why do you want a 70-cm-wide oven?"

"Because I can't fit my large baking dish in my current 60-cm-wide oven."

"Why do you want to fit that dish in the oven?"

"To cook large birds like geese and turkeys."

"When was your oven installed?"

"Twenty years ago."

"Since then the technology has changed, the internal walls of modern ovens are much thinner. I suspect you could fit the large baking dish into one of the new 60-cm-ovens. That would be less expensive because then we would not need to completely redesign that side of the kitchen to allow for the extra-wide oven."

The architect has asked the "Why" questions so he can understand what is really behind the new requirement. He has asked the "When" question to try and understand the householder's mental model of what he believes is possible. His persistence has paid off because he has uncovered the real requirement from the original solution. And by so doing he has been able to come up with a better, in this case cheaper, solution.

When you are trying to understand a new requirement remind yourself everyone has his own mental model of the world and naturally we tend to talk to other people as if they have the same model. It is very tempting to think just in terms of a solution. But in order to make changes that improve the value of that software, we need to think further and discover the reasoning behind making the change.

Some considerations when trying to uncover the real requirement are:

- What is the real goal behind this requirement?
- What are the socio-technical boundaries of the investigation?
- Do I understand the requirer's mental model?
- Why does the requirer have this requirement?
- Does the requirer have preconceived ideas about the solution?

It's a requirement, not a solution, if you can state it in technologically-neutral terms.

One question we are often asked is how does one know one has a requirement and not a solution? The answer is when you can state the requirement in technologically neutral terms within the boundaries of the problem you are trying to solve. For example take the statement "I want a 70-cm oven." By asking the "Why" questions we arrive at the real requirement—the product shall be able to roast a goose or turkey. This technologically neutral statement means we can now come up with the most appropriate solution within the constraints.

2. Understand the Inside

The inside of the system we intend to change—we are talking about all the elements of the system, not just the software—is usually made up of a combination of designed physical systems and human activity systems. For example, suppose you have a requirement to report on the relative profitability of a pharmaceutical company's product range. To be able to effectively implement the new requirement in the existing system, without upsetting anything, you need to understand the details of how the system works now.

Understand Existing Software

From the point of view of existing software systems, you need to understand which parts of existing software may be affected by the change you are proposing to make. The relative difficulty of answering this question is affected by:

- The age of the software
- The quality of the original design
- The number of people who have made changes
- The change-control procedures that have been used
- The quality of the documentation
- Your familiarity with the software system
- Access to people who are familiar with the software system
- The degree of systems thinking applied in making previous changes

The longer the software has been around and the more people who have modified it (without using systems thinking) the more time-consuming it will be to understand it.

> *Program documentation is notoriously poor, and its maintenance is worse. The solution is to incorporate the documentation in the source program. Such programs are called self documenting.*
>
> —Fred Brooks, *The Mythical Man-Month*

You have to learn enough about the existing program or programs to identify the parts that are concerned with the company's product range and its profitability. You are trying to answer questions like: Which parts of the program refer to the product range? Does any part of the current program calculate profitability? If you change this calculation are other parts of the program affected? You are using your understanding of the new requirement to guide you to the relevant parts of the code.

If you are lucky, previous maintainers have left you a trail by documenting what they learned when they changed the software. If you are extremely lucky, the trail they have left is up to date. As Fred Brooks pointed out, it makes sense at the beginning of a program's life to incorporate the documentation in the source code. Then it is much more likely subsequent maintainers take the trouble to keep the documentation up to date.

When you change an undocumented or inaccurately documented program the tendency is not to bother with documenting the change. After all it has never been documented before, so why start now, especially when it is such a mammoth job?

You will never have time to document the whole program, but it does subsequently save time—and add very little to your time—to document what you have learned by making your change. By leaving a trail you save the next person—and there will be a next person; whatever you are changing will be changed again—having to redo the investigation you have already performed. And the next person may well be you. There is little point kidding yourself you will remember all the details.

Understand Existing Human Activities

Apart from the software we have to understand existing human activity systems that are inside the system boundaries. In your investigation of human activity systems you take exactly the same approach as investigating the software. But this part of the system looks very different: Instead of the implementation being realized in lines of code it lies in human activities such as procedures, documents, emails, phone calls, meetings, and job responsibilities as shown in Figure 7.2.

In our pharmaceutical products example it is necessary to discover who is interested in the profitability of the product range and for what they intend to use the information.

Investigation of human activity systems is usually more complex than investigation of designed physical systems. Whereas code is static while you investigate it, human activity systems are dynamic and often inconsistent. Similar to a software system, human activity systems are often changed in a fragmentary way. When this happens the overall system is not understood by anyone and acquiring an understanding often neces-

Figure 7.2

Software and Humans. A software system and a human activity system are both a complex combination of nodes and interfaces. The human activity systems are more complex to understand because the nodes are human beings who do not necessarily behave consistently.

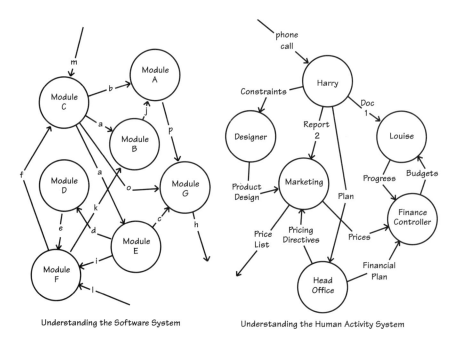

Understanding the Software System   Understanding the Human Activity System

sitates talking to a number of different people and gradually piecing together the details.

The inside of the system you are going to change, both the software and the human elements will always be complex because they reflect reality. Your task is to expose that complexity so you can decide how best to change it and it satisfies the new requirement without upsetting anything.

3. Understand the Outside

Process 3 of the model shown in Figure 7.1 calls for some exogenous thinking; you have to consider all the other systems that may be affected by, or may affect your new requirement. So push your investigation outward and look outside the obvious boundaries of the new requirement.

In the case of the new requirement for reporting on profitability of pharmaceutical products consider the rest of the world. Are any other parts of your organization potentially interested in the profitability analysis? Do any other people, organizations, software, or hardware in the outside world influence your organization's profitability? For example, does the national health authority (FDA, National Health, Health Canada, etc.) have rules or charges you should take into account when analyzing profitability? How about suppliers from whom you buy the raw material for making your drugs: Have you taken all the costs into account?

Go back to Peter Checkland's system types shown above and consider whether any *Designed Physical Systems, Designed Abstract Systems,* or *Human Activity Systems* have any sort of connection with the new requirement.

By asking this set of questions you are ensuring you consider external factors that can affect the new requirement.

4. Question the New

Now that you understand the new requirement and the systems affecting it, you can consider its value to your organization. Consider the following checklist of questions.

- What is the real business advantage of making this change?
- What is the priority of this change?
- Can we improve the advantage?
- Have we considered the impact on existing systems?
- What are any unintended consequences of making this change?
- Do alternatives exist for realizing the advantage?

This is when you consider how making the change will affect other parts of the overall system that is your organization. At this point it helps to build a systems dynamics model—we will discuss how to do this later in the chapter.

5. Choose the Strategy

Now you consider your analysis of the change and determine whether you will implement the new requirement. Have you proved it has enough benefit and is relevant to the project? Does it have a high enough priority? Alternatively, does it suggest unacceptable consequences?

If you intend to go ahead, what strategy will you use for specifying and implementing the requirement? Does it need further investigation? Regardless of its size, treat this change as a project in its own right. Once successful, this new project (the change) has to be integrated with the rest of your project.

We normally use our Volere template as a checklist, quickly going through each of the sections to see if anything remains we need to investigate and/or specify. In the pharmaceutical products profitability analysis, we would consider each of the 27 points on the template as a trigger for asking questions. For example, Section 10 refers to *Look and Feel*. Do any requirements pertain to the presentation and appearance of the report? Does it have to appear as a company product? Do public relations requirements apply necessitating the use of branding, or are there any special appearance requirements relating to the pharmaceutical industry? If so, have those requirements already been specified elsewhere, or do you need to do further investigation to define what they are? Please take a moment to look through the template's table of contents in Appendix B to see how the process works.

System Dynamics

Systems dynamics models help you to evaluate whether the change you propose to make is going to have the effect the requirer wants.

When you make a change to an existing system you are trying to solve some kind of problem. Part of our five-step process for making changes to existing systems is to try to predict whether the change solves the problem and other effects it may have. With a simple change predicting effects may not be too difficult. But if one takes a systemic view of each change, one realizes very few simple changes exist. And due to the complex dynamics of interrelated systems you can easily underestimate the far-reaching effect of a change. Systems dynamics modeling helps to evaluate whether the change you are making is actually going to have the effect the requirer wants.

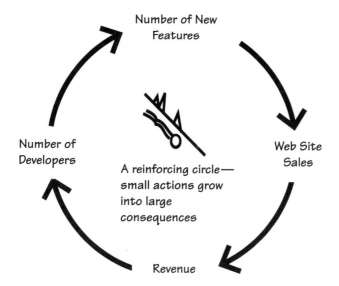

Number of New
Features

Number of
Developers

Web Site
Sales

A reinforcing circle—
small actions grow
into large
consequences

Revenue

Figure 7.3

Dynamics Model 1: This reinforcing loop shows how the number of new features has an effect on Web site sales. This in turn has an effect on revenue. Greater revenue enables more developers to be hired. This in turn has an effect on the number of new features.

In *The Fifth Discipline,* Peter Senge writes about organizations that have used systems thinking skills to realize untapped potential. To find these opportunities, these organizations look past obvious everyday views of their company and take the much wider view—how their company relates to the outside world. A systems dynamics model is a device for exposing this wider view of a system.

Systems dynamics models as we are using them here are made up of reinforcing loops and balancing loops. A reinforcing loop indicates exponential growth or collapse, while balancing loops generate forces of resistance that eventually limit growth. Let's look at some examples.

Dynamics Model 1, shown in Figure 7.3, illustrates a reinforcing loop, symbolized by the snowball rolling down the hill. The model tells us revenue is growing and the company decides to hire more developers. The more developers there are the more new features they can add to their Web site. More features generate more Web site sales that in turn generate more revenue.

However, this happy growth situation at some stage reverses itself—Web site sales start to decline causing a decline in revenue, which in turn leads to laying off developers and reducing the number of new features. To understand why this collapse happens, we need to look at Dynamics Model 2 in Figure 7.4.

The company becomes a victim of its own success. Revenue increases because it has lots of developers to build new features that attract Web site sales. But the huge number of Web site sales causes a decline in response time, and after a while people become frustrated with the delay,

Systems dynamics models as we are using them here are made up of reinforcing loops and balancing loops. A reinforcing loop indicates exponential growth or collapse, while balancing loops generate forces of resistance that eventually limit growth.

Figure 7.4

Dynamics Model 2: The balancing loop at the right helps us to understand the reason for the decline in revenue. The increase in Web site sales eventually causes an increase in response time. After a period of time this makes customers more conscious of delay and causes them to reduce their visits to the Web site that in turn reduces Web site sales.

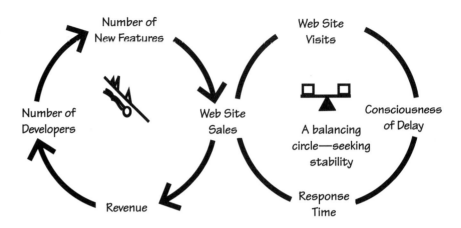

ceasing to visit the site. Becoming a victim of success is a problem that does happen from time to time. People Express is a now-defunct airline that was at one time the fifth largest carrier in the United States. This low-cost carrier became so popular with its customer that demand began to outstrip supply, and the need to introduce extra staff quickly led to a decline in standards the airline was not able to arrest. Five years after founding, People Express went out of business.

The third model, shown in Figure 7.5, exposes the real problem; a systems thinker will see the response time is at the heart of understanding variations in this system's behavior.

The additional balancing loop in shown in Figure 7.5 shows how the difference between response time and expected response time suggests the need to improve the response time. The addition of a long-term plan based on the perceived need to improve the response time identifies planned improvements. The implementation delay indicates a period of time transpires before the Web site capacity can be increased. But when it is, it reduces the response time, which in turn reduces the consciousness of delay and increases site visits leading to increased site sales.

We have found dynamics models useful to predict consequences of changes, and to help plan strategy for making and monitoring changes to systems. Going back to Figure 7.5 for a moment, suppose this is your project and the implementation delay looks longer than you planned. You expect the resulting decline in Web site capacity will affect the response time. What can your organization do to avoid losing customers? Maybe warning them and telling them what you are doing about it will help—most people respond well when you tell them the truth. Maybe you can devise some special loyal customer benefit that will encourage

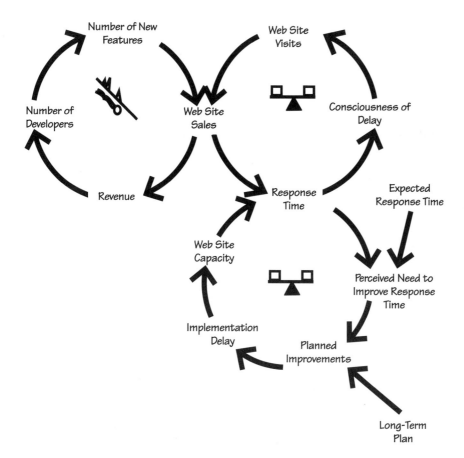

Figure 7.5

Dynamics Model 3. The recognition of the difference between the response time and the expected response time identifies the perceived need to keep the two in synch. Management actions need to be directed towards keeping the model in balance.

them to stay with you during the difficult period. Lots of ideas come about when you understand the real problem.

These models are not prescriptive. Their purpose is to try to understand why systems behave as they do. Also, they make it possible for people to understand the mental models of others. They are a powerful tool for making management decisions and planning changes to existing systems.

What Do I Do Right Now?

Consider the project success indicators we describe in Chapter 1. The following PSIs are affected by your practices for dealing with new requirements for existing systems:

- No excessive schedule pressure
- On-budget delivery

- Lack of creeping requirements
- Control of changes
- Completion not cancellation
- Product adds value
- No misunderstood requirements

The longer a system exists the more likely changes in customs, people, and technology obscure its original purpose.

New requirements have an impact on many PSIs because they affect the size, complexity, and stability of your project. New requirements for systems that have existed for some time are particularly likely to have unforeseen consequences due to the archaeological effect. The longer a system exists, the more likely changes in customs, people, and technology obscure its original purpose. So, depending on the number of layers, every change to that system requires more "dig time" to understand the consequences of a change.

Take some time—even two minutes per success indicator—to ask yourself:

- How do our new requirements affect our ability to meet that success indicator?
- What changes can we make to our new requirements practices to improve that success indicator?

For example, if you are suffering from excessive schedule pressure—ask yourself why. Many possible reasons exist, one of them might be because the effect of new requirements is not reflected in the project plan. Maybe some of this is caused by the "just one more tiny thing" effect. It's only one tiny thing, just add it—it's not worth going through changing the scope and the plan and assessing the impact. And it might really be just one tiny thing the first time, but if it happens once it will keep on happening and the cumulative effect creates schedule pressure. What you have to deliver (due to all the new requirements) and the schedule you planned are no longer in synch.

If you recognize this as one of your problems then maybe you can improve things by having more rigour in the process for identifying, analyzing, and implementing new requirements.

Or perhaps the PSI you want to focus on is whether the product is adding value. Maybe you have lost some customers lately or people have been making complaints about your product—perhaps your help desk is swamped with unhappy customers.

What's the Least I Can Get Away With?

Encourage your project team to treat every change to an existing system as a miniature project in its own right. Any change is not just a change to

CHOCOLATE

Your authors live in London in a terrace or row house we thought unremarkable until we looked into its history. The house was built in 1834, with a certain George Gutch as the architect. Gutch was also the architect of the Grand Union Canal that runs at the end of the street. He designed our row of houses and several similar terraces in this district.

The five floors of the house are linked by a staircase at the back. This rear-staircase design was invented by George Gutch for our row of houses and was subsequently used in many other London terraces. George lived in our house, and his sister Mrs. Colville lived next door. According to the indenture document we uncovered, we know George rented out part of his property in 1869 to a Mrs. Purvis for the sum of sixty-four pounds per annum. The property has been bought and sold many times since then. Our friends Roddy Taylor and Tony Maitland bought it from an Irish lady called Mrs. Doyle before selling it to us. The colorful Mrs. Doyle ran a brothel on the top floors, and to ensure an orderly house, let the basement to a policeman from nearby Paddington Green police station. She had the rooms all painted pink with a pattern of powder puffs. Mrs. Doyle was a religious person and pictures of the saints covered the stairwell walls—no doubt for the spiritual well-being of her customers.

Existing systems: When we bought this house it was much as George Gutch had designed it. During our renovations, we planned to cut a new doorway. When work started on this the builder made a startling discovery. The area where we wanted the door was held up not by a steel beam as we had assumed, but by a brick arch. Readers with a keen eye for history will have spotted that this house

continued

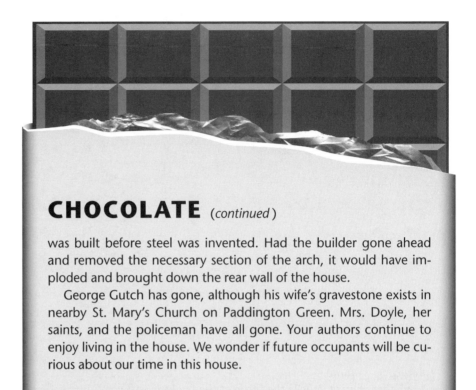

CHOCOLATE (*continued*)

was built before steel was invented. Had the builder gone ahead and removed the necessary section of the arch, it would have imploded and brought down the rear wall of the house.

George Gutch has gone, although his wife's gravestone exists in nearby St. Mary's Church on Paddington Green. Mrs. Doyle, her saints, and the policeman have all gone. Your authors continue to enjoy living in the house. We wonder if future occupants will be curious about our time in this house.

software; it is a change to a larger system that may be composed of many designed physical systems and human activity systems.

We have described a five-step systematic approach to making changes to existing systems. As a project manager you can use the approach as a checklist for managing both small changes and large ones.

Systems dynamics models are a tool for predicting and understanding the behavior of a whole system. Use them to assess the impact of changes and to communicate with other project managers.

Resources for Requirements for Existing Systems

The following sources, in addition to those already referenced, have useful information on requirements for existing systems.

- Brooks, Fred. *The Mythical Man-Month.* Addison-Wesley, 1975—*This book is worth reading for the wonderful insights from his time as project manager for the IBM System 360. This collection of essays knits together experiences with the technical and sociological systems involved in doing a complex project.*

- Checkland, Peter. *Systems Thinking, Systems Practice.* John Wiley & Sons, 1993—*This book explains the details of the soft systems theory and how you can apply to understand and make changes to any system. The taxonomy of types of systems is particularly useful.*
- Senge, Peter M. *The Fifth Discipline. The Art and Practice of the Learning Organization.* Doubleday, 1990—*This is Senge's classic on how organizations should use systems thinking as a tool for business planning and making better decisions by looking at the whole system.*
- Senge, Peter M., et al. *The Fifth Discipline Fieldbook. Strategies and Tools for Building a Learning Organization.* New York: Doubleday. 1994—*Comprehensive exercises and tutorials on how to build and apply systems thinking models.*
- Weinberg, Jerry. *Quality Software Management.* Dorset House, 1992—*Volume 1 Systems Thinking, 1992, looks at the problem of thinking about the correct "system"—the system for doing business, and not just the computer system. Volume 2 First-Order Measurement, 1993, tackles the subject of how measurement is part of any quality movement. Volume 3 Congruent Action, 1994, solves the problem of acting together to solve problems. Volume 4 Anticipating Change, 1997, discusses the idea of managing change. While the focus of the books is software management, the content is applicable to any kind of development project.*

Measuring Requirements

An all-too-often failing in software projects is the inability to estimate the resources and time needed to deliver the product. Projects run late, often because we do not know the size of the task. Without measuring the task, it is close to impossible to make accurate predictions. This chapter is a primer on counting function points as a way of measuring the size of the work area under study and using its size to estimate the effort needed for gathering its requirements.

One of the most common problems facing project managers today is being asked to give a firm estimate of the time needed before knowing how much effort is involved. For some reason, you are supposed to be able—on day one of a project—to say precisely, categorically, and irrevocably how long it will take. Keep in mind all you may know about the project at this stage is its name, and it might be similar to a project you undertook several years ago.

What is wrong with this? The answer is you had no opportunity to measure. It stands to reason before you can know how long it will take to study a piece of work and derive a product to improve that work, you have to know the size of the piece of work. Obviously, the larger and more complex the work area, the longer it takes. But how big is "large"? To answer that, we have to be able to *measure* the size and complexity of the work.

Measuring is neither new nor unique. The building contractor estimating the right amount to charge is quite careful to measure the size of

> " *Function Points are aimed specifically at what users care about, and they are first calculated during the requirements phase.* "
>
> —Capers Jones, *Assessment and Control of Software Risks*

the task before committing to a fixed-price contract. The catering contractor makes sure to know how many people are to be fed and what they are to eat before agreeing to a price for services. It seems every mature industry measures as an integral part of its project work.

The Limited Aim of This Chapter

This chapter gives you enough on function point counting to measure the size of the work area and, from that, estimate the effort needed to complete requirements activity. It is not a full treatise on function point counting, and we have somewhat simplified the process. If you would like to learn more about the subject, please explore other more complete sources of function point counting. We cite several at the end of the chapter.

Measure the functionality of the work area, and from that project the requirements effort.

The limited aim of this chapter is to show you how approachable function point counting can be, and to demonstrate easy ways of using the technique to measure and estimate the effort necessary for your requirements project.

What Do You Measure?

Although function point counting was originally developed to measure the functionality of software, we can use the same technique to estimate the requirements activity. To give you an idea of function point counting, we are borrowing an analogy from Carol Dekkers of Quality Plus Technologies. (At this stage the authors wish to acknowledge the help given by Carol Dekkers in writing this chapter. Any remaining errors are due to the authors, and are definitely not Carol's.) Carol points out if you want to know how much it will cost to build a house, you ask the architect. Suppose rough sketch plans have been drawn and, from them, the architect measures the area of the building. "That comes to 2400 square feet," he tells you, "and this style of building runs to about $100 per square foot." Now you have a good idea of the projected cost.

Using this analogy, if you wish to estimate how much your requirements project will cost, measure the work area you are about to study. While the architect measures the number of square feet the building will occupy, you measure the number of function points—the functionality—within the work you intend to study.

The functionality is the work that is done—the calculations, the reporting, the storing, and retrieving of data, and so on. Keep in mind you are measuring nonrepetitive work. Nonrepetitive means you measure a piece of functionality once regardless of how many times it is performed in a given time period.

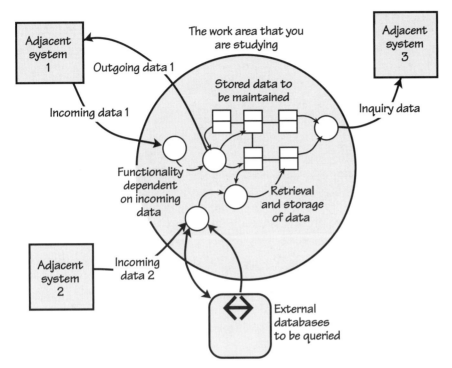

Figure 8.1

The work you are studying contains functionality and stored data. The functionality is triggered by incoming data, and the nature of the functionality is directed by that data. The stored data also needs functionality to maintain it. Queries on the stored data require yet more functionality. Function point counting measures this functionality.

As an example of functionality, look at the many mobile telephones on sale. You immediately notice the significant variation in price among models. Why? Because more expensive phones have more features. In other words, they have more functionality, or do more work. (We are ignoring the premium that manufacturers charge for exotic materials and "coolness.")

In the same way, you are measuring with the objective of estimating the effort needed to study a work area. The variable from one project to another is the functionality of the work area under study. Simply put, the more functionality contained in the work area, the more effort needed to study the work area and write the requirements for a product to accomplish some or all of that functionality.

Measuring functionality is the role of function points (see Figure 8.1).

The basis of function point counting is the amount of functionality within the work area is in proportion to the number of data items being processed and their complexity. Each data flow that enters and leaves the context carries data that requires an amount of processing to be performed upon it. To put it another way: If a flow contains many different data elements, sufficient functionality must exist to produce and process each element of data. Similarly, if data stored within the work has many

The basis of function point counting is the amount of functionality within the work is proportionate to the amount and complexity of the data being processed.

attributes and has a complex arrangement, it requires a lot of functionality to maintain and retrieve it.

This relationship between data and functionality means we can measure functionality, in other words count function points, by measuring the data in the data flows entering and leaving the context and by measuring the stored data used by the work. The latter is measured whether contained in the scope of your work area or held in databases maintained outside yet referenced by the work.

Having measured the functionality of the work area in function points, you apply a metric representing the time or effort needed by your organization to study and specify the requirements for one function point's worth of work. Given the independence of function points from type of system, this metric is valid regardless of the nature of the project you are about to undertake.

If function points are completely new to you, it may be useful to consider the following examples of software systems and their sizes. These figures come from Capers Jones of Software Productivity Research. Jones counted the function points after these systems were installed.

- Airline reservation—25,000
- Insurance claims—15,000
- Telephone billing—11,000
- Visual basic—3,000
- Word 7.0—2,500
- Aircraft radar—3,000
- Unix v5—50,000

Jones also gives us the average cost in the United States of specifying and installing a single function point. Although he (correctly) gives a range, we find it convenient to use a midpoint number of $1,000. Please do not rely on this figure—it is intended only to show the kind of projections that are possible using function points.

If your project is not for in-house development, but rather for other types of projects, the principles of function point counting still apply. If, for example, you are about to build a software product for sale, simply revert to the original idea of counting the function point for the software. The only difference is the metric of the effort needed for determining its requirements. Similarly, you can use function point counting for maintenance or enhancement projects. In these cases, the count measures additional functionality to be provided.

Count function points by measuring the data flows that enter and leave the work area, and the stored data used by the work.

Counting the Function Points

You are measuring the functionality of a business or work area. Start by defining the scope of that area. As part of your initiation routine we suggest you build a context model to provide the basis for the function point measurement. The context model can be created, literally, within a few days of the project getting under way, giving you an early indication of the amount of requirements analysis to come. See Figure 8.2 for an example.

Note the context model at this stage is a model of the *work area* you are about to study. It does not matter whether this work is automated or manual, the context simply defines the scope of your study. You are measuring this scope with the intention of determining how long it will take to complete your study.

Stored Data

Every piece of work you study contains stored data. The databases, files, archives, and so on that our work areas maintain and reference all add to the functionality of the work. During the requirements activity you may already know you will be using established databases. Alternatively, it may be part of your project to design and install them. In either case, all

See Chapter 4—Learning What People Need for information on how the work context diagram relates to the gathering and specifying of requirements.

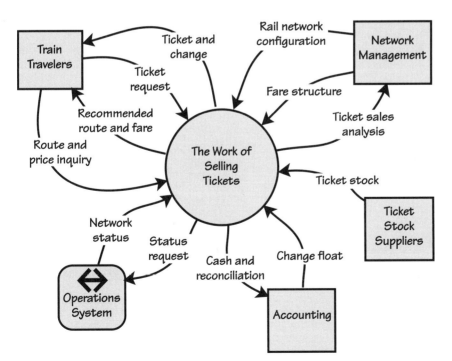

Figure 8.2

A context model for the business of selling tickets for a commuter rail system. The model shows data that enters and leaves the business area. These flows, together with the data stored and retrieved by the work, are used to estimate the effort needed to study the requirements. Data stores do not appear on this model but are the subject of their own model. The *Operations System* is an external system that maintains stored data used by the Ticket Selling work.

you need to know for function point counting is the data to store—in the abstract sense.

It does not matter if you are using databases or other means to store your data; it should be a relatively simple matter to have a member of your team with a working knowledge of data modeling to assemble a first-cut model for the data stored within your context. This model shows the classes, or entities, of stored data. We do not need an extreme degree of precision to count function points; it suffices to know the approximate number of attributes for each of the classes. This should not be a time-consuming exercise because the data modeler's first attempt should be close enough for our purposes here.

In Figure 8.3 we show a data model for the ticketing business we showed in Figure 8.2. These are the entities you would expect to find. Each *Station* is part of a *Line*—travelers use lines to navigate the system. The station falls into a *Zone* that determines the *Fare*. This organization wants to know how many of different ticket types were sold and the amount for each, so each is recorded as a *Fare Sale*.

Each of the classes contains attributes. (By now it should be apparent we are using the terms "class" and "entity" interchangeably. Please think in whichever term is common in your organization.) Attributes are the actual data elements. That is, they have an alphanumeric value. For example, the entity *Fare* would have attributes of:

Fare type—adult, child, concession
Journey type—one way, round trip
Price
Time of day restrictions—some fares are not available in peak hours
Perhaps one or two others

RESOURCE NOTE

Suzanne and James Robertson's *Complete Systems Analysis,* Dorset House, 1994, contains a detailed tutorial on how to build work context diagrams.

Figure 8.3

This model of the stored data shows the subjects of the data stored by the ticketing work. Each of the classes or entities on the model represents a collection of attributes. We use these to count the function points attributed to the stored data.

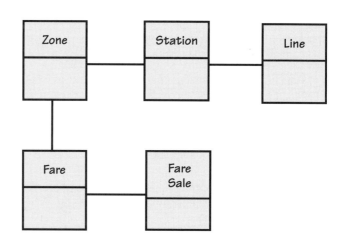

The classes shown on the model should be in second or third normal form. If that term is unfamiliar to you—and no good reason exists why you should know it—it means all the data attributes belonging to the entity pertain to the subject of the entity, and not to anything else. For example, all of the attributes for the *Fare* entity describe a fare. No attributes exist for the *Fare Sale* or the *Zone* stored in the *Fare* entity.

The need is for a model that reasonably represents the data stored in the work context regardless of the medium or technology used to store it. We prefer to use a class model to represent it, but if you already use another data modeling notation it will give you an equivalent result.

Stored data contributes to the functionality of the work area, but we defer counting it until after we have looked at counting the business use cases.

Business Use Cases

We discussed earlier in this book how any piece of work can be partitioned into business use cases. To briefly recap, business use cases are the processing that is done by the work area in response to some external stimulant—a business event—that is usually demanding a service provided by the work. The business use case includes some processing, and some data stored and/or retrieved by the process.

If we take the context model for the ticket-selling work shown in Figure 8.2 and partition it into its business use cases, the resulting list would be as shown in Figure 8.4.

Looking through the table you see that two kinds of business use cases exist: those that originate outside the work (*Sell ticket to traveler*) and those triggered by time (*Produce ticket sales analysis*). This difference is important to function point counting as it counts the business use cases slightly differently depending on whether they are an *input,* an *output,* or an *inquiry*. We show examples of each of these as we work through the counting process.

Measuring the Business Use Cases

Let's take one of the business use cases triggered by an event—the *business event*—that happens outside of the work context. The result of this business event is that a flow of data appears at the boundary of the work signaling the event occurred.

In Figure 8.5 we show a model of one of these externally-triggered business use cases, in this instance *Sell ticket to traveler*. We have used regular data flow notation here as it is appropriate at requirements time and

Figure 8.4 These are the business use cases we derive from the context model. Note that the input and output flows are all shown on the context model in Figure 8.2.

Name of Business Use Case	Input or Triggering Data Flow	Output Flow	Processing
Sell ticket to traveler	Ticket request	Ticket and change	Check that destination is reachable; calculate fare; dispense ticket; record sale
Answer travel inquiry	Route and price inquiry	Recommended route and fare	Find available route; calculate fare; advise traveler
Update rail information	Rail network configuration	None	Change data about rail network
Update fares	Fare structure		Change the fare data to reflect the new structure
Update supplier delivery of stock	Ticket stock	None (they do not appear to give a receipt)	Install the stock in the ticketing outlets
Update accounting delivery of the float	Change float	None	Add the money to the cash dispensers
Produce ticket sales analysis	None (this is triggered by time)	Ticket sales analysis	Retrieve and report all sales data
Count the takings	None (this is triggered by time, probably the end of shift)	Cash and reconciliation	Count the money and compare it with the ticket sales

convenient for function point counting. What you measure in function point counting is shown on these models.

However, we hasten to add you may not actually build these until some time after you need to measure the size of the work. It is possible to carry out the measurement from the context model with a shrewd guess at the data to be stored therein. We are illustrating the counting process using the business use case models to make it easier to explain.

The primary intention of this business use case is to get the output flow. That is, the traveler wants a ticket (and change if necessary), and the input he provides is whatever is needed to get the ticket. In function point counting terminology this business use case is called an *output* or, to be completely precise, an *external output*. Along with the significant output flow, this kind of business use case must also contain processing that makes some calculations, or updates stored data, or both.

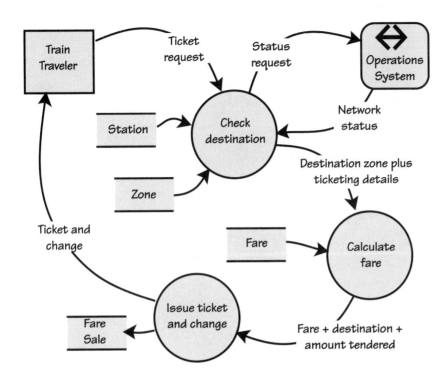

Figure 8.5

This business use case is triggered by the event of a traveler wanting a ticket; the work learns of this event by arrival of the input *Ticket request*. Note also the data entities used and the resulting output *Ticket and change*. The *Operations System* is an external system containing a database. This is queried by the business use case to determine if the destination station is operational and reachable. This external data store is counted by the function point computation.

Because it is an output business use case, we start with attributes of the output data flow *Ticket and change:*

Origin station
Destination station
Price paid
Type of journey
Fare type
Date
Change

That makes seven data elements. Hold on to this number for a moment.

At this stage it is not vital you know precisely what all the elements are, but you should know how many of them there are in the flow. We realize you are counting very early in the development cycle, so it is permissible—providing you are being sensible and no measurement purists are watching—to guess at some of these. You will see in a little while why you can guess.

Now we look at the stored data used by this business use case. Figure 8.5 shows the *Station* entity is referenced to determine the traveler has

Figure 8.6

This is the table showing function point counts for business use cases where the primary intention is to provide an output. The correct terminology for these is *external outputs*.

Data Elements

	1–5	6–19	20+
<2	4	4	5
2–3	4	5	7
>3	5	7	7

Data Entities Referenced

elected a valid destination. The business use case also checks that the station is operational and can currently be reached. It does this by interrogating the database belonging to the *Operations System*. Then it has to calculate the fare, which it does by referencing the *Zone* of the station and looking at the *Fare* entity. Finally, it records the sale in the *Fare Sale* entity. So five entities are referenced or written to by this business use case.

These counts are converted to function points by referencing the table in Figure 8.6. The 7 *data elements* of the output flow put us in the middle column, and the 5 *data entities referenced* means we are on the bottom row. The intersection gives us 7 function points.

We mentioned before it is permissible to guess a little about the number of data elements in the data flow. The table in Figure 8.6 shows ranges for the number of data elements. Providing you can guess to within these ranges, we see no reason to specify precisely each of the flows around the context at this stage.

Add the count for this business use case to the accumulated function point count for the work and then count the next business use case. Continue the process until you have counted all of them.

Not all of the business use cases are of the same type. That is, some of the externally-triggered ones are classified as *external inputs*. These are counted slightly differently. And we have yet to discuss how we count the temporal business use cases.

Counting Input Business Use Cases

There is a business use case called *Update fares*. This qualifies as an external input because its primary intention is to update some internally stored data. Outputs from this kind of business use case, if any, are trivial. In this example, the incoming flow *Fare structure* causes changes to some

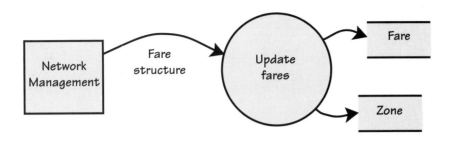

Figure 8.7

The primary intention of this input business use case is to alter internally stored data.

of the data stores within the scope of the work. This business use case is shown in Figure 8.7.

Earlier we discussed the stored data and said the entity *Fare* had about six attributes. So it is reasonable for any of these to be updated. Thus, the data flow *Fare structure* must have at least six attributes. Let's guess and say it contains three more attributes used to update the *Zone* entity.

The next part of the method is to count stored entities or classes referenced by the input. When counting function points for inputs, you count any data stores read or updated by the processing for the input. The example in Figure 8.7 shows two entities are referenced by this business use case.

The next part is to convert those two counts to function points. For that we use the table shown in Figure 8.8.

So far we have said that the input flow *Fare structure* contains 9 data elements or attributes. We have also seen that to process this input flow, the work accesses 2 data entities. The cell at the intersection of these counts gives a result of 4 function points.

These function points are added to the aggregation, and you continue with the rest of the business use cases.

Data Elements

	1–4	5–15	16+
<2	3	3	4
2	3	4	6
>2	4	6	6

Data Entities Referenced

Figure 8.8

The function point counts for an input business use case. Note the input must come from an adjacent system. The correct function point counting terminology for these is *external inputs*.

Temporal or Time-Triggered Business Use Cases

Two of the business use cases shown in Figure 8.4 happen because it is time for them to happen. These are called *temporal* or *time-triggered* business use cases. You find these periodic happenings in every piece of work. For example:

- It is time to report on the week's sales.
- 30 days have elapsed since the invoice was sent and it is still unpaid.
- A holders policy is due to expire in 60 days.
- It is 1.5 seconds since the system checked the altitude.

Temporal business use cases usually provide some kind of reporting. For example, in the ticket selling work, an example of a temporal business use case (triggered by the temporal event *Time to produce the ticket sales analysis*) is called *Analyze Ticket Sales*. Figure 8.9 shows how this appears in data flow notation. Note because this is a time-triggered business use case, there is no incoming flow of data to get the processing started. By convention we do not show a time trigger—it would be something like an alarm clock reminding the work of the time—so the process simply starts up and reads the stored data.

Temporal business use cases can also be triggered by someone outside the work who wants some information. If that person were to select it from a menu—or in the case of a manual system yell "Hey, Bert! Can I have the ticket sales analysis now?"—we consider "it is time" the work produced it.

The name given to this kind of business use case in the function point counting method is *inquiry*. As the stored data within the work is being inquired upon, this is a reasonable name for it. If, however, the processing is more than just the simple retrieval of stored data then it is classified as an *output*. The latter comes into play if stored data is updated or nontrivial calculations are involved. The count must reflect this by allowing for its greater complexity.

If the business use case shown in Figure 8.9 were an on-demand report, it would be possible for someone in *Network Management* to enter parameters to get the analysis they wanted. Unless non-trivial processing goes on as a result and/or data stores are modified, this is still considered an inquiry type business use case. In this case, you count the data elements in both the input parameter flow and the resultant output flow. However, if a data element appears in both input and output flows, only count it once.

Temporal business use cases are either outputs—where non-trivial calculations take place and/or stored data is updated—or inquiries where

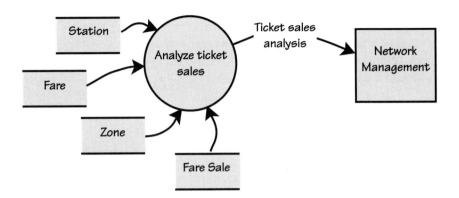

Figure 8.9

The temporal business use case of *Analyze Ticket Sales*. Note this use case is triggered by time, and so no input comes from the outside world. This business use case is an *inquiry* type. That is, stored data is simply retrieved and not modified; no calculations are performed.

the intention is to present information to the outside world and no significant processing occurs.

To count the function points for the business use case shown in Figure 8.9, use the inquiry table shown in Figure 8.10. This business use case refers to 4 data entities, which puts us on the bottom row of the table. Now, all you need is the number of data elements in the flow *Ticket sales analysis*. Note these are *unduplicated* elements. You are counting unique data elements or what may be called *data element types*. In any event, if you look at the table you see you have two options: 5 or more than 5. No contest. Even without talking to the people in *Network Management*, there must be more than 5 elements in the report that they want. (If there were to be some input parameters, it would not make any difference.) So this output adds 6 function points to our accumulation.

Again, add the function points from this business use case to the accumulated total.

Data Elements

Data Entities Referenced	1–5	6–19	20+
1	3	3	4
2–3	3	4	6
>3	4	6	6

Figure 8.10

The table showing the function point counts for *inquiries*.

The Stored Data Are Also Counted

The data stored in the work area must be maintained. This naturally requires an amount of functionality and it, too, is counted by measuring the amount and complexity of the data.

The first of the stored data to be measured is the data held inside the work area. Function point counting manuals refer to these as *internal logical files*. These are the databases, flat files, paper files, or whatever else is part of the current work area. Keep in mind any files having to do with implementation are not counted, for example, backups and manual files that are identical (or close) to automated files.

Again, use the entity or class model of the data to count from. This time, for each entity count the *attributes* or *data elements* (the terms are synonymous) it contains. Skip any attributes that are stored for purely technological reasons but count foreign keys (pointers from one class to another). The count should be accurate enough to assign the class to one of the three columns shown in Figure 8.12.

The next count is *record elements*. These are subtypes of entities. As an example, let's make a change to the stored data for the ticket-selling system. Suppose *Stations* in the ticketing work can be of different types. Some stations are located where buses stop right outside, and for these stations the system sells transfer tickets. The fare structure is such that commuters can buy a combined ticket for train and bus if they are travelling to a transfer station. Some of the stations are wheelchair accessible—not all, as this is an old rail network. So the *Station* entity would be changed to look like Figure 8.11.

In function point terms, the *Station* entity counts for 2 record elements. You count only the subtypes, and not the parent entity. For the other entities in the class model, count them as having 1 record element.

Figure 8.11

The *Station* entity has two subtypes. One contains attributes about transfers available from this station, and the other has attributes describing the degree of wheelchair and other handicapped access. These subtypes are necessary, as transfer attributes do not apply to all stations. Neither are all stations accessible, and so accessible attributes are not stored if not needed.

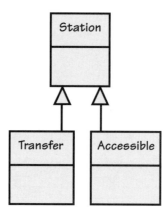

Data Elements or Attributes

Record Elements	1–19	20–50	51+
<2	7	7	10
2–5	7	10	15
>5	10	15	15

Figure 8.12

The function point counts for internally stored data, or *internal logical files* as they are known in function point terminology.

As an example, let's go back to the *Fare* entity we mentioned earlier. You can see this as part of the stored data model in Figure 8.3. (By the way, you can call this a data model, a class model, or an entity model. For our purposes they are all the same thing.) We said that the attributes of *Fare* are:

Fare type—Adult, child, concession.
Journey type—One way, round trip.
Price.
Time of day restrictions—Some fares are not available in peak hours.
Perhaps one or two others.

The "perhaps one or two others" may seem a little cavalier. But look at the table in Figure 8.12. You need only to know if there are between 1 and 19 attributes to the class, or between 20 and 50, or more than 51. Given the range of these numbers, and given the need to do this relatively quickly, it is permissible to make some inspired guesses as to the number of attributes for the entity.

So let's say *Fare* falls into the first column. It has no subtypes (no need exists for specialist attributes) and so it counts for 7 function points. You do this for the remainder of the stored data. Most of them also have a count of 7, as none of them has more than 19 attributes, and only *Station* has 2 subtypes, and even has few enough attributes to count for 7 function points. There are 5 entities in the stored data model, so the *internal* stored data attracts 35 function points.

Externally Stored Data

Most of the work you study relies on externally stored data. By this stage our organizations have automated so much of their data, and there is so

Figure 8.13

The *Operations
System* is an external
system that maintains
a database of the
operational status of
the network. The
ticket-selling work
queries it.

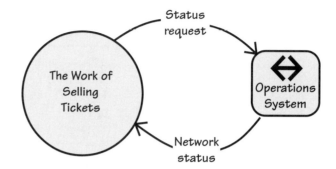

much of it, it is almost impossible to find a piece of work that does not
have to go outside to get some needed data. Most organizations have a
customer relationship management (CRM) system where you send a request if you want to know anything about a customer. Similarly, if your
work area needs any accounting information, then it gets it from the accounting system.

In the ticket-selling work, the Operations System holds all information about the operational status of the network. So when the work is
selling a ticket, it sends a *Status request* and gets back *Network status*. Figure 8.13 is an extract from the context model that shows the flow.

Although external data does not have to be maintained by the work,
the need for the data adds functionality to the work. So it too is counted.
Do it the same way as you did for the internal data; however, instead of
building a data model let's use educated guesses to size the data.

You are selling a ticket for a train system. You are querying a database
to determine if the destination station is operational and if it is reachable
from the origin station—you'll have very unhappy commuters if you sell
them a ticket and they can't get there. Taking an educated guess at the
data entities gives the following.

A Station—You need to know if it is open.
Line—All stations are on one line or another.
Track section—Trains can break down and you would need to know which
part of the network is blocked.
External influences—You would not sell a ticket to a station if a fire were
raging next door.

None of these has more than 19 attributes—again this is an educated
guess, but you can confirm it by talking to the program manager or database people for Operations. Using the table in Figure 8.14 we see 4 entities, each in column 1, yield 20 function points.

Data Elements or Attributes

	1–19	20–50	51+
<2	5	5	7
2–5	5	7	10
>5	7	10	10

Record Elements

Figure 8.14

This shows the function point counts for *external interface files,* or data stored in an adjacent system.

A small aside: Figure 8.14 shows use of an external file. The flows to and from the adjacent system are *not* counted for function point purposes. The adjacent system in this case is a *cooperative* system. That is, it provides some service in collaboration with the work area. So the flows to and from the cooperative adjacent system are the parameters needed for the inquiry against the database and the resultant information extracted from the database. In both cases their attributes would be the same as the stored data. For function-point counting, think only about the use of the adjacent system's database (in this case it is providing database access) as if it belonged to the work area.

The Story So Far

Use the flows entering or leaving the context model to determine the business events. Each event has a response from the work which we refer to as a business use case. For each of these, ask whether its primary intention is to

- Process the input, update the stored data, make calculations, and produce no significant output—an *input* business use case.
- Use the input flow to produce an output flow, as well as make calculations and update stored data—an *output* business use case.
- Retrieve or report on stored data without making calculations—an *inquiry.*

Count the data elements in the flows, the entities of stored data, and use the appropriate tables to convert to function points. Add these to the accumulated total.

Count the stored data entities and their attributes. Determine if they are stored internally (*internal logical file*) or externally (*external interface file*). Use the appropriate table to convert your counts to function points and add them to the accumulated total.

At this stage the function point counting method calls for an adjustment called *general system characteristics*. This is calculated according to complexity and the technical environment of the work area. The adjustment multiplies the function point count by a factor between 0.65 and 1.35. If you are undertaking the study of a complex work area, consider a complexity multiplier along the lines of the above. On the other hand, if you, like many project managers, are involved in more or less the same kind of work area for each project—and when it comes to requirements the technical environment is practically constant—then the multiplier does not make a lot of sense.

It is becoming common practice for function point counters to ignore general system characteristics. Studies have revealed most people are not getting any benefit from this additional step. So we suggest you skip it.

Adjust for Lack of Data

You are measuring early in the project, and you may not have all the data you need for a completely accurate function point count. We have shown above how you count the function points using the inputs, outputs, inquiries, internal files, and external files. However, even if you do not have all five of these, you can still count function points. The count is simply adjusted according to how many of these parameters you *have* counted.

The table shown in Figure 8.15 gives the *range of uncertainty* depending on the number of parameters you used in your count. For example, if you used only three parameters—say the inputs, outputs, and inquiries (these are easiest because they show up as data flows on the context model)—then your function point count is accurate within a range of +/– 15%.

Figure 8.15

This table comes from Capers Jones. He calculated these uncertainty ranges based on history gathered from many projects in different industries.

Number of parameters used	Range of uncertainty
1	+/– 40%
2	+/– 20%
3	+/– 15%
4	+/– 10%
5	+/– 5%

What Do You Do with Function Points?

The function point count for the requirements activity for the project is simply the addition of the counts for all of the business use cases and the stored data. This is probably a depressingly large number, but we assume you are interested in trying to get to the truth here.

At the beginning of this chapter we used Carol Dekkers' analogy that a function point count of a work area is similar to an architect's count of the number of square feet in a building. The architect has historical figures (cost per square foot) he uses to convert the number of square feet into total estimated cost for the building.

Our equivalent in a requirements project is to convert the function point count into effort needed to gather the requirements by multiplying the number of function points by the time or effort needed by your organization to complete the analysis and requirements for one function point. If you do not know the number for your organization, we suggest starting with somebody else's metric.

Capers Jones of Software Productivity Research gives us the following rule of thumb formula:

$$\textit{Effort in staff months} = \textit{(function points / 150)} * \textit{function points}^{0.4}$$

Thus for a 1000 function point work area (a substantial, but not overly large area) the effort in person hours is $(1000 / 150) * 1000^{0.4}$, which results in 105.66 staff months.

Jones includes in his metric the effort needed for the software developers, the QA personnel, the testers, technical writers, database administrators, and project managers. Keeping in mind Jones is looking at typical software development in which about half the effort is spent debugging, it is safe to say if you take one-third of Jones' number that would cover a thorough requirements effort.

Other people in the field confirm Jones' formula, but remember it is for an entire industry. Your organization is different, and the productivity for requirements gathering at your organization is dependent on many factors. The skill and availability of the business users has an impact, as does the skill of the requirements analyst. You should consider whether your analysts are being asked to work on several projects at once (this slows down all the projects) and whether their physical accommodation is suitable for what they are doing. Your own management skills also have an effect on the morale and productivity of your team.

Despite these variables, it is advisable to start with Jones' metric and work toward your own metric for the rate at which you gather requirements, thus getting consistent estimates of the requirements effort.

Several organizations can provide metrics for productivity rates, and sometimes these can be specified for your particular industry or project type. We have listed some of them under Resources at the end of this chapter.

In Conclusion

We have by no means given you a complete dissertation on counting function points. Our intention was to demonstrate how it is fairly easy to make an accurate measurement of the size of the work to be studied.

You might also be tempted to check out some of the alternative methods of sizing work areas. Mark II function points are available; Tom De-Marco's *Bang* metric is a natural extension to modeling business use cases; Barry Boehm's COCOMO method is the best known of the many automated tools and methods.

Please consider throughout this description we have been using some fairly cavalier terms: "educated guesses," "in the range of," and so on. This does not diminish the usefulness of counting function points as a way of estimating the requirements activity. However, it does mean that any projections you make based on your function point count must have the same degree of reliability. If your function point count is accurate to within +/– 15% then any further calculation you make cannot have a greater degree of accuracy.

You can count function points on day three of the project and give yourself a reasonably accurate guide as to what lies ahead. And you can do this before concrete has set around the deadline.

Early in the project we feel it is far better to have an estimate *accurate* to within +/– 15% than to have a guess in all probability wrong by 100% or more. It is also preferable to have this estimate sooner rather than later.

We do not claim that function point counting is a panacea for all estimation needs, but we would like to point out that most of the Fortune 500 companies use function point counting, as do thousands of other organizations around the world. Most important, you can count function points on day three of the project and give yourself a reasonably accurate guide as to what lies ahead. And you can do this before concrete has set around the deadline.

What Do I Do Right Now?

In Chapter 1—Requirements and Project Success we listed a number of PSIs. The ones to which function point counting contributes are

- No excessive schedule pressure
- On-budget delivery
- Completion, not cancellation

To realize the contribution made by function point counting you naturally have to perform the task. We suggest you start by building a context model and count the function points for the inputs, outputs, and inquiries on the model. Use the tables of function points and accumulate your count. Build a data model for the *internal* stored data, and count function points for that.

Then count the external stored data. Now that we have automated so much of our data, it is likely more external stored data exists than internal. At least, that has been our experience for most of our projects. Building a model for all of it is time consuming and not really profitable. Instead, work as we suggested above and ask the database administrators, programmers, and project leaders to tell you about the data. Let them give you a list of the entities or classes and their attributes, or just the database tables and columns. This will usually be enough for your purposes.

Start with the Jones metric. Measure the performance of your team and derive your own metric for requirements effort needed per function point. This should be gradually refined over the course of several projects. Until you have a metric derived from multiple projects, build an uncertainty factor into your estimates.

What's the Least I Can Get Away With?

Estimation of the effort needed is such an important part of product development, and such a neglected one, we urge you to do more than the minimum. However, try this:

- Build a context model; you cannot get away with less than that.
- Count the flows that enter and leave the context model as part of an external business use case. This is the one where a data flow arrives from outside and triggers a response. The output flow is the product of that response. Count these but do not count those that go to cooperative adjacent systems solely for the purpose of extracting or storing data on their databases.
- Assign five function points to each input and six function points to each output. These are the medium counts. If the flows around your work area are significantly simple or complex, use the low or high counts.
- Don't count the stored data. Just allow that your minimalist function point count has an uncertainty of +/–15%.
- Use the Jones rule of thumb to convert that number to staff months.
- Refine the results over several projects.

CHOCOLATE

Measurements in the world vary. Most nations measure in grams, meters and liters, and some—noticeably the United States and the United Kingdom—still drive miles to their destination and drink pints or fluid ounces of a chosen liquid. If you buy shoes outside your own country, you find your foot is measured differently. The months in the Islamic year start with the sighting of the first crescent after the new moon and therefore do not coincide with the Gregorian calendar. The Chinese year starts at a different time from the Gregorian calendar used in the West. All of these measurements have a foundation in the past.

Global measurements do exist, however, and paradoxically, their origins are unknown. The entire world uses 24 hours in the day, 60 minutes in the hour, and seven days in the week.

The duration of the day matches (more or less) one rotation of the Earth. The ancient Egyptians divided their day into ten parts, with two hours in the morning and the evening set aside for the twilight. During medieval times, there were 12 hours of daylight and twelve of darkness. Thus the duration of an hour varied according to the season. There was no need to tell time as the work day started at dawn, and finished when the sun went down. Nobody needed to know the time. Clocks appeared in the 14th century, and now the day became divided into hours, minutes, and seconds. The number of hours became 24 but nobody knows why.

Similarly, the seven-day week. The Christian Bible explains that God created the world in six days and rested on the seventh. However, a seven-day week was known in Rome before the advent of Christianity. Experts fail to agree on the origin of the seven-day week, with places such as Babylon, Persia, and others being mentioned as its birthplace.

If you want to do even less than that, count around the context of the work; again omit counts for data from external databases. Allow 90 burdened hours of requirements analytical time for each flow. This number is not exactly a random number; several organizations have used it as a starting point. But be sure to adjust it as you complete projects and gather your own numbers.

Resources for Measuring Requirements

There is a lot of material available on the Web, a lot of it free. We mentioned the following organizations earlier in this chapter, and all are good places to start for more information on function points, as well as productivity metrics.

- The David Consulting Group: www.davidconsultinggroup.com
- The Gartner Group: www.gartner.com
- International Software Benchmarking Group: www.isbsg.org.au
- International Function Point Users Group: www.ifpug.org
- META Group: www.metagroup.com
- Quality Plus Technologies: www.qualityplustech.com
- Software Productivity Research: www.spr.com
- United Kingdom Software Metrics Association: www.uksma.co.uk/

The following sources, in addition to those already referenced, have useful information on measuring requirements:

- Dekkers, Carol. *Function Point Counting and CFPS Study Guides, Volumes 1, 2, and 3.* Quality Plus 2002. http://www.qualityplustech. com—*In addition to case studies, all study guides provide logistics/hints for the IFPUG Certified Function Point Specialist (CFPS) Exam.*
- Dekkers, Carol. *Demystifying Function Points: Clarifying Common Terminology.* http://www.qualityplustech.com—*This is used internally at IBM as one of its definition standards.*
- Fenton, Norman, and Shari Lawrence Pfleeger. *Software Metrics—A Rigorous and Practical Approach,* 2nd edition. Thomson Computer Press, 1996—*This looks at several ways of measuring the software development process. The case studies—H-P, IBM, the U.S. DoD—alone, are worth the price of the book.*
- Garmus, David, and David Herron. *Function Point Analysis—Measurement Practices for Successful Software Projects.* Addison-Wesley, 2001— *This book provides a thorough treatment of function point counting using the IFPUG rules.*

- *IFPUG Function Point Counting Practices Manual, release 4.1:* IFPUG, Westerville, OH, 1999.
- Jones, Capers. *Assessment and Control of Software Risks.* Yourdon Press, 1994—*Jones looks at more than 50 of the major problems that can afflict software projects with particular attention to measurement and metrics risks. He also discusses the prevention and therapies for these risks.*
- Pfleeger, Shari Lawrence. *Software Engineering—Theory and Practice,* 2nd edition. Prentice Hall, 2001—*As the title suggest, this is a more general text on software. However, the words on measurement are relevant to this chapter.*
- Putman, Lawrence, and Ware Myers. *Five Core Metrics—The Intelligence behind Successful Software Management.* Dorset House, 2003—*Not function points but other very good ways and things to measure. The authors demonstrate how the five core metrics—time, effort, size, reliability, and process productivity—are used to control and adjust projects.*

Managing the Requirements

*Requirements are the foundation of system develop-
ment. It takes management to build this foundation
correctly and in good time. Here we present how
requirements analysts and project leaders can take
charge of their requirements and ensure they get
the best value from their requirements efforts.*

Getting Management Value from Requirements

This book is based on our experience that products (software or any
other type of product) cannot be built unless the requirements for that
product are known to the builders. How you discover the requirements is
not so important—but it is supremely important you do. This chapter
looks at ways you can manage the team as it goes about finding the requirements.

The requirements question is not whether you are going to find the requirements. You are going to do that either by doing it before you build
something or later during the maintenance of the product. The latter is
far more expensive so it makes sense to do the former. The question is,
how much do you want to invest in requirements? This chapter is about
managing the balance between not knowing the requirements and
spending so much time discovering them the project loses relevance.

Keep in mind when we are talking about requirements we are not necessarily talking about producing the complete requirements specification

*66 It will take too long
to get the requirements
for this product. Why
don't we start building so
that it looks like we are
getting somewhere. 99*

—Dilbert's boss

"Requirements is perhaps the most misunderstood part of systems development. But it is an absolutely critical function. We don't need to eliminate requirements; we need to sharpen and refine them. Good analysts find out things that are not obvious. Sometimes this takes time, but the results are always better systems."

—Ken Orr, *Cutter Executive Report "Agile Requirements"*

before writing a single line of code. While arguments exist for doing it that way, it is possible, often desirable, to produce the product in iterations. This means gathering a small number of requirements, implementing them, getting the client's confirmation, and then proceeding with the next iteration.

Regardless of the approach you take—we discuss your process in Chapter 11—Your Requirements Process—some management factors contribute to successful requirements projects. In this chapter, in no particular order, we tell you about the management factors we have found most useful.

Early in the Project

Getting convergence on the requirements early in the project is one of the most beneficial requirements activities. A recent survey[1] carried out by Cutter Consortium showed the highest reported problem (35%) is the lack of sufficient requirements information at the beginning of a project. This tallies with our personal observations that insufficient attention to the requirements activities early in the project results in projects that expend considerable time and effort before arriving at an understanding of the objective of the project.

A few key deliverables must be established as firmly as practical at the outset—scope, stakeholders, and goals. Figure 9.1 shows these as targets chasing each other.

The *Scope* defines the boundaries of the investigation and the boundaries of the product to be built by the project. We have learned that it minimizes confusion if we build two scope models: one for the investigation and one for the product. The investigation scope determines which stakeholders to include in the requirements study.

Stakeholders define the human society that affects the success or otherwise of the project. A project stakeholder is someone who gains or loses something (functionality, revenue, status, compliance with rules . . .) as a result of the project. These people in turn decide what benefits or goals they want for the project.

Goals define success criteria for the project. They answer the question: "How will we know if this project is or is not a success?" Goals are used to guide the project and to help the project team make choices about where to concentrate their efforts.

Each of these should be able to be established in the first few days of any project. If they can't then it is an indication that insufficient ground-

---

1. Bennetan, E.M. *Requirements: The Eternal Moving Target.* Executive Update Vol 3 No 15, Cutter Consortium, Massachusetts, U.S.A. 2002.

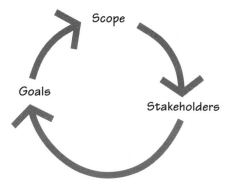

Figure 9.1

The elusive targets. The *Scope* of the requirements study determines which *Stakeholders* become involved. Stakeholders determine the *Goals* of the project, which in turn has an effect on the *Scope*.

work was done before investigating the requirements. The intention of these early deliverables is first to confirm with your client you are about to solve the right business problem, and second to enable you to start assembling the right team to complete the job. We discuss these items in this chapter.

Scope of the Project

We define scope using a context model. This model shows the work you are about to study and its relationship with the outside world. We have already talked about this model in Chapter 4 and discussed how business analysts use it when they elicit requirements. We bring it up again here, as several management issues warrant a closer study.

Figure 9.2 shows an example context model. This is the model you build if you are about to develop a software product to be deployed by employees as they go about their work at this sales company.

The first thing to note is the central bubble is labeled "The Work of. . . ." In this instance, all activity relating to managing personal information is contained within this bubble. This work may include activities performed by humans as well as the work expected of the eventual automated product. The reasoning here is you build products to help people do work. Therefore, you have to understand the work in order to build a relevant product. It might seem a waste that your team is setting out to study things they have no intention of automating, but look at it this way: If they understand the work fully, they will almost certainly build a better product—one that fits right in with the way people work. On the other hand, if they start with the *assumed* product only, the risk is not only of building a product that does not fit into established work practices, but also of missing opportunities for beneficial automation and ideas for improvement of work.

You build products to help people do work. Therefore, you have to understand the work in order to build a relevant product.

Figure 9.2

The work context model for managing personal information for employees.

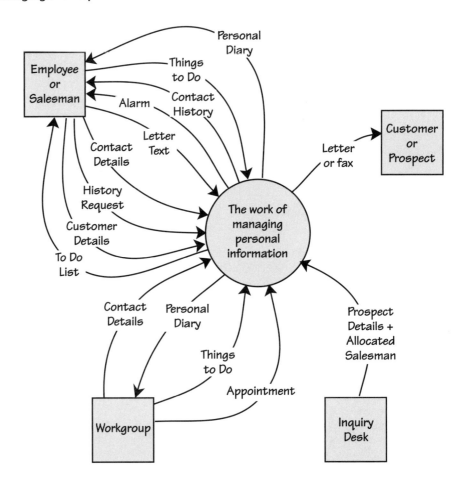

When your business analysts investigate a work scope, they are looking into a *business area*. At some stage, when their understanding of the work is more developed, and they have a much better idea of what is needed by the stakeholders, they define a *product scope*. The product scope is the result of decisions they make about how much of the business area can be profitably made into the eventual product. The product can be a piece of software or it can be a machine, a consumer item, a set of procedures—anything you intend to build. Whatever it is, we call it your product.

In the first few days of the project, you are unlikely to be completely certain of the work scope. In common with many models, this act of modeling helps you firm up your ideas and the ideas of your client, to arrive at a mutually acceptable agreement of the scope of the work area. The context model shows scope by highlighting data connections between the work to be studied and adjacent systems (the squares around the periphery). These connections—data flows to give them their correct name—are collections of data items passed to or from the work. It takes functionality to produce a flow of data, so the flows indicate where that functionality exists. To state the obvious, if a flow leaves the work bubble, some function inside the bubble must have produced it.

It is vital you get a consensus on the context. Part of your task here is to negotiate with the stakeholders (more on this in a moment) as to what should be included, and what specifically excluded. You show these by adding or deleting boundary data flows and/or adjacent systems. The project goals are a useful guide and the context should show that the functions that contribute to delivering the goals are included in the investigation. Naturally the context is somewhat fluid in the early stages as each stakeholder puts forward his claim for inclusion (or otherwise) of features. You may be called on to mediate in disputes and turf wars that sometimes occur. This is often accomplished by facilitating trades between the parties—"We leave out automatic customer checking but include account balancing."

Each flow is produced by some functionality, so the flows indicate where that functionality is.

Your management role here is to strike a balance between keeping the context down to manageable size and including enough functionality to guarantee your project delivers a useful product.

The context is the most useful input to the estimation process. We talked about this in Chapter 8, which includes a demonstration of how the context is the starting point for function point counting. Even if you are not using function points, the context model gives a good visual clue as to the complexity of the task. You can almost eyeball the context model as it develops and make educated guesses as to how much you can accomplish in the available time.

You can almost eyeball the context model as it develops and make educated guesses as to how much you can accomplish in the available time.

The context model should reflect the project goals. Although the output data flows are not specifically mentioned in the goal statement, it is obvious they are contributing to the goals. For instance, if you look at the context shown in Figure 9.2, the project goals include something about managing customer and contact information, as well as provision of a personal diary to the employees.

The context is also a clue to the identity of the stakeholders. As stakeholders are anybody with some interest in the product, it stands to reason that they are identifiable from a model of the business area of the product. Again, refer to the context model in Figure 9.2. Some obvious stakeholders are employees, salesmen, and inquiry desk operators. Customers can be considered stakeholders, since it is possible the product can provide some extra service for them—which can affect their relationship with the sales people. Also, consider the sales manager as a stakeholder. Perhaps the sales manager is the client or sponsor for this project. We also include scheduling experts, usability people, and possibly security people. Finally, because this product probably holds personal information, we also include the company lawyer to ensure we comply with privacy laws.

How do you know if you are getting close to an agreed context of investigation? From the start of the project keep track of the rate of change in the context model. We do this by taking a snapshot each day and noting the number of additions, changes, and deletions to the flows and adjacent systems. Not perfect. However, if the model shows honestly named flows, it does provide an effective management indicator of whether the scope is starting to stabilize.

Before proceeding too far with your project, we urge you to review the context model with your client or sponsor and your project team. At this early stage it is vital everyone sign on to the context. This is the model that by and large determines product scope, becomes the arbiter of scope creep, the basis of estimates, the authority for features either included or excluded, and generally the guide for your project for most of its duration. Make sure it's right before investing much more time.

At this early stage it is vital everyone sign on to the context.

The Stakeholders on Your Project

The reason for paying attention to the stakeholders is very simple: Missed stakeholders mean missed requirements. It is better to spend a short amount of time looking for all relevant stakeholders rather than a long amount of time undoing and redoing because stakeholders have been missed.

Stakeholders are the people with some interest in the product, which does not necessarily mean they have a financial stake. Stakeholders may be the ultimate hands-on users of the product, the managers of the users, they may be people who buy the product, have some special knowledge needed to build the product, or have some influence on the success of your product. You are a stakeholder—you have an interest in the product—as are the members of your team. The client paying for development is a stakeholder, as are government bodies, professional associations, pressure groups, and a seemingly endless list of other people.

In Chapter 3—Project Sociology we discussed stakeholders at length and explained how to perform a project sociology analysis to ensure you have the right people on board, as well as identify any gaps in your stakeholders. The project sociology analysis should be a fairly early activity because it affects how soon your business analysts can get to work.

A management issue here is the willingness of the stakeholders' participation. Once you have identified stakeholders, individually contact them and advise them why they are stakeholders, what you need from them and why their participation is to their advantage. Naturally you want willing participation and we go so far as to suggest if you are not getting willing participation (within reason) then consider asking yourself if this project is worth doing. If nobody is signing on to it, perhaps no one really wants it.

The stakeholders are your most valuable resource during the requirements activity. Make sure you know who they are and make the most of them.

Estimating

Accurate estimating is impossible unless you have something concrete on which to base your estimates. When you build a house you do not start construction until you have a firm quote from the contractor. The contractor is obliged to put up the building for the fixed quote—if he underestimates the cost of construction the extra comes out of his pocket. In this industry he has to *know* the cost of construction before starting work.

In the building industry, a quote is prepared by measuring the cost and labor associated with each component. The architect draws up the plans for the building, then a quantity surveyor measures each component in the building—so many cubic yards of concrete, so many windows of this size, and so on. The contractor looks up the cost of buying the concrete from a ready mixed company and adds that to the labor costs of pouring and setting each yard of concrete (he has industry standards for this). Finally, he adds his profit margin. The building industry has a couple-of-thousand-years' head start on the software industry, so doesn't it make sense to learn something from it? How about measuring rather than guessing the estimate? How about knowing how much it costs before starting construction? These are not difficult to achieve, but they require discipline and seem to be lessons we (the software industry) are still struggling to learn.

Early in the requirements process you have the work context diagram as input to estimating. You can use this model to size the work by estimating the number of function points. However, the size of the work has to be converted to some measurement of resources needed.

Units of Estimates

To give yourself a starting point you need to know what resources are needed in your organization to take one function point's worth of work area through the requirements activity. (You could of course use the same technique to measure how much resource you need to take one function point's worth of work all the way through implementation.)

Use your project history to come up with an average time or cost per function point (FP) from previous projects in your environment. If you have not already counted previous projects, you can perform a retrospective function point count for a completed project by drawing its context diagram and going through the function point counting procedure we describe.

The aim is to have an average cost of one FP. We suggest you plot the averages to see the comparison among projects in your environment and consider which projects have the most factors in common with yours. Then use that average as the starting point for estimating your project. Figure 9.3 shows such a plot.

You can record the meaning of your function points as cost per function point, or you can of course make this into person-days, or burdened days, or almost anything that is suitable input to your estimating. In *Planning Extreme Programming*, Kent Beck and Martin Fowler make the observation that "It doesn't actually matter what units you express the estimate in. The only important thing is that you always use the same unit." They go on to suggest "ideal days." That is, if a developer can put in a full day on a task, and not be distracted by other duties or meetings, then it counts as an ideal day. This is a useful unit, because developers are reasonably good at guessing how long a task might take them, however they are not good at predicting whether they will get the uninterrupted time needed for it.

Naturally, ideal days are rarely possible in an organization because few people get completely uninterrupted time. Similarly, if the task takes more than one person's effort, having two, or more, people able to put in an ideal day is unlikely. Beck and Fowler use the term "velocity" to measure the amount of availability and the work rate of a team. They also acknowledge ideal time and calendar time are different.

Chapter 8—Measuring Requirements is a detailed discussion of how to count function points.

RESOURCE NOTE
Software Productivity Research, founded by Capers Jones, has applied function point counting in many different industries. Look at http://www.spr.com/ for more information.

Figure 9.3

This is a plot of function points against time taken. Usually some scatter occurs because different project teams work at different paces on different projects. However, it's likely similarities exist between projects in your organization because they are operating in the same environment.

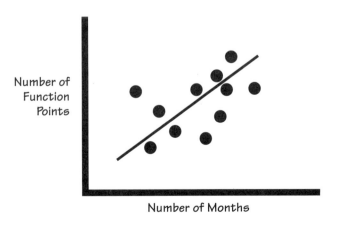

Number of Function Points

Number of Months

Some project managers make use of a "burdened day." That is, how much work can people actually accomplish after breaks, vacations, personal telephone calls, time for administrative overheads, and so on.

An Estimate Is a Prediction

Software is a young industry and has yet to learn some lessons. One of these is an estimate given on day one of a project is not accurate. Time and again we see project managers criticized because they fail to deliver by the deadline that was cemented in place *before* they (or anyone else) could possibly know what has to be done. The dilemma facing managers is one of being required to produce realistic estimates based on supposition and guesswork.

Tom DeMarco said, "An estimate is a prediction that is equally likely to be above or below the actual result." He went on to suggest that rather than submit a firm estimate we submit a range. If your estimate is a probability curve rather than one number, a much greater likelihood exists that people will understand the truth of your estimate. If you have a history of time and cost per function point for projects in your environment, use the variations between projects as the basis for determining the probability range.

Time and again we see project managers criticized because they fail to deliver by the deadline that was cemented in place before *they (or anyone else) could possibly know what has to be done.*

Defend Your Scope

One of the most common problems a project manager faces is scope creep. Earlier in this chapter we talked about the work context diagram as a tool for negotiating and defining the scope of your investigation. We are not pretending that once defined, the scope does not change—we know from experience it does. What we need is some way to manage the inevitable change.

A lot of scope creep happens because people are working enthusiastically on their part of the project. One of the authors (James) participates in a requirements mailing list. I recall a proposal that the contributors to the list write the requirements for an open source requirements tool. This was greeted by great enthusiasm, but before more than a dozen messages had passed the scope had already grown from a requirements specification handler to a general-purpose document handler. The proposed enlargement (we should be honest here and call it bloat) would have made the barely nascent project unworkable. And this was a group of requirements practitioners working without a client.

When people get new ideas they naturally want to add them to the scope of the product. Because it is so easy to add new ideas at requirements time, products often end up being fatter than they need to be. Your requirements management task is made more difficult because on the one hand you do not want to quell enthusiasm; on the other hand you need to be able to guide the project to a successful and timely conclusion.

We advocate you put both your work context and product scope diagrams on the wall of the project office and use them as a central communication point for all the stakeholders. Encourage people to look at each change in terms of how it will affect the intended work context and product scope. Each change to an interface on the work context has an effect on the size and thus effort needed for the requirements investigation. It also usually means a parallel change occurs in the scope of the product. Instead of a bureaucratic procedure ask people to consider the relative benefit of each proposed change. If the change is incorporated, what does it cost and what do you gain from it?

Each change to an interface on the work context has an effect on the size and thus effort needed for the requirements investigation.

Mastering Change

The bugbear of most requirements analysts is change. "The requirements keep on changing, we can't get anything finished unless we freeze the specification." However, experience has proved again and again that freezing specifications does not work. During the time the specification is frozen and the product is built, the business continues to change. So when the product is delivered it does not fit into the world.

Changing the business goals, changing technology, changing one's mind, changing the scope, changes from outside . . . there are plenty of reasons for change. Sadly, wishing they would go away does not work. But driving changes into the open as early as possible does have a beneficial effect.

Many changes are not really changes, they are requirements that people do not think of until they see something that looks close to reality. However, you obviously cannot wait until the product is a reality to discover the missing requirements. So the requirements analysts need to use techniques that encourage and value changes as early as possible in the requirements process.

Encourage your team to use a variety of techniques to trawl for requirements. Encourage the use of scenarios and low-fidelity prototypes early in requirements gathering. Before focusing on all of the little details, take a broad brush through the project and see if you can drive changes out of the woodwork early. Put your work context diagram on the wall and question it every day. Should you push your investigation boundary further out? Remember it does not mean you have to investigate everything to the same depth, it means you are taking a true systems-thinking approach and trying to understand the world that potentially contains your requirements.

We are not saying this "flush out early" approach stops you having any requirements changes. But the changes you do have are more likely to be things that cannot possibly have been known earlier—like a change in the law.

Requirements Buffer—Dealing with Uncertain Requirements

Suppose you have a project for which the aim is to do research and find out as much as you can about a given subject. In this case you really do not know when you have finished because you do not have any way of knowing where you are going. In a case like this all you can say is you're finished either when you run out of time/money or when you discover something your sponsor says is wanted. These sorts of projects are very common in research laboratories and universities; it is the raison d'être of these institutions to do research. And this situation relates to every business project to some degree.

Every project has some degree of research and development because it is the first time that particular project has ever been undertaken. True, similar projects have gone before, but this project has its own unique conditions and the effect of these conditions is unknown until some experimentation has been done. The situation is extreme in cases where people say "I do not know what I want but I will know it when I see it." Not an ideal situation in which to gather requirements—unless you expose it as a project with a greater than normal degree of research.

Universities and research institutions allocate budget to research, but business projects appear to think that it is free. But that is not true, we need to spend some of the project budget in order to research the uncertain, unconscious, and undreamed of requirements. And we need to allocate some of the budget to this work.

We use a *requirements buffer* as a way of helping the requirers to own the uncertainty (see Figure 9.4). The larger the client buffer the greater the research element of the project.

Every project has some element of research—think of this as an element of uncertainty—so every project should have some kind of client buffer. This is part of the budget that is put aside for things nobody has yet thought of. But keep in mind the buffer is a finite amount. As the project proceeds, items arise that were previously not considered and these are candidates for the buffer as they represent extra effort or cost to be expended. Now the client (or whoever controls the money supply) decides whether to spend part of its buffer on this item, or whether it is more prudent to wait in expectation of some more important or dramatic item to arise. It is useful to keep in mind the amount of functionality the

> 66 . . . we must not strive for certainty before we act for in so doing we will surrender the initiative and pass up opportunities. 99
>
> —Warfighting: The US Marine Corps Book of Strategy

Figure 9.4

The client buffer is that part of the project budget that has not been allocated and is available for the client to spend.

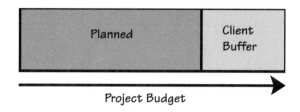

buffer buys early in the project is not the same as later when you have already done some implementation and consequently every change has a greater impact.

The buffer should be visible to everybody. One way to do this is to have a wall chart and gradually shade in the buffer as it is spent. Make the shading into a ceremony that involves both business and development stakeholders. This helps to keep people aware of how much flexibility you have planned. We have found how the sight of a gradually decreasing buffer restrains the suggestions for "nice to have" features to the product. It also helps you and your client to work more smoothly and to collaborate on the most advantageous ways to spend the buffer.

Using Requirements for Version Planning

One of the many advantages a consistent requirements language provides is the ability to do incremental, phased or versioned development. This relies on the ability to partition a complex whole so you can work separately on the pieces, and to keep track of how the pieces affect one another.

Figure 9.5 illustrates a whole project broken into business-related chunks each of which has well-defined boundaries. While each business chunk can stand alone, it can also be related to other chunks and to the entire project. Rather than implementing the whole project in one go, the decision has been made that version 1 implements the requirements for business chunk 1, which is implemented by product chunks 1, 2, and 3. On the right of the diagram we see which of the requirements are implemented by each of the product chunks.

Figure 9.5 illustrates how, in order to be able to plan and manage phased implementation, we need to be able to partition the whole project scope into business chunks, product chunks, and atomic requirements. And we need to be able to keep track of the relationships among them.

Rather than talking at the abstract level of "chunks," we have applied systems engineering principles to develop the generic requirements

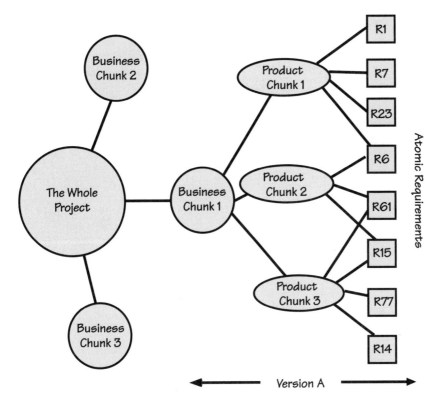

Figure 9.5

Chunks and Versions. Management of phased development relies on keeping track of which requirements are implemented in each version and how those requirements are related to the implemented product, the parts of the business, and the whole project.

knowledge model (see Appendix A). This model is a guide to which business chunks and product chunks are most commonly useful to managers. We have explained how to use the business event as a way of breaking the project into business chunks—each of those chunks is represented by a business use case. We discuss these in Chapter 4 where we talk about eliciting the requirements. If you consider that a business chunk is a business use case, then the associated product chunk is a product use case. Then, as you start to investigate the detailed requirements you discover one atomic requirement might be associated with a number of different product use cases.

You can find more ideas about versioning and chunking in Chapter 10 where we discuss how you can use the generic knowledge model.

How Much Are You Risking?

If you are building a kidney-monitoring machine, an aircraft guidance system or a baby's seat restraint then it is clearly unacceptable to *not* get the right requirements. Failure of these kinds of products can result in injury to humans, possibly loss of life. But suppose you are building a customer-billing system or an inventory control system. What risk are you taking if you do not get the right requirements?

It is true that flaws in a customer-billing system are not putting human life at risk. However, as Tom Peters says, companies are known by their systems. Suppose you build a poor customer-billing system that does not provide for convenient payment methods, produces unfathomable bills, fails to provide commonly available facilities, and is a major irritation to your customers. What happens? Your customers depart for a rival service that is prepared to provide systems that make their life easier. Daily life has enough irritations without poor systems adding to the annoyances.

An example of this kind of system-generated annoyance recently happened to your authors. We visit Australia frequently as we have work there and our families live there. We maintain an Australian bank account for convenience. The credit cards connected to this account were recently reissued and the bank told us they could not be sent to our home in London. Instead, they told us to pick them up next time we were in Australia. But then on the subsequent trip to Melbourne we were told that sending the cards to a branch of the bank near to where we were staying was impossible and (Catch-22) the cards could only be sent to our London home address.

This is poor requirements work—in all our many conversations with the bank, the information we were given was being read from a screen by a real person who wanted to help. But different employees had different versions of the rules, causing frustration both to the bank employees and to us, the customers. If the bank's system cannot get two plastic cards to us, we wondered, what else can they *not* do, and why should we continue to bank with them? Consider when something like this happens to you. You make a request of a bank, shop, supplier, service provider . . . how many times have you been told, "the system does not let us do that." This is simply a requirements failure—nobody bothered to investigate all the requirements before building the product.

Quite a few risks are associated with requirements. However, the one we want you to consider now is the risk of not getting the right requirements. If your product does not do what it is needed, what happens? Will lives be lost? Will it be a minor inconvenience? Will it need extensive rework? Will the product be shelved and never used? Will you lose customers? One of the most valuable things you can do for your project is to assess the impact of incorrect requirements—impact in terms of both time and money. This relatively simple exercise will probably give you more insights on how much effort to expend on requirements than far more elaborate risk management efforts.

Consider the risk of not getting the requirements.

The People on Your Team

Smart people cooperating with each other make a more effective team than a centrally controlled one. Your task as team leader is to assemble the best and brightest you can find, give them a project that interests them, provide what they need, and let them get on with it. The previous sentences may sound like tree-hugging, Kumbaya-singing, sandal-clad, new-age pop philosophy, but take a minute to examine them.

Plenty of evidence supports the fact that smart humans behave better when they act in mutual self-interest, as opposed to being centrally organized by some super-authority. For example, the collapse of communism around the world showed the inability of any central control to regulate such complex things as the economy and industrial production. Consider the quality of software produced by the open source movement. Linux has far fewer errors than any commercially produced operating system. This is mainly due to its being built and cared for by programmers whose main motivation is to do good work and be a part of the cooperative that develops Linux.

While an individual is capable of thought, a collection of cooperating individuals is capable of collective thought where the whole is greater than the sum of the parts. If one person does all the thinking, then the team is limited to the capability of that person. By giving your team members room to think, you relieve yourself of having to think for all of them. Your task instead is one of setting goals and guiding the team toward them.

As an illustration of the individual versus central control, consider the cleanup work on the World Trade Center site after the terrorist attack. This kind of work, on this scale, had never been done before—the ruins were unstable and massive, fires were still burning, and heavy wrecking equipment had to perch precariously on top of building ruins and demolish from above. The authorities on the site had no work rules for this kind of chaotic environment. When it came to work safety, it was a case of every man for himself. And yet, not a single recovery worker was killed, and the injury rate was about a half of the average for the American construction industry. It seems the individual workers were very capable of thinking for themselves and at the same time looking after fellow workers engaged in the same task.

> *. . . our philosophy of command must be based on human characteristics rather than on equipment or procedures.*
>
> —Warfighting: The US Marine Corps Book of Strategy

Don't Fragment Your People

When fragmentation of people increases productivity decreases. By fragmentation we mean when people are not full-time members of your team but work for a few hours at one task and a few more at another. The

Figure 9.6

Fragmented people are not as productive as people who are allowed to get on with one task. The fragmentation always results in inefficiencies due to having to reestablish communication links and pick up the threads of previous work.

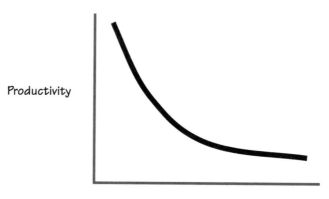

Productivity

Fragmentation of People

main problem here is each time the fragmented person rejoins the team, he has to reestablish the lines of communication with the other team members. Similarly, permanent members of the team feel that this is an intruder disrupting the rhythm and personality of the team.

Of course, for the fragmented person, life is also difficult: concentrating on one task, then moving to another, picking up any relevant advances made by the team, reestablishing links and lines of communication, and finally doing some real work . . . provided that by now the fragmented person is not being asked to cut himself into another piece for yet another unrelated task (see Figure 9.6).

See Chapter 3—Project Sociology for details on stakeholder maps.

Fragmentation applies only to your core project team. There are many stakeholders who are not expected to be on the project full time. Of necessity, their involvement is fragmentary. Use your stakeholder map (see Chapter 3) to help you consider where and when you run major risks from fragmentation.

Fragmentation also has a detrimental effect when your people are working on a project but located in more than one place. And the place can be another building or another town or another country. The immediate and obvious effect is the lack of eyeball-to-eyeball communication. We have also noticed the "us and them" feeling that creeps into geographically fragmented teams. We have a human tendency to think anybody from another place is not as smart, competent, or well informed as we are. For example, do you make jokes about your nearest neighbor country? Are they complimentary? But if you meet people from that country every day, if you have lunch with them and chat, you cease to make uncomplimentary generalizations.

"Adding People to Late Projects Makes Them Later"

This famous quote from Fred Brooks (*The Mythical Man-Month*) is a piece of wisdom we would do well to heed. Brooks is describing his project to build an operating system for IBM, and, because they're behind schedule, he decides to double the number of people on the project. He realizes later—and admits to this in his book—that a better course would have been to halve the number of people.

The problem of adding people means disrupting the rhythm that your existing team has established. Figure 9.7 shows how it also increases the number of communication paths.

New people penalize the existing team. When new members arrive, they almost certainly have to ask questions. And the most obvious people to ask are the most skilled—and therefore the most valuable to you—people on the team. So you end up with the least knowledgeable people preventing the most knowledgeable from working.

As it is likely you will change team members during the course of the project, we suggest you buy yourself an insurance policy—appoint a person to take the role of project knowledge guardian. This role has three purposes: to train a novice in the details of the project, to provide a person responsible for keeping the documentation trail coherent, and to know enough to be able to provide answers to questions.

On one of our projects we hired Sue, a recent graduate with no project experience, to be the project knowledge guardian. We explained the project knowledge model and the process we were using and made it her responsibility to keep track of progress and to add new models, documents, and requirements to the knowledge base and, most important, to maintain a coherent trail.

Although she did not have project or subject-matter experience, the total immersion allowed her to absorb the required knowledge without the need to devote significant resources to training her. Quite quickly she

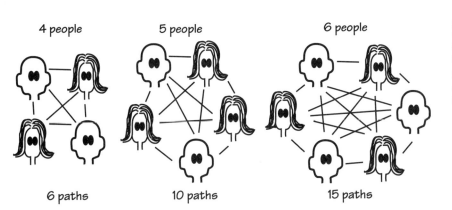

4 people   5 people   6 people

6 paths   10 paths   15 paths

Figure 9.7

As people are added to the team, the number of lines of communication increases out of proportion.

was able to answer most questions about the project. When new analysts joined the project, Sue was able to bring them up to speed quickly without disrupting the established team members. Naturally enough, she eventually acquired enough knowledge to become an analyst herself, which she did as soon as we were able to hire another project knowledge guardian.

Finding the Best Requirements Analysts

Analysts are the conduit between the requirers and the builders. The task is one of understanding both camps. This simple statement points to the skills that characterize a good requirements analyst.

Listening	The ability to be in input mode. To listen to what someone is saying and to be able to reflect it back to them.
Understanding	To work at understanding the real meaning behind what is said or observed. To keep asking questions until the real reason is exposed.
Translating	To be able to translate the same subject matter into the form that best suits a particular communication. For example, sometimes a very abstract model will be suitable to communicate understanding of a requirement. Sometimes it will be necessary to build a prototype or several scenarios in order to communicate with a particular person.
Modeling	The ability to build models that take a variety of *different viewpoints*. Analysts should be able to build models that focus on the data of the subject matter. Similarly they should know how to model processes, activities and states. They should have models in their toolkits for looking at the big picture or one small detail. Most of all they should not be limited by one form of notation. A good analyst is able to distinguish between flavor of the month and good systems engineering principles.
Inventing	A good analyst does not expect a requirer to think of everything that he wants. Requirers ask for what they believe is possible or what occurs to them at the time. Once the analyst starts to understand the subject matter he is in a position to invent and suggest requirements that will make a better product.
Negotiating/ mediating	To be able to listen to a number of conflicting points of view and help people to converge on a solution.

| Iterating | To be prepared to look past the first answer in search of the best answer. To accept that it is okay to be wrong early. |
| Organizing | To be able to keep track of a number of seemingly disconnected facts and to progressively weave them into a connected and coherent specification. |

We have learned domain knowledge is not the key attribute of a requirements analyst. If an analyst has knowledge of the subject matter domain it's an added bonus as this usually makes the analyst more confident and likely to be inventive. However, it is far more important for an analyst to have the skills listed above and to be ready to learn about new subject matter.

> *. . . a good analyst should be able to distinguish between flavor of the month and good systems engineering principles.*

Auditioning New Team Members

At one stage of our careers, your authors worked with a highly regarded New York training company. To join this company a potential instructor underwent an audition. The existing instructors assembled and the candidate instructed them. The instructors evaluated the candidate's competency and knowledge. We observed that there was an additional unspoken factor playing a major part in the hiring decision: whether the candidate would fit in with the culture of the organization. The auditioning process worked extremely well for many years and made for a tight-knit group of like-minded, competent instructors.

Perhaps the most significant factor influencing the success of your project is the people staffing it. Simply put, the better the people the better the chance of success. Therefore it makes sense for project managers to optimize their hiring process. We have seen many approaches to this, and the most successful ones always involve existing team members being part of the hiring process. Competent team members want to hire other competent people. They also want to hire someone who fits with the team personality. (It is also true to say that any incompetent team members want to hire other incompetents.)

Most successful hiring processes take a day or more to put someone through the interviews, auditions, tests, and other sessions. While this is taking valuable project time away from your team, it also ensures you are getting the right people.

Most successful hiring processes involve several work aptitude tests. These can be requirements problems set by your requirements analysts, or programming problems set by programmers. We have found team members are usually good at setting tests designed to reveal the people they want to work alongside. We have seen some programmers

> *We have found team members are usually good at setting tests designed to reveal the people they want to work alongside.*

set wonderfully challenging—you might even say diabolical—tests to find like-minded programmers and eliminate the not-so-goods. But the value lies in having your team participate in the hiring process it means you only hire people the team respects.

Communication within the Team

One significant attribute of a manager is the ability to communicate effectively. One of a team's most effective capabilities is to be able to communicate so each team member can make the others aware of what the member is doing. And when it comes to communication, simple is best.

66 *Stick with simple tools, like pencil, paper, and whiteboard. Communication is more important to success than whizbang.* 99

—Kent Beck and Martin Fowler, *Planning Extreme Programming*

We ran several requirements projects that started each day with a project meeting. These were short (maximum of 30 minutes) and sharp, and team members reported what they were doing, whether they had problems or needed help. On some occasions, we devoted the forum of the meeting for one of the members to make a presentation of some topic—business-oriented or technical—we felt the rest of the team should know about. Part of our management role was to keep the meeting to the point and tactfully cut short any speakers who were speaking as if they had the rest of the day to explain some trivial point. We all enjoyed the meetings and learned much from one another.

In most organizations today the team works in cubicles rather than individual offices. We recognize cubicles are one of the great productivity destroyers due to almost constant interruptions and high levels of non-relevant conversations. Unfortunately, many upper managers see only the cost of floor space, not the cost of lost work. If you are forced to work in cubes then we recommend you acquire a war room for your project (we leave it to you as to how you achieve this, but bribery and blackmail are possibilities). The war room is a meeting room for the project team and a place for the project leader to publicize records, charts, decisions, and other information on the progress of the project.

Linguistic Integrity and Consistent Requirements

The Tower of Babel—where everyone was speaking a different language and no useful work could get done—is an extreme example of the effect of the lack of linguistic integrity. Suppose someone on your team speaks to you in Italian. Unless you are a fluent Italian speaker you need to make sure you have heard correctly—perhaps by writing down what you think you heard and verifying it with the speaker. Then, you need to look up the words you do not know in a dictionary. Then you need to parse the sentence and put it into context based on what you know about the person who spoke to you. Making this sort of translation is clearly time consuming. But at least if you are aware that someone is speaking a different language, you are conscious you don't know what it means. In the Tower of Babel story, people did not have dictionaries available and because they were all speaking different languages communication very quickly became impossible.

A more dangerous situation is when you *think* everyone is speaking the same language, but each speaker has a different meaning for the words. We often hear requirements analysts complaining that no common agreement exists about requirements terminology. What one person calls a constraint another person might refer to as a goal or a nonfunctional requirement. One person uses the term "requirement" to mean a one-sentence description, another uses the same term to mean a set of attributes that includes a rationale and fit criterion. This problem is typical of a young discipline. We do not hear doctors arguing about what they mean by *antero-lateral border* (part of the fibula, or calf bone), architects and builders know what is meant by a *corbel* (a stone bracket projecting from a wall or corner to support a beam), and we are grateful all airline pilots know what *runway 29 right* means.

In contrast, the software industry has not been around long enough for people to converge on terminology and achieve linguistic integrity.

The problem of linguistic integrity is not confined to the meaning we ascribe to terms we use to manage our work like *constraint* and *requirement*. Business subject-matter terminology, unless consistently used, can cause significant and expensive misunderstandings. One of your authors (Suzanne) worked on a project where people used the term *net pay*. Everyone thought that everyone else had the same meaning for the term. When I started asking questions I discovered five quite different meanings for the term. And yet everyone had been proceeding convinced they were talking about the same thing.

The good news is that you can do several things to improve the linguistic integrity of your project.

The price we pay for lack of linguistic integrity is significant in terms of the cost of rework it causes. The good news is you can do several things to improve the linguistic integrity on your project.

Your Project's Language

At the beginning of your project make an agreement on the terminology that you, the developers, are going to use to communicate your progress. Here we are talking about the language of planning and progress of the project. You are looking for terms that consistently describe the way you will talk to one another in order to plan and define tasks and to communicate progress. You might refer to this as the language of your method.

Another way to think about it is the project language is irrelevant to the actual subject matter of the business problem you are solving. For example a business user does not need to know you are building context diagrams, class diagrams, atomic requirements. These ways of packaging your knowledge are present simply to facilitate communication and progress within the project team. Some of the terms may prove to be useful ways of packaging progress and running reviews—but the business people understand the business subject matter without *needing* to know about the way you choose to organize it.

For example, what term are you going to use to talk about a business-related grouping of requirements? Do you have a consistent agreement about precisely what you mean by requirement? What is the relationship between a requirement and your unit of implementation? What is your term for a product-related grouping of requirements? Without this agreement you spend a lot of time mopping up misunderstandings. You do not have to start from scratch to determine your requirements knowledge terminology. Our suggested way of doing this is to start with the generic requirements knowledge model (Appendix A) and modify it to incorporate the terms you intend to use (see Chapter 11—Your Requirements Process for a detailed description on how to tailor the knowledge model).

Apart from the improved communication within the team, the project management advantages of having a consistent requirements language are immense. You can assign responsibilities related to groups of requirements. Helen will investigate all the requirements for business use case number 7, John is concentrating on business use case 23.

Review progress by looking at the requirements themselves, rather than asking repetitive questions of your team. How many requirements have an agreed fit criterion? Can we plan a first version of the product for the first fifteen product use cases?

Use requirements groupings from your business, product, type, or implementation to communicate with different stakeholders depending on their interests. While one stakeholder is interested in the requirements relating to a specific product use case, another stakeholder is interested in the security requirements. Yet another needs to know the business use cases affected by a change to a particular atomic requirement.

Your Subject Matter Language

Investment in your project's language pays off in many ways. Once you have established it and used it for one project you can use it as a starting point for another project. But you also need to have a consistent language for the subject matter of the project.

Your Contextual Consistency

A business analyst cannot expect every project stakeholder to talk about his work using consistent terminology. It is true that people in the same field have some common terminology—for example the insurance industry uses terms like policy, claim, benefit. But within the world of insurance different meanings are assigned for these terms depending on who is using the term and under what circumstances.

We could try to define one meaning for every term used within an industry. However, due to the number of people, projects, and companies involved, this is close to impossible. Given the difficulty of imposing one meaning for a term within an entire industry—or even within one organization—it is a better idea to limit ambition to defining the meaning of the subject matter within the boundaries of a project.

The boundaries of the project are defined by the work context model discussed in Chapter 4. This model provides a visible statement of the boundaries of your interest. The data flows that enter and leave the work boundary contain much of the subject matter and hence the terms used in your project. When this model changes, you need to reflect any new subject matter in your definition of terms.

Your Subject Matter Language

The interfaces on your work context model declare the subject matter terms that need to be defined. And these need to be defined to elementary level in your project dictionary. For example, if you have an interface called Customer Details on your work context, then your project dictionary should contain a definition like:

Customer Details _____

Defines everything a salesman knows about a customer

Composed of: *Customer Name, Customer Address, Customer Sex, Customer Credit Rating, Customer Age Grouping, Sales Region, Buying History.*

Then each of the elementary data items would also be defined in the project dictionary when we know enough about each one to give it a defined range of values.

Customer Age Grouping _____

The age grouping of a customer used for targeting marketing campaigns

Values are: *Teenager, Young Adult, Middle Aged, Elderly*

The context model draws boundaries around the investigation and the dictionary defines all the terms used within the boundaries. All terms

RESOURCE NOTE
On the Volere requirements template we define subject matter terms in Section 5—Naming Conventions. It does not matter whether you call these your naming conventions, glossary, dictionary, or definitions. It does matter that terms your project uses must be unambiguously defined and consistently used.

used in individual requirements must conform to the terms defined in the dictionary.

Each of the elementary data items within the boundary of your context of investigation is an attribute of one of the business classes. As you start to understand more about your data you can make this understanding communicable by drawing a business class model.

For example, we defined an attribute called *Customer Age Grouping* as having a range of values. But what does this attribute describe? The answer depends on the meaning of the data item within the work context. But it would not be a surprise to know *Customer Age Grouping* is an attribute of a class of business data called *Customer*. And the better you understand the work and what it does, the better you are able to attribute each elementary data item to the class that it describes and to identify the connections or associations among the classes.

Your business class model (see Figure 9.8) is a summary of all the subjects of data (classes) and links (associations) between them that are important to the work you are studying. The processes that use the business classes to carry out the work are the source of the functional requirements. Note we have used the same notation—in this case a UML class diagram—to build a business class model and also to build the requirements knowledge model referred to earlier in this chapter.

Figure 9.8

This business class model captures knowledge about three classes of business data—Account, Customer, and Salesman. Each class has a number of attributes—for example Salesman has Salesman Name and Salesman Quota. The lines between the classes indicate associations—there is an association called Billing between Customer and Account. And the * and 1 say that there are potentially many (*) Accounts for each Customer but each Account will only be for one (1) Customer. The range of values for each attribute is defined in your data dictionary.

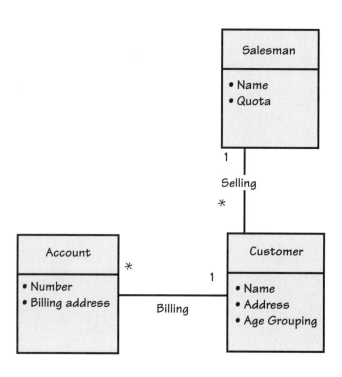

Using Templates for Consistent Specifications

Over the years, your authors have written many requirements specifications. We realized fairly early a certain amount of repetition existed in each specification. This led us to develop the Volere Requirements Specification Template as a generic template that can be used on almost any project. Since the first version in 1995, we have refined and augmented the template with feedback from users in many different industries. Most people using it report they tailor it to their specific needs and use it as a guide for gathering their requirements.

We have included the template table of contents for the Volere template in Appendix B. The complete contents can be downloaded from www.volere.co.uk. Whether you use ours or some other one, we urge you to use a template. We have found having a consistent specification document is of immense help in gathering the requirements and communicating them. If developers know what to expect, then they welcome the specification instead of putting it on the shelf and ignoring it. However, when we suggest using a template, please also consider what we have said elsewhere in this book about versioned releases and partial specifications.

Testing the Requirements for Better Products

There is little doubt the fastest way to develop software is to pay attention to its quality at every stage of development. This has been documented enough that it is common knowledge (not necessarily common practice) among project managers. The question is not whether managers want to build quality into their products, but how to do it.

Informal Quality Gateway

The purpose of a quality gateway is to start testing the quality of requirements as soon as you gather them. The gatekeepers test each requirement for compliance with the quality criteria established for the project. We find it useful to establish the requirements quality criteria at the outset of the project and ask analysts to keep these criteria in mind as they are recording requirements.

Quality Gateway Checklist for Requirements

We have found that checks like the following serve to ensure that the requirements are syntactically correct, and almost always reveal weaknesses in the analysts' understanding of the requirements.

- Does the requirement have a meaningful and comprehensible description?

- Does the requirement have a rationale that truly justifies its existence?
- Does the requirement have a valid fit criterion, and does that fit criterion make the requirement testable?
- Is the requirement relevant to the product context?
- Is the requirement viable both from a technical and budget standpoint?
- Does the requirement have a customer value and is it honestly rated?
- Does the requirement have a source?
- Is the requirement gold plating?
- Is it a solution and not the real requirement?
- Is the requirement uniquely identified?
- Is the requirement cross-referenced to its product use case(s)?
- Is the terminology within the requirement defined?
- Does the requirement use terminology consistently?
- Does the requirement contain all the attributes established by the quality criteria?

In Chapter 3—Project Sociology we recommend your stakeholder list contain testers. Providing you have well-defined quality criteria for your requirements, then testers are extremely skilled at spotting requirements that do not conform.

Once the quality gateway checks become a natural part of the analysts' work, you find they record better requirements. Naturally no analyst wants his work rejected by the gatekeepers, and so attention is paid to the wording, clarity, and content of the requirements.

Most projects have some points (often called phases or stages) where all or part of the requirements are handed over to another group of stakeholders. Typically this handover occurs when the requirements are deemed to be well-specified enough for them to be able to be translated into software, machinery, or organizational procedures. Each of these communication points needs some agreed-upon quality gateway check to ensure all parties understand the requirements in the same way.

The reason you sometimes need formal quality gateway checks is because some kind of division of responsibilities is present. The more complex your project sociology, the more people who are involved, and the more fragmented their roles, the more formality you need. However, be careful not to turn this into a bureaucratic exercise containing meaningless signoff procedures.

Sign *On* not *Off*

Documents are often accompanied by a request like "We need you to sign off on this by Friday." Consider the message of this statement: You sign it and get it off your desk so it won't bother you any more. The image arises of ridding oneself of something bothersome. But that's not what you really want. Instead you want the signer to care about the contents of the document and to be involved rather than viewing the request as a nuisance. These observations about the negativity of sign *off* have led us to experiment with the alternative concept of sign *on*.

The request "Will you sign on to this document?" sends a very different message. The person is drawn into the subject matter. You are asking: Given your knowledge of this subject matter, can you give us some guidance—a much more human way to ask for input at various checkpoints. When we started to use the idea we discovered something else: You can use the idea of *sign on* at all levels of the project and it opens up an opportunity for a more meaningful way of approving requirements.

You can use the idea of sign on *at all levels of the project and it opens up an opportunity for a more meaningful way of approving requirements.*

Your requirements come from many different stakeholders with many different specialities. There is no one person who can approve the accuracy of every detailed requirement. So asking one person, or even a review committee to approve in the entire contents of a requirements document is patently absurd. It's much more effective to have the relevant stakeholders sign on to the details they are qualified to approve. So where does this leave the manager when asked to approve a set of requirements?

Asking one person, or even a review committee to approve all the details in a requirements document is patently absurd.

The manager is not asked to sign on by reviewing the details of each requirement. Instead the manager signs on by reviewing whether the person who signed on to the details is qualified to do so. In other words, did these requirements come from the right source, and have the right people been involved? Thus the responsibility for sign on is shared between the relevant parties. This appeals to sensible human beings and makes the concept of quality tangible rather than words from an inspirational poster.

Prioritizing Requirements—Don't Build What Is Not Needed

Given the pressure of time, a problem that occurs with most projects is there always seem to be too many requirements. Something else immediately observable is not all requirements are equal. Some are important, some are frivolous, some belong in future releases, some are pure gold plating, some are of such value the client will not want the product if they are omitted.

We all use the term "requirements," and the inference to be drawn from this word is that a requirement specifies something that is required, and therefore must be included in any implementation of the product. This is a terminology problem. What we really by "requirement" is an intention, a desire, or a wish. For example, if you have a requirement that

What we really mean by "requirement" is an intention, a desire, or a wish.

appears to be reasonable but then discover it costs $500,000 to implement, your client may say that it is no longer a requirement. Similarly, you may have 500 requirements but time to implement only 300. Suddenly the other 200 are no longer "requirements."

This means you need some way of choosing the important over the trivial and the urgent over what can be delayed. Prioritization means many things and it is worthwhile considering what you need to achieve by prioritizing your requirements.

Let's start with the simplest case of prioritization. In almost all systems, there are a few crucial business events. These are the ones most closely tied to the goal of the product. We refer to these as "mother lode" events. We suggest you isolate these early in the project, have your team do the business analysis and then design and build the part of the product that supports them. The intention here is to first get a "proof of concept" preliminary version of the product, and second to have a "serious prototype." This is a working version of the product that serves as a model for the rest of the development. The priority in this case is alignment with the project's goals.

When your analysts are writing requirements, we suggest they attach what we call a *customer value* to a requirement. This is a two-part scale we adapt from the work of William Pardee. The value is expressed as a score of one out of five for how happy the client will be if you successfully implement the requirement, and a contra score of how *un*happy the client will be if you do *not* implement the requirement. The second score, called *customer dissatisfaction* is revealing because trivial and gold-plated requirements usually get low dissatisfaction scores.

RESOURCE NOTE

For more on customer satisfaction and dissatisfaction refer to *To Satisfy and Delight Your Customer* by William Pardee. Dorset House, 1996.

One way of making comparisons between requirements is to add the satisfaction and dissatisfaction scores together, sort in descending order and pick as many as you have time to implement. This is not an organized prioritizing technique. It is more a way of keeping everyone aware that choices have to be made—and it helps to highlight this from the start of the project.

Prioritizing requirements gets more complex when we look deeper into the basis for making choices. You may have reasons to consider one or, more likely, a combination of the following bases for prioritization:

- Minimal cost of implementation
- Value to customer
- Time to implement
- Ease of technical implementation
- Ease of business implementation
- Value to the client's business
- Obligation to some external authority

Not all factors are relevant to every project, and the relative importance of the factors is different for each project. Also, within a project the
relative importance is not the same for all stakeholders. Given this com-
binatorial complexity you need some kind of agreed prioritization procedure to provide a way of making choices.

Let us move to the scenario in which you have too many requirements
to fit into the time allowed for the next release. At this stage we recommend triage—sorting the requirements into three groups:

- Those requirements that must be part of the next release; their
  customer value scores are high and you recognize them as being
  urgent.
- Disposable requirements: those nobody will miss if they are absent.
  A low dissatisfaction score is an aid here.
- Requirements you would like to fit in if time permits.

And to finish setting the scene, let's say you have the resources to
build the "must haves" but not all of the "would likes," and so these are
the ones to be prioritized.

You can use a spreadsheet to prioritize the "overflow" requirements.
Ideally, especially if you have done a good job on progressive prioritization, these requirements fit into the Medium or "would like if possible"
category. If you cannot fit all the High priority requirements into your
budget, then prioritize the High priority requirements and either drop
the Medium category and Low category or tag them for future releases.

The *prioritization factors* we show in Figure 9.9 are the factors mentioned above, or ones that are important your project. The *% Weight*
applied is the agreed percentage importance of a factor. You arrive at the
percentage weight by stakeholder consensus. The total percentage
weights for all factors must of course be 100%.

Column one shows the "would like" requirements you want to prioritize. These may be atomic requirements or they may be clusters of requirements represented by product use cases, product features, or
business event responses. For each requirement/factor combination you
give a score out of 10. The score is assigned based on how much of a positive contribution you think the requirement makes to this factor. For
example, requirement 1 has scored 2 for the first factor because it does
not make a very positive contribution to *Value to Customer*. On the other
hand, the same requirement scores 7 because it does make a positive contribution to *Value to Business*. The score for minimizing cost of implementation is 3 because we think this requirement is relatively expensive
to implement. We think requirement 1 is easy to implement, so for that
factor it scores 8.

RESOURCE NOTE
Alan Davis writes about
triage in *The Art of
Triage: A Report from the
Trenches*. University of
Colorado Springs, 2002.

Figure 9.9 A table of prioritized requirements. The column headings are factors you consider important to the project. Each one is weighted to show its relative importance. Each requirement gets a score out of 10 based on how much it contributes to that factor. The score is adjusted by the percentage importance rating and the adjusted total is the priority of the requirement. This prioritization spreadsheet is downloadable from www. volere.co.uk. The spreadsheet contains some examples you can replace with your own data.

		Volere Prioritization Spreadsheet									
Requirement/ Product Use Case/Feature	Number	Factor— Score out of 10 **Value to Customer**	% Weight Applied **40**	Factor— Score out of 10 **Value to Business**	% Weight Applied **20**	Factor— Score out of 10 **Minimize Implementation Cost**	% Weight Applied **10**	Factor— Score out of 10 **Ease of Implementation**	% Weight Applied **30**	Total Weight **Priority Rating**	**100**
Requirement 1	1	2	0.8	7	1.4	3	0.3	8	2.4	4.9	
Requirement 2	2	8	3.2	8	1.6	5	0.5	7	2.1	7.4	
Requirement 3	3	7	2.8	3	0.6	7	0.7	4	1.2	5.3	
Requirement 4	4	6	2.4	8	1.6	3	0.3	5	1.5	5.8	
Requirement 5	5	5	2	5	1	1	0.1	3	0.9	4	
Requirement 6	6	9	4	6	1.2	6	0.6	5	1.5	6.9	
Requirement 7	7	4	2	3	0.6	6	0.6	7	2.1	4.9	

For each score, the spreadsheet calculates a weighted score by applying the % weight for that factor. The *priority rating* for the requirement is calculated as the total of the weighted scores for the requirement.

You can use a variety of rating systems to arrive at the weights for the factors and the scores for each requirement. Of course the spreadsheet is merely a vehicle for making it possible for a group of people to review and arrive at a consensus for prioritizing the requirements. By making complex situations more visible you make it possible for people to communicate their interests, to understand other people's opinions, and to negotiate.

The Waiting Room

One of the authors (Suzanne) was consulting on a banking project. One of the key stakeholders was a banking expert who was very enthusiastic about the possibilities of the product we were planning to build. Every day this banking expert would appear with another new idea—"and we could provide that interface to the branch officers and we could sell it on the Internet. . . ." We were in a quandary; we did not want to stop her being enthusiastic and having ideas. On the other hand if we kept adding new features we would never get the product built. So we resorted to the requirements waiting room.

Every time a new requirement emerged outside the scope of the product we noted it down and put it in a file we called the waiting room. All the stakeholders knew about this file. From time to time we would visit the waiting room and have a look at the occupants. For future versions of the product we started with the waiting room and together with the business people we decided which of the requirements should be liberated and included in the next version.

Although the waiting room can be used very informally it can also be set up as a formal way of managing requirements for version control. One of our clients who builds operating system software has a waiting room divided into compartments labeled with version numbers. Each new requirement is assigned a version number and all the stakeholders can see the planned content of each version.

The requirements from the prioritization exercise above that do not make it into the next release are added to the waiting room. We have found that having a waiting room means you are not discarding requirers' wishes, just putting them aside for later consideration. But suppose you do decide a requirement is definitely *not* going to be included in the product. You record this—we have a section in our template (6: Relevant Facts and Assumptions)—so everyone knows the decision has been made. This helps to prevent people wasting time by reviving issues that have already been decided.

Avoiding Litigation

"You didn't build what I wanted."

"Yes I did, it's exactly what you said you wanted."

If this happens on a large project and it cannot be resolved then, increasingly often, litigation erupts. This is happening so frequently now for software being built on contract we wonder if lawyers' fees are built into the budget.

The problem almost always comes down to poorly written and in some cases nonexistent requirements. In a dinner conversation with a prominent lawyer, we mentioned we were writing a book on software requirements; he did not exactly turn pale, but he made the point quite strongly if more people wrote better requirements documents his income would decrease dramatically.

We know of one case in which a contract referred to the requirements specification, and this was said to be an appendix of the contract. When our arbiter friend asked to see the appendix, both sides went very quiet. Apparently, the requirements for the product were never written and yet this was a $20 million contract. The cost of discovering the requirements would have been far cheaper for both sides than the amount they spent on lawyers.

The message here is simple: Regardless of whether you are the contractor or the contractee, ensure your contract is based on measurable, unambiguous requirements.

There is another side to litigation that needs to be considered. In the Volere Requirements Specification Template we include a section for legal requirements. These are the requirements that come about because of laws or statutes that cover the business area of the product. For example, if your product is to hold personal data, you must ensure that it protects that data and complies with privacy laws. Similarly, laws exist that deal with credit, consumer rights, and so on. It is worth including the company lawyer as a stakeholder to avoid having your product hauled off to court by an angry customer. This never looks good on your resumé.

What Do I Do Right Now?

We have discussed a number of requirements practices that help project managers and team leaders to manage requirements analysts. A common thread connecting all these factors is the need to have a consistent way of communicating and recording requirements knowledge. The following is a summary of requirements practices and the management advantages they can provide.

Requirements Practice	Management Advantages
Linguistic Integrity	• Communication between requirers and developers • Less rework caused by misunderstandings
Work Context Diagram	• Communication of the overall project • Basis for early estimates • Promotes early feedback
Separate Work and Product Contexts	• Ability to communicate with different stakeholders • Ability to plan changes and assess the effects
Project Sociology	• Early discovery of who should be involved • Insurance against missing requirements • Basis for decision-making framework

Requirements Template	• Guide for discovering requirements • Guide for communicating requirements knowledge • Formality helps to avoid litigation
Testing Requirements	• Creation of feedback loop between stakeholders • Early involvement of testers' expertise
Quality Gateway Checks	• Promotes early discovery of misunderstandings • Creates feedback loop • Promotes early commitment to quality
Sign On not Sign Off	• Appropriate allocation of responsibility • Promotes thorough review rather than rubber stamp
Prioritization	• Expectation management • Basis for negotiation
Waiting Room	• Helps to address scope creep • Trapping good ideas for the future
Requirements Input to Version Planning	• Traceability and change management
Requirements Input to Estimating	• Early estimates based on measurables • Vehicle for communicating progress
Requirements Input to Risk Management	• Early, more comprehensive identification of risks
Requirements Buffer	• Ability to deal with uncertainty
Recognition of Analyst Skill Set	• Help in finding the right people • Identifying strengths and weaknesses in the team

What's the Least I Can Get Away With?

If you are not already doing so, start to use requirements deliverables—even if you just start with a minimal set—as a way of assessing progress, planning and communicating with your team.

The requirements deliverables are all the classes of knowledge (like atomic requirements, business use cases, stakeholders) and all the other components of the knowledge model in Appendix A. Success relies on the consistency of your deliverables. If you have this consistency you can gain many management advantages.

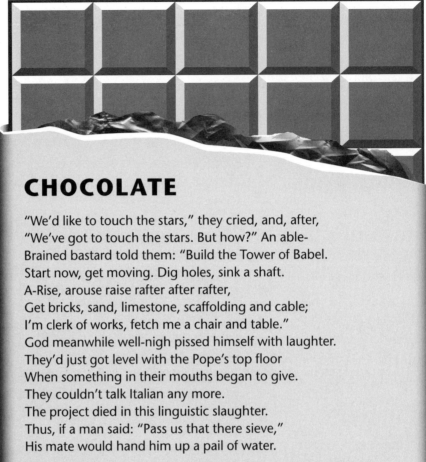

CHOCOLATE

"We'd like to touch the stars," they cried, and, after,
"We've got to touch the stars. But how?" An able-
Brained bastard told them: "Build the Tower of Babel.
Start now, get moving. Dig holes, sink a shaft.
A-Rise, arouse raise rafter after rafter,
Get bricks, sand, limestone, scaffolding and cable;
I'm clerk of works, fetch me a chair and table."
God meanwhile well-nigh pissed himself with laughter.
They'd just got level with the Pope's top floor
When something in their mouths began to give.
They couldn't talk Italian any more.
The project died in this linguistic slaughter.
Thus, if a man said: "Pass us that there sieve,"
His mate would hand him up a pail of water.

Translation by Anthony Burgess (*A Mouthful of Air*) of a poem
by the Roman poet Guiseppe Gioacchino Belli (1791–1863).

At the start of the project to build the Tower of Babel the project
team had one common language with a minimal set of words. They
were confident they could build a tower that would touch the stars.
God, annoyed by this arrogance, scuppered the project by replacing the common language by a mixture of tongues.

Resources for Managing Requirements

The following sources, in addition to those already referenced, have useful information on managing requirements.

- Beck, Kent, and Martin Fowler. *Planning Extreme Programming.* Addison-Wesley, 2001—*This explains how extreme programming projects are planned by breaking them into sequences of one to three week mini-projects. Regardless of whether you are doing extreme programming you can benefit from the many good ideas for iterative planning.*
- DeMarco, Tom, and Tim Lister. *Waltzing with Bears: Managing Risk on Software Projects.* Dorset House, 2003—*This takes the positive view of risk—if you take a risk it will provide great rewards. Part of this is to be able to make risk visible and quantify it so it can be managed. Provides many practical techniques, worth reading for the risk diagrams alone.*
- Garmus, David, and David Herron. *Function Point Analysis: Measurement Practices for Successful Software Projects.* Addison-Wesley, 2000—*A significant work. It provides a thorough treatment of function point counting using the IFPUG rules.*
- Highsmith, Jim. *Adaptive Software Development: A collaborative approach to managing complex systems.* Dorset House, 1999—*A wealth of techniques, tools, and approaches for helping people to collaborate on personal, cultural, and structural levels. Adds discipline to iterative and rapid development methods.*
- Jones, Capers. *Conflict and Litigation between Software Clients and Developers.* Software Productivity Research, 2001—*The results of many years' study on the causes of litigation on software projects. Valuable advice on how to write contracts that avoid expensive litigation.*
- McConnell, Steve. *Professional Software Development.* Addison-Wesley, 2004—*Gives some compelling arguments for how we can produce software that satisfies requirements, on time and within budget. The focus is on what we need to do to achieve professionalism of individuals, organizations, and the software industry. Important insights into why we need a software engineering code of ethics.*
- Peters, Tom. *The Circle of Innovation.* Alfred A. Knopf, 1997—*An ideas handbook that gives guidance—with lots of examples—on how organizations can take advantage of continual change.*
- Thomsett, Robb. *Radical Project Management.* Prentice Hall, 2002—*Project management techniques for today's complex environments. A flexible process that expects change. Lots of good ideas, especially on the subject of how to keep the appropriate stakeholders involved throughout the project.*
- Weinberg, Jerry. *Quality Software Management Volume 4—Anticipating Change.* Dorset House Publishing, 1997—*The fourth volume in the series analyzes change and looks at how to become an organization that anticipates and profits from change.*

Requirements Meta-Management

Most projects have multiple parts. They involve several distinct units of software, more than one hardware device, many people in a variety of roles, multiple locations, and other components that are different enough to warrant each of them being treated as a separate project. Each of the projects has its own management, so we look at how to manage the requirements for dependencies among interrelated projects.

Almost all projects involve multiple technologies: Part of the development may be implemented as software on a mainframe or server, part on the Web, some of it as a COTS package, some custom stuff on personal computers, some changes to job responsibilities, maybe a scattering of mechanical and electronic devices, and some changes to existing products. Other parts of the development may be implemented as part of a physical consumer product and some parts may be implemented as business procedures. Each of these technologies represents a separate system and each of the systems is at a different stage of its lifetime. Yet all of them have to be made to work harmoniously as one integrated system. Here we look at how to manage requirements for multiple parallel systems, a multi-technology project.

> *The real leverage in most management situations lies in understanding dynamic complexity.*
>
> —Peter Senge,
> *The Fifth Discipline*

What Is Meta-Management?

We can view any organization as one big system that exists in order to meet its business goals. The supermarket sells goods to its customers, the

We can view any organization as one big system that exists in order to meet its business goals.

bank provides financial services, the opera house provides entertainment for the public, and the motor manufacturer makes vehicles. But the big system is always composed of many smaller systems. Look inside any of these organizations and you see several projects in progress concurrently. The supermarket is satisfying each customer's request and at the same time producing orders to send to suppliers, along with updating its Web site. This is happening at the same time as the installation of a new checkout system along with investigating a new payroll package for its employees. Each of these individual systems needs to be managed so it meets its own goals. But we also have to manage the connections among the individual systems and the projects that are building, running, and maintaining them—that's where meta-management applies.

Meta-management is the activity of managing the progress, integrity, and change among a number of individual systems that affect one another and the overall aims of the organization (as shown in Figure 10.1). A meta-manager is concerned with managing the progress of parallel systems throughout their lifetimes and ensuring the combination of projects contributes to the overall goals of the organization.

Why Do We Need It?

When a project is in trouble—lateness, budget problems, customer dissatisfaction, nondelivery of supplies, and so forth—a common factor is always present: At least one external influence is behaving unexpectedly. Even if you have been diligent in identifying external influences, you still need to monitor their dynamic behavior in respect of your own project.

If you are an individual project manager, you naturally focus on the details of the product your own project is building. It is quite difficult to monitor the dynamics of surrounding projects when your responsibility and reputation lie within your own project. Inevitably the external influences are not recognized or the influences change and the impact of that change is not anticipated. This points to the need for managing interproject interfaces and highlights the need for a *meta-manager*.

The meta-manager is concerned with predicting and defining the influence of one product on another.

The job title "meta-manager" is unusual. Your organization might call this role "program manager" or "interface manager" or "change manager" or possibly "release manager." The title does not matter; the important issue is you have someone concerned with predicting and defining the influence of one project on another and with keeping individual project managers aware of any changes that affect their projects. We refer to this person as a meta-manager.

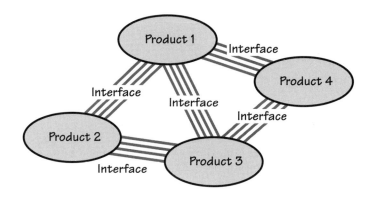

Figure 10.1

Meta-management is the activity of managing the progress, integrity, and change among a number of individual products that affect one another and the overall aims of the organization.

Defining Interproject Interfaces

The integrity of the interfaces among projects is the responsibility of the meta-manager. Interfaces by definition are the individual links between projects, so the task naturally is to coordinate information about the interfaces from representatives of the involved projects. The task for the meta-manager is to provide agreed-upon definitions of the interfaces to all interested parties and to ensure that every involved party understands it in exactly the same way.

Each interface has a number of constituents that need to be defined and managed (see Figure 10.2).

The meta-manager needs to make sure all these questions are answered from the perspective of people at both ends of the interface. The manager should be looking for conflicting answers, which indicate problems between projects.

The Project View

We have suggested each project has a product scope diagram. Figure 10.3 is a simplified illustration showing product scope diagrams for three concurrent projects. The problem is this: the project manager for project A has two interfaces to manage (we said this was simplified), one output to product C and one input from product B. Product A does not work correctly unless it gets the information it needs from B. Thus it falls to A's manager to negotiate with B's manger for the interface he needs, and negotiate with C's manager as to what C has to supply. Any failure to agree or to understand the interface means one or the other product does not work correctly.

Figure 10.2

This table summarizes questions a meta-manager uses to ensure the integrity of interfaces among products. You can use the list to identify details of product dependencies and to analyze any changes that occur throughout the life of the product.

Interface Constituent	Questions to Ask
Systems	Which systems—any mixture of automated, mechanical, or organizational—are linked by this interface?
Who	Who is responsible for each end of this interface?
Data Content	A detailed definition of the elements of data and/or control, along with their defined ranges of values.
Technological Content	A detailed definition of any elements that exist because of the implementation of the interface.
Form	What technology (digital, paper, voice, touch, radio beam . . .) is used to carry the contents of the interface?
External Influence	Which external organization/s (a COTS producer, outside supplier) can unknowingly make changes to this interface that may have an effect on our implementation expectations?
Control	How do we start/stop this interface?
Periodicity	When does this interface become active? And how often is the interface active during some predefined period?
Volume	What amount of data does the interface have to handle per unit of time?
Speed	What is the transmission and reception speed of this interface?
Protocols	What protocols or standards apply to this interface?
Cost	How much have we invested, or will we invest in this interface?
Value	What is the benefit of this interface?
Beneficiaries	Who gets something of value from this interface?
Progress	Has the interface been implemented? What stage of implementation has it reached? What is the planned implementation date?
Risk	Are there any risks related to this interface?
Expectations	Are there any other expectations held by people at either end of the interface?

One of the prime aims of requirements analysts is to discover as many requirements as possible as early as possible in the project life cycle. But despite our best efforts, we know some requirements will change and new requirements will be discovered well into the project. Suppose the analysts working on product A decide that they have to make some non-trivial changes to their product's requirements. And further suppose the changes affect the interface with product C. Whose responsibility is it for these changes to be communicated and agreed upon? Team C has already agreed that the interface and proposed changes have nothing to do with its product. Team A needs to make changes, but this means disrupting the work of Team C.

The above scenario is simplistic. You rarely find a single interface between products, usually you find not only many interfaces, but also they have complexities and subtleties that make changing them fraught with risk. Naturally, they need to be changed frequently following the discoveries characteristic of all requirements projects. And also naturally, the individual project teams have enough to contend with without the extra burden of constant renegotiation of their interfaces with adjacent projects.

The Meta-View

The meta-manager keeps track of interfaces among projects. The meta-manager is also responsible for the interface definitions—either by defining them himself, or ensuring that they are defined by the project teams

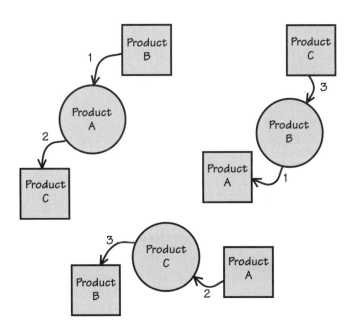

Figure 10.3

The manager for Product A uses his product context diagram to keep track of how product A relates to the outside world. In this case, he has interfaces to two projects running at the same time. Because the three projects are inter-related, we see a similar situation in the product scopes for the other projects.

Figure 10.4

A meta-project. The meta-manager keeps track of the interproduct inter-faces. Monitoring starts at the birth of a project and con-tinues throughout the lifetime of each product.

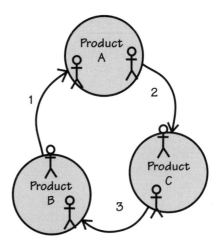

as part of the normal project work—and monitoring the interfaces for change and ensuring the definitions are current and all participating projects are in agreement.

Who Does What?

Each interproduct interface has two owners, one at each end of the inter-face. For example in Figure 10.4, product B produces interface 1 and product A receives it. To manage the constituents of the interface, spe-cific people from each of the involved projects should jointly own the interface.

We use joint ownership to mean the two owners are responsible for agreeing upon the interface. To do this they must jointly define the con-stituents of the interface. We set the constituents out earlier in this chap-ter. The owners, in conjunction with the meta-manager monitor the interface for changes; this may seem laborious but keep in mind a change to one product may well have a knock-on effect on another that is not immediately adjacent to the two in question. In any event, the meta-manager is ultimately responsible for ensuring the interface defini-tions are an exact description of the current reality.

Now suppose one end of the interface is connected to a system—a ma-chine, company, human, or automated product that lies outside your organization. For example, a banking system with an automated teller machine. An interface exists between the ATM and the human banking customer. Obviously you cannot ask the bank's customers to be the guardians of this interface. Instead it requires a customer representative who understands the customers' view of the interface—a marketing per-son, an ergonomics expert, or a requirements analyst with skills in this

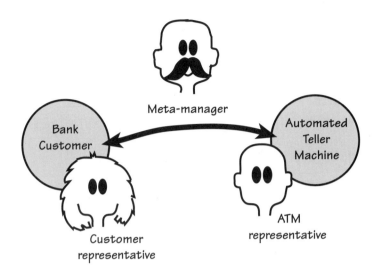

Figure 10.5

To understand and maintain the interfaces, representatives have to see the interface from the point of view of their end of it. The meta-manager has the responsibility for integrating the different viewpoints.

subject. The point is these people see the interface from "their end." They have to take the view of the interface as it affects their own view of the whole system (see Figure 10.5).

Early in the life of a project, the interface owners and the meta-manager communicate often. Once the project settles down and the product is implemented, communication becomes necessary only when a change occurs that affects an interface. The inference here is the meta-management does not stop when a product is implemented, but continues throughout the lifetime of that product.

Something we have found useful is for the meta-manager to maintain an interproduct interface map centrally available to anyone who needs to understand dependencies among projects. Clearly the interproduct map is a complex model and is best maintained using some kind of automated tool. Many tools exist on the market with the capability of recording system boundaries and defining the interfaces among them.

In Chapter 7—Requirements for Existing Systems we discuss how to manage new requirements throughout the life of a product.

RESOURCE NOTE
Visit www.volere.co.uk/tools.htm for a survey of requirements tools.

Each Component Is a Separate System

When we start a new project, the product to be built is often thought of as "the system." That is, a system that seems to exist by itself with little thought given to how it fits into the larger scheme of things. The first step toward putting "the system" into its place in the real world is to surround it with other systems (people, technology, software, organizations) and to declare the resulting interfaces.

To see how this works, consider Figure 10.6. Here we look at a typical project and its relationship with other systems. The inner circle is the

Figure 10.6

Your project is a number of interconnected systems. When you have investigated sufficiently, you identify the boundary for your intended product and its interfaces with the rest of the world—as illustrated by the lines between the central circle and the two outer rings. Then, as you start to make technical design decisions, you identify subsystem boundaries—as illustrated by the interconnected ellipses within the intended product.

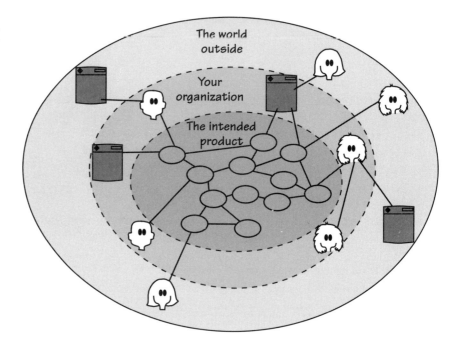

See Chapter 3—Project Sociology for examples of drawing stakeholder maps to identify the investigation, organization, and product boundaries.

product the project is to build. However, functionality cannot exist in isolation, it needs inputs from outside. And, of course, it must have some output. You see these interfaces represented as lines between the intended product and the ring that represents parts of your organization and also between the intended product and the outer ring that represents the world outside.

The more your team learns about the business requirements for the product, the better it is able to identify boundaries of the product to be built. Part of this task is to define the interfaces between the product (represented by the inner ring in Figure 10.6) and other systems in the organization (represented by the middle ring).

However, the product is likely to be made up of more than one component—represented by the interconnected ellipses inside the inner ring. Obviously, the larger and more complex the product the more components or subsystems are likely to compose it. Bear in mind each of these subsystems can be implemented using different technology. And the implementation of one business requirement can be divided among a number of subsystems. Part of the skill of meta-management is to help people communicate and keep track of the interfaces among subsystems.

The Continuing Task

The meta-management job continues throughout the lifetime of a product. Whenever a change occurs to business or technical requirements, it is likely changes also occur to attributes of some of the interfaces. Or perhaps the change results in the introduction of a new interface. Staying aware of new and changed requirements helps a meta-manager to monitor changes to interproduct interfaces.

Another advantage of investing in meta-management is the ability to prevent duplication of effort. We were consulting on how to implement meta-management with a large organization that builds operating system software. By identifying and analyzing the interproject interfaces, we discovered six separate projects in the organization were working on the same or a largely overlapping set of requirements. This situation arose because of the piecemeal way the organization had grown. Every part of the company thought of itself as quite different and tended to produce their products in a vacuum. It was not that people did not talk to one another, but when they did communicate they were always under time pressure and they used far from common terminology that made it very difficult to recognize commonality. Given the nature of day-to-day pressures, nobody on the individual projects had time to take a wider view and discover duplications among the different projects and the duplication of human effort.

The steps this company went through to apply the principles of meta-management are:

- Analyze the interproject interfaces.
- Recognize duplication of effort.
- Repartition projects to minimize duplication.
- Appoint a meta-manager responsible for monitoring interproject interfaces and facilitating necessary communication among projects.

The meta-manager is likely to be aware of requirements that have already been implemented. If a change or a new project is planned, the meta-manager is likely to be able to direct the project group to relevant sources of knowledge.

Refer to Chapter 7—Requirements for Existing Systems for more on defining requirements for systems that have been in existence for some time.

What Do I Do Right Now?

The project success indicators particularly affected by meta-management practices are:

- Control of changes
- Control of configuration
- No nasty surprises

Every time you have a change to your project, analyze the change from the point of view of your project and then consider the meta-management implications. Use the list of interface constituents shown in Figure 10.2 to ensure you ask the questions that identify effects on other projects. In other words make meta-management part of your change-control procedure.

Look for the most likely leakage points among your interproject interfaces. You can do this by comparing the list of interface constituents (again Figure 10.2) with your stakeholder list and asking the question: "Which stakeholders may unknowingly do something that has an effect on the integrity of this interface constituent?"

For example consider the interface constituent we have called *External Influence* and described as "Which external organization(s) (a COTS producer, outside supplier) can unknowingly make changes to this interface that may have an effect on our implementation expectations?" This is a likely leakage point because a COTS producer has many customers and is likely to make a change to its product without realizing it may affect the integrity of one of your interfaces.

Treat meta-management as a real job. To get the benefits, unless you are a very small organization, you need an individual (or individuals) whose job is to manage the interfaces among projects. In other words, meta-management does not just happen—it needs devoted resources.

What's the Least I Can Get Away With?

Educate your project team to publicize the interfaces between their project and other projects in your organization. Make an interproject interface map (see Figure 10.7 for an example) and put it in a visible place. Encourage people to write comments and questions on the map. Redraw the map to reflect the growing knowledge. Publicize the insights (some will always be present) that have made a difference to your project.

On one of our projects the manager put such a map on the wall outside her office. This was located in a narrow corridor but didn't prevent people from clustering around. And people from different projects within the meta-project became knowledgeable enough to raise significant questions early in the project.

Resources for Meta-Management

The following sources, in addition to those already referenced, have useful information on meta-management.

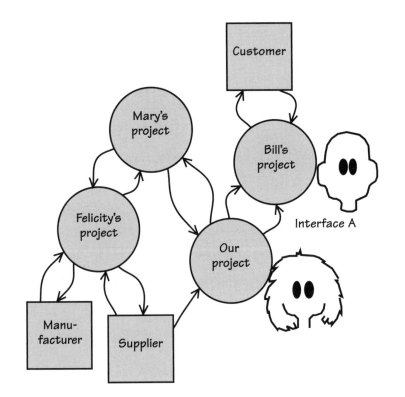

Figure 10.7

This map exposes the interfaces—and thereby the overlapping requirements—among projects. The map shows our project needs to talk to Bill about Interface A. It is necessary to establish that both projects have the identical understanding of their attributes.

- Burgess, Anthony. *A Mouthful of Air*. Random House Group, 1992—*An analysis of the differences and similarities among languages from the point of view of words, character sets, and sounds. This book is an inspiration for anyone who would like to learn another language.*
- Hayakawa, S.I. *Language in Thought and Action*. George Allen and Unwin, 1970—*This guide to language and meaning helps the meta-manager address the question of how to pool knowledge to converge on a common meaning.*
- Senge, Peter M. *The Fifth Discipline. The Art and Practice of the Learning Organization*. Doubleday, 1990—*We include Senge here for his advice on how to understand the dynamics of the complete system.*
- Weinberg, Jerry. *Quality Software Management Volume 4—Anticipating Change*. Dorset House, 1997—*The section on protecting information assets, in particular the discussion of data dictionaries and standards, contains helpful guidance for meta-managers.*

CHOCOLATE

A part of any manager's task is to measure and monitor his or her workforce. However, the act of measuring often distorts the measurements. This is known as the "Hawthorne effect" after a series of productivity measurements done at the Western Electric plant in Hawthorne, Illinois, during the late 1920s. Management was interested in determining the optimum level of lighting in the plant. It measured productivity, adjusted the lighting, then remeasured. At each change of lighting the managers noticed productivity increased, regardless of whether the lights went up or down, including a remarkable increase when the lights were so low that workers were almost in the dark. The conclusion later reached was that because the workers knew their productivity was being measured, they modified their behavior to suit the measurement.

Naturally, when managers start measuring and the project team is aware of the measurements, members of the team (consciously and subconsciously) adjust their behavior so their output conforms as much as possible to the measurement. This usually results in unexpected results that are not what was intended. There is a famous Soviet cartoon that satirizes the failure of measuring output by showing the manager of a nail factory being given the Order of Lenin for exceeding his tonnage. The manager was standing in front of the two cranes that were needed to hold up one giant nail.

Your Requirements Process

Requirements processes are sometimes document-heavy, time-consuming activities that result in specifications that are largely ignored by the developers. It does not have to be this way. In this chapter we look at how to get the best impact from your requirements and spend the minimum time doing so.

What Are *You* Doing?

Each day, pilots fly airplanes from one city to another. If you were allowed to visit the cockpit you would see the pilots sitting calmly while they preside over the airplane. It is routine: the pilots have flown this route and this plane hundreds of times before. However, occasionally something goes wrong and the pilots rapidly take the necessary corrective action. They can do this because they are trained to react to these exceptions. This leads us to say that flying an airplane is, although highly skilled, a routine process with the occasional exception.

Projects that build new products are different. There are almost no routine projects. Each project builds a product different from all others: It uses different technologies and solves different problems with different time frames and different sets of people to do the work. Each project is full of exceptions, and the only way to deal with them is to adapt to each new set of circumstances.

Ask yourself, "What am I trying to do and how shall I do it this time?"

Your objective is to get the right product in the least practical amount of time with the least practical number of errors in the product.

What you are trying to do is to get the right product in the least practical amount of time and cost, with the least practical number of errors in the product. The right product is one that satisfies the business need, is attractive to its intended users, and at the same time fits into the organization's overall product lines and objectives.

Chapter 2—Requirements Value provides guidance on how to perform a project value analysis and choose whether or not to invest in the project.

Ignoring quality in the hope of delivering your product sooner never works. Unlike manufactured goods, software is cheapest when it is free from defects. Software errors are so expensive to fix and the ramifications of errors so disastrous that taking steps to avoid them results in a cheaper product delivered earlier. It has been the experience of our clients the fastest way to deliver software is to get it right the first time.

Consider also that in most projects about half the errors are requirements errors. This is illustrated in Figure 11.1. The inference to be drawn is by paying attention to requirements gathering, you reduce errors significantly and thereby reduce your time and cost to complete the project. This does not mean spending month after month producing the perfect requirements document. But it does mean requirements play a pivotal role in your development process.

Unlike manufactured goods, software is cheapest when it is free from defects.

In this chapter we discuss some aspects of development processes. Along the way we hope you pick up on several you can include in your own process. At the end, we bring the pieces together.

Figure 11.1

Most of the errors in software projects stem from the requirements activity. This is also when it is cheapest to correct any defects. Yet many software projects rush through requirements in the hope of saving time. The result is always poor requirements, faulty products, and expensive maintenance costs.

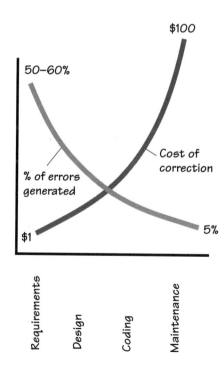

Agile Development

Agile development, like every other advance in systems development, contains some good ideas and is monstrously overhyped. We would like to look at the good ideas, and suggest how you can make best use of them.

Agile development is based on having minimalist, incremental requirements and constant redesign of software to accommodate new requirements at any stage. The requirements can change as often as needed. Agility also demands you develop the product for what you know at the moment and do not try and build in predictions about what may be needed in the future. The programmers are tasked with building "just enough" to satisfy the current requirer request.

One of the underpinnings of agile development is that documentation is unnecessary—code is all that is needed. The business user must be part of the team and communicates directly with programmers who build software to satisfy the user. This means you must have programmers both willing and capable of listening to the requirers, as well as requirers willing to work full time with the programmers as they explore the needs by building software increments for each new request.

Whenever the programmers consider a new requirement, or a change to the existing ones, and this does not seamlessly integrate with software written to date, the whole of the code is redesigned. This redesign—it is known as *refactoring*—is done so any new addition does not leave the code in an unmanageable state. This idea of constant redesign is one of the most valuable ideas to come from agile development. Needless to say, refactoring should be performed using automated tools that can put all the objects back into their correct hierarchies.

Pair programming is another of the good ideas to come from the agile school. This works by having two programmers sharing a keyboard. Before code can be installed at least two programmers have to agree that it is the most elegant and workable solution they can find. The usual result is better, more readable and reliable code. Each programmer in a pair acts as the other's conscience. The quick fix, the cheap hack, the untested alteration, the dirty trick, and other shameful acts are banished. The effect of having two programmers at the one keyboard is increased productivity and better-quality code.

Along with pair programming, *small increments* are another of the foundation stones of agile development. Although this is not new, the agile school has perfected it. The programmers build whatever they know at the moment and make it work. This can mean releasing an increment each week, or each day in some cases. Some proponents even advocate a few hours between releases. Each increment should contain enough new functionality to allow the requirers to assess it and agree it

Agile development proposes that rather than sticking to some institutionalized way of developing products, you concentrate on doing those things that provide the best value.

satisfies their needs. Then more requirements are introduced, and those are added to the existing code for the next incremental delivery.

Requirements are never optional—the delivered product has to work to suit the requirers' needs. Agile development does not exactly advocate skipping the requirements part, but it does advocate programmers learn the requirements by building proposed solutions at the keyboard. But note here they are building solutions. These may or may not be a solution to the real requirement.

It is safe to say that this approach is not suitable for large projects. The problem is that there is never a single requirer, but many stakeholders each of whom has demands on the product. To build what one requirer asks for at the keyboard is probably impacting others' needs.

Perhaps the most valuable contribution that the agile movement has made is the idea that rather than sticking to some institutionalized way of developing products, you concentrate on doing those things that provide the best value to the customer. This means assessing at the beginning of the project what you need to do this time, and what activities provide the best payback. We heartily endorse this.

Your Process Is a Chart of the Terrain

Instead of a pedantic step-by-step process, consider giving your team a chart of the terrain they are to navigate. You tell them where you want them to go, and they find the best way to get there. Along the way they may find they have to take a diversion or two, but the chart shows them how to get back on track.

> *In preparing for battle I have always found that plans are useless, but planning is indispensable.*
>
> —General Dwight Eisenhower

While we do not advocate rigid processes, nor institutionalized processes, nor proprietary processes, nor anything mandated by someone who has very little to do with the work of your project; we *have* learned some things must be done—requirements, architecture, designing, implementation, testing—to achieve the right product. We also know that it is impossible to manage a project unless the members of your team know what you want them to do and, most important, how you assess progress. For convenience we refer to this as a process.

It goes without saying that any process you use must be as dexterous as possible and include only those activities that give value to this project. This implies that for each project you consider the *output* of each activity. Some outputs can give you good value: They make a downstream activity significantly easier or more effective. So when you consider your own process, pay attention to defining outputs of activities, then it becomes easier for your team to understand and plan what it has to do to produce that output.

Almost all software is built by teams. Any team needs some kind of process (you can call this a game plan or roadmap or whatever) so that all team members are aware of what they have to produce, individually, and what their team mates are doing. Without this, team members run the risk of leaving out important activities, duplicating work, or worse, doing work that does not have to be done.

There is no doubt the process you use for conducting your projects is your own. Why? Because no other person in the world faces the same issues you face, knows the resources you have at your disposal, or knows the scope and objectives of your project. Any off-the-shelf methodology, any edicts handed down from ivory towers, cannot be what you need. However, you do not have to build a process from scratch, and you do not have to spend several months documenting in minute detail the process you intend to use.

We are going to show you a way of designing your own process by using a generic requirements knowledge model and a generic requirements process model. So instead of talking about what your project needs to *do,* we start by talking about what you need to *know.*

> *Don't fight a battle if you don't gain anything by winning.*
>
> —Field Marshall Erwin Rommel

Requirements Knowledge—What Your Analysts Have to Discover

It is the responsibility of the requirements analyst to discover what the requirers need the product to do and to communicate those needs to the builders of the product. A requirements analyst has to be able to learn the requirements by translating ideas, wishes, feelings, observations, and assumptions into measurable requirements. From these requirements, builders (including designers, programmers, architects) must be able to understand what has to be built. And understand it well enough to be able to raise questions rather than making assumptions. The distinction between analysts and builders becomes a little unclear at times when you have job titles like analyst/programmer; however, the role distinction holds good regardless of people having multiple roles. Three separate roles still need to be represented on any project: the requirer, the requirements analyst, and the builder.

Requirements, if useful, are not simplistic. But neither do they have to be overly complex. We have put together a requirements knowledge model, based on the Volere requirements template, that shows the subject matter for the requirements activity. This is shown in Figure 11.2. The full knowledge model including definitions of all the classes and associations is in Appendix A. Your requirements analysts collect this information (not always at the same level of detail) as they are trawling for

A requirements analyst has to be able to learn the requirements by translating ideas, wishes, feelings, observations, and assumptions into measurable requirements.

Figure 11.2

The requirements knowledge model identifies information to be gathered by the requirements activity. The requirements knowledge model uses UML symbology. Rectangles with a name inside them represent classes of knowledge and associations between the classes are represented by lines with a name to give the reason for the association. The multiplicity is shown as 1, meaning a single instance of the class, and * meaning many instances participate in the association.

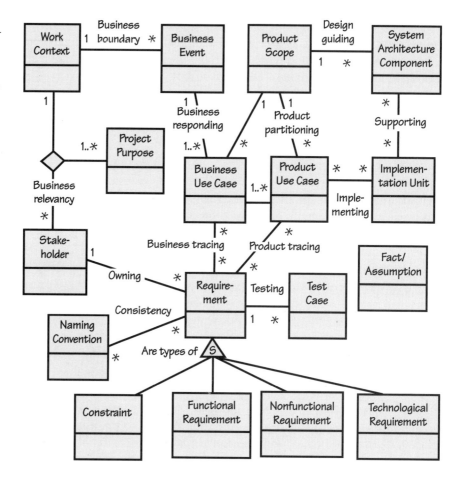

requirements. Think of this model as a guide to your repository of the requirements and associated knowledge. Let us explain it.

The knowledge model is based on experience in using the Volere requirements template (discussed in Chapter 9—Managing the Requirements). Each of the classes on the knowledge model corresponds to one or more sections on the template's table of contents. For example the class called *Work Context* maps to Section 7: Work Context on the requirements template. The class called *Stakeholder* maps to Sections 2 and 3 on the requirements template.

Each class in the generic requirements knowledge model (shown as a rectangle) represents a different type of requirements information. For example, the class *Project Purpose* is information that defines why you are doing the project. There is an obvious need to understand and record this information so you can come to a consensus with the key stakeholders on the reason the project exists. Similarly, a need exists to communicate the project purpose to all interested parties, keep the business analysts on track, and ensure all the requirements are relevant. We call this a class of knowledge because there are facts—we correctly call them *attributes*—you must gather in order to understand it in detail. Attributes for the *Project Purpose* are as follows:

A description of the purpose so you can communicate the background of the project and the reason for the business investment in this project.
A description of the business advantage or benefit expected from the investment in this project.
A measurement of the advantage that allows the delivered product to be objectively tested to determine whether the benefit has been achieved.

Another class, the *Work Context*, is discussed elsewhere in this book. We usually represent this class of knowledge using a context model. The *Stakeholder* class represents all the stakeholders identified as either having requirements for the product or having skills or knowledge needed for the product's requirements. The *Project Purpose* relates to, or associates with, the *Stakeholders* and the *Work Context*. We have called this a *Business Relevancy* relationship because these three pieces of information are considered together to ensure the project is relevant to the business.

Note the *Product Scope* class is different from the *Work Context*. This is because the business analyst studies the product users' work and then, with the help of other stakeholders, decides how much of that work can be done by the product. The *Product Scope* class represents the physical incarnation of the product. To provide a convenient grouping, it is *partitioned* into *Product Use Cases* as a convenient unit of implementation. The *Implementation Unit* class is information about what you and your system architects decide is the appropriate amount to implement in one release cycle.

The *Owning* association between *Stakeholder* and *Requirement* is present because the business analysts need to know which stakeholders requested which requirements. The *Requirement* can be one of four types. A *Constraint* is some physical limitation on the product or a predetermined design decision with which the designers must comply. A *Functional Requirement* is something the product is required to do, and a *Nonfunctional Requirement* is a quality such as usability, security, or operability the product is required to have. *Technological Requirements* come about because of the technology the designer chooses to implement the requirements. These four are all requirements, but we have found it useful to categorize them to help with their discovery.

Making Use of the Knowledge Model

This section of the book is about deciding your own process. Let's look at this from a different perspective. Instead of starting with the activities in the process, we suggest you start with the information that your process has to accumulate and derive the activities from that. In other words, what you do and how you do it is driven by what you have to learn.

By inspecting each of the classes in the knowledge model, you determine the most appropriate information content for that class. Once you know the type of information to be collected, decide who must be involved and how that information is to be collected.

We have described a model of the information you are investigating during the requirements process. But the model we described is a generic model, and generic is not going to get you through your next project. You need to make this into *your* model.

The remainder of this section makes use of the detailed generic Requirements Knowledge Model in Appendix A. We are assuming you have a few fingers in its pages and are referring to it along with this description.

Each class represents information your team must learn and communicate. However, classes are not necessarily synonymous with documents. While *Work Context* is probably a separate diagram—hopefully on public display—use cases and requirements are probably bundled in an automated specification. You choose how you wish to package and disburse this information, but first it is useful to consider what the classes of knowledge mean to you.

For each of the classes, consider the following.

- What is this thing called in your organization? If you already have a different name for it then change it to use your existing name.
- Is this thing relevant to your project? For example, if your project is to build an embedded product with well-defined boundaries, then *Work Scope* may not be a relevant deliverable.
- Does the given definition adequately describe this deliverable in your organization? The intention is for you to change our definitions to suit your own project and organization. However, please check the definitions of the adjacent classes to ensure the overall integrity of your model remains.
- How is this information recorded? If it is part of a document or file, is that the appropriate home for it?
- Who is assigned to gather this information?
- What does that person (or do those people) have to do to get the information? Are any special techniques called for?
- What is the source of this information? Does it require consensus or is it from a single source?

Consider whether there are any other classes of knowledge you need in order to relate the model to your own organization. Typically the additional classes of knowledge are concerned with tracing the business requirements into your implementation environment and/or into your marketing environment.

- The knowledge model contains a class called *Implementation Unit.* This is typically a module of code or a class or logical grouping of classes. You might also use the term *Feature* to describe this. If you are outsourcing your development you might have need of a class called something like *Outsourced Unit.*
- If your product is machinery of some sort this may also be a component of the machine.
- What about the class called *System Architecture Component?* Is this a meaningful piece of information in your own implementation environment? Does it help you communicate with the appropriate people or should you change its name or partition it into a number of classes?

The answers to these questions will to a large extent mould your process. Each piece of the information has to be gathered, understood, and recorded. The task is to ensure that each of the pieces is put into place and the *association* between the classes is understood and made.

Associations link the classes and play a part in your process. For example, an association exists between *Product Use Case* and *Requirement* called *Product Tracing.* The existence of this association means requirements analysts need to know which requirements belong to which product use case, and for any product use case, the requirements it contains. The need here is to be able to test that all of the necessary functionality is present for each of the use cases, and to check the completeness of any use case. This association is actually implemented by recording the use case identifier on each of the requirements as they are captured.

Each of the associations in the model is explained in Appendix A. Having considered the need for the association, you must include in your process a way of implementing it. This means having some way of recording the association, and the classes at either end of the association can be retrieved.

For each of the associations:

- Is the association necessary in your environment?
- Is the name of the association and its description consistent with what you call it in your organization?
- Should you enhance or change the description?
- Are there other associations useful to you?

When you add or change classes or associations in the model remember to also modify the supporting class and association definitions.

The intention of this tailoring exercise is to mould the knowledge model so all the business analysts to have the identical and consensual understanding of what information has to be collected.

Our normal way of working with our clients and this requirements knowledge model is to start with the generic model shown in Figure 11.2. We make it clear our objective is not to have them adopt our model wholesale, but to understand what each of the classes represent. Then to change the names to suit local naming and to change the attributes to fit with what they already have, or what they would like to have. This generally results in additions to the model. We try and involve different parts of the organization: marketing people usually add other groupings of requirements ("features") while engineering folks usually go for a smaller collection called something like "component."

The point of the exercise is that when it is complete—and it does not take very much time—the whole organization has the same understanding of what information is needed, what individual contributions are to be, how it will be packaged and published, and what to expect from the requirements activity. This way all of the affected business comes to a common understanding of what information needs to be learned to support the building of the correct product.

Expect your own knowledge model to significantly vary in size from our generic one. We have seen up to 28 classes and as many associations on one model. This was mainly due to differences between the functional grouping of the requirements, how the marketing people grouped the requirements, and how the requirements were grouped for implementation.

The knowledge model represents the requirements information you have to collect. However, it does not show you how to collect it. In Chapter 4—Learning What People Need, we discuss techniques requirements analysts use as they go about collecting this knowledge. However, we wish to stress not all of the knowledge has to be discovered before moving on to downstream activities. We can discover and build in short cycles. Let's look at that.

A Cyclical Process

We have spoken elsewhere in this book about the desirability of having a process that delivers partial versions of the product at fairly short intervals. To be effective, such a process includes requirements and implementation releases in each cycle. Figure 11.3 shows such a cyclical process. As we discuss it, keep in mind that there are factors—known

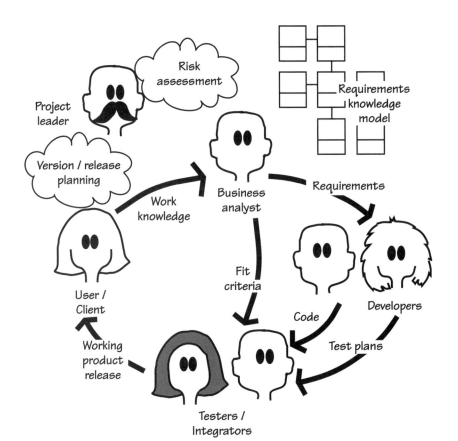

Figure 11.3
The cyclical process. The cycle starts with the client or the chief business user agreeing to a release with the project leader. Each release should include some functionality the business users consider to be a useful addition. Generally this is a number of product use cases. The project leader assesses the risks involved and communicates these to the business analysts. The requirements are gathered for just those use cases and the developers implement the increment.

only to you—that make your project different from all others. These factors influence the degree of effort you put into each part of the cycle.

As with most things, the key activity is the earliest. The project leader, together with the client or chief business user, or possibly marketing, decide what the next release is to be. Use your knowledge model to ensure you have a consistent understanding of what will be included in the release. If you have a consistent connection between the agreed release and one or more product use cases then your cyclic process is easier to manage.

When you choose the product use cases to include in the release, include enough additional functionality to demonstrate an advance of the product. This might mean some sparkling feature that will be attractive to customers, or perhaps a new screen the user community wants. You can look at several aspects: The value the customer places on the new work is a good guide, as well as the complexity of the new use cases. Developers should be allowed to implement some of the most difficult stuff early on. Obviously they do not want to get to late stages of the project to find that there are some technical problems they cannot solve, or at least not without extensive rework.

Paradoxically you might also give consideration to some of the easy stuff so you can allow your team and your client to see the cycle at work. Teams need reinforcement to demonstrate the effectiveness of what they are doing, and there is nothing better for this than to produce a working version shortly after commencing the cycle.

Business analysts trawl for requirements only for that part of the product that is to be the next release. Once those requirements are stable enough, they are communicated to the developers. Thus the business analyst is a conduit to get the needs and wants of the business to the people who build the appropriate software for them. The *fit criteria* flow shown in Figure 11.3 is the measurement the business analyst attaches to a requirement for two reasons. One is that the analyst must have the exact same understanding of the requirement as the requirer. The other is so testers can run objective tests to prove the delivered product exactly *fits* the requirement.

Once the new code is proven to be working as needed and integrated into the existing product the user takes delivery and then starts the next cycle.

Linking Requirements to Testing and the V Model

No matter whether you are using short or long release cycles, testing must be part of your process. The V model was originally derived to organize testing. Our colleague Dorothy Graham, who is a specialist in the field of testing, points out how the V model is an excellent tool for involving testers in testing requirements. Once again, if you are familiar with this way of seeing development and testing, you might want to skip the next few paragraphs.

RESOURCE NOTE
Dorothy Graham, "Requirements and Testing: The Missing Link," *IEEE Software,* September 2002.

The V model is shown in Figure 11.4. The model shows the activities of software development and how they can be organized to maximize the deliverable of a quality product. Down the left side of the V are the activities that define the product to be built, culminating with *Implement Code.* Note that each of the activities generates tests that have to be run to determine the implementation has correctly delivered the output of that activity.

Note also this is *not* a waterfall method. Your project is run using as many or as few incremental cycles as you decide. Each incremental cycle (whether it is represented by one product use case or a much larger chunk of functionality) goes through all the activities in the V. The *feedback* flows are present so each activity can let the previous one know whether its output was satisfactory. This kind of model for development

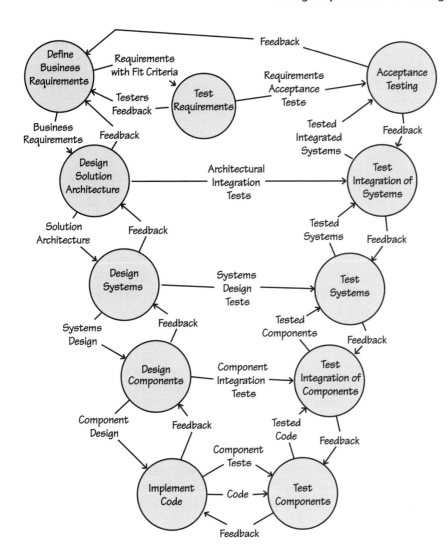

Figure 11.4

The V model of systems development. This model shows development and testing activities, and the interfaces between them. Note each activity generates test plans later used to test for compliance. Note also the feedback mechanism. This means the V model is not intended to be a waterfall model, but rather an iterative one.

is only effective if a certain amount of feedback goes to the previous activity. The absence of feedback indicates that an activity was performed too perfectly. That is, it *overspecified* to the point people working on the subsequent activity had absolutely no questions.

The part of the V model we are concerned with here is at the top left. The *Define Business Requirements* and *Test Requirements* are included in the main thrust of this book. However, it does fall to the business analyst, with the help of others, to determine the product's scope. This is part of the *Design Solution Architecture* and *Design Systems* activities. The *Test Requirements* activity is what we would normally call the *Quality Gateway* we defined in *Mastering the Requirements Process*. Briefly, each requirement is given a quick test to determine it is relevant to the project, that it does not contribute to scope creep, that it is testable, unambiguous, not gold plating, and so on. Requirements that pass this syntactic check are added to the specification, while rejects are returned to the initiating stakeholder.

Fit Criteria for Creating Feedback

In the V model shown in Figure 11.4, the *Test Requirements* process means testers' expertise is introduced early in the project. This testing activity enforces the convention that each requirement has a *fit criterion*. The fit criterion is a measurement of the requirement that allows the eventual implementation to be tested to determine if it meets, or fits, the original requirement. For example, a requirement such as "The product must be attractive" might be a valid requirement but is not testable. The fit criterion in this case is a measurement of "attractive." Let us suppose that your requirer says that it must be attractive so that his workers will voluntarily start using it right away. Then the fit criterion is something like "70% of the target users will be using at least 50% of the delivered functionality within two weeks of delivery." This measurement is what the delivered product will be tested against. The designer is also party to the fit criterion and now must design a product that is "attractive" enough to entice people to use it. Note the fit criterion is purely a measurement of the requirement, and does not attempt to say how the product is to be made attractive. It exists purely to make the requirement testable.

In the *Test Requirements* activity, the testers test the fit criterion to determine whether it is possible to write a cost-effective test for that requirement. There are also other tests to determine the suitability or not of the requirement. (We are speaking of "requirement" in the singular here as we advocate testing the requirements one by one before testing them as functionally related groups.) The tests you run on your requirements are derived from attributes of a requirement you decided in your requirements knowledge model. We have suggested attributes (in keeping with the Volere requirements shell) in the model shown in Appendix A.

The end result of the *Test Requirements* activity is you test the requirements to determine if they fit their purpose. The V model shows how the requirements are the foundation of all other activities. If requirements errors or omissions are made—many projects report that 50%–60% of errors originate in the requirements activity—then the ripple of corrections could go all the way through all the activities in the model.

So it stands to reason they should be tested, and tested early. By doing so, you are creating early feedback. The importance of "early" cannot be

Creating early feedback on quality of requirements should be a major consideration in the way you implement your process.

overstressed, as early errors are the cheapest to correct. If an incorrect requirement is allowed to make its way to later activities, chances are all previous activities will be affected when the error is eventually discovered. This can be expensive, and at times downright embarrassing.

Mapping the V Model to Your Environment

The V model is a generic model, but one that serves well to ensure you get a quality product. Keeping in mind that concentrating on quality delivers the product in the shortest time, we look at how you can make this model serve for your project.

Start with any process on the V. Consider its interfaces. Let your team know what they need to deliver by specifying these inputs and outputs. Do this by determining the content of the interface by referring to your requirements knowledge model:

- What knowledge classes should be in this interface?
- What associations are inferred by this interface?
- Precisely what attributes should be in the interface?
- What other information should be in this interface? The answer to this question sometimes causes you to make changes to the knowledge model.
- Are all the sources of the interface aware of the above?

Determine the form of the interface by referring to your Project Sociology (Chapter 3) and either the process you currently have or the Volere generic process.

- On what medium (email, Web, database, paper, phone) does this interface travel from one process to another?
- When does this interface travel from process to process?
- How often?
- Who is responsible for the interface, from the point of view of each process?
- How do you test the quality of the interface?

Note what we are doing here. We are not specifying an elaborate process, just the things that have to get done. We are looking at the deliverables, not the way in which to get them.

Now look at the people involved. Using your project sociology analysis—summarized in your stakeholder map—determine which stakeholders need to be involved in each process. This is striking a balance between ensuring enough stakeholders are present to ensure all the requirements are found and minimizing the number of people involved, thus improving communication.

- Which stakeholders are involved in this process? This includes both members of your core team as well as interested stakeholders who are requirers.
- Is the stakeholder involvement full or part time?

This should be an iterative process. The V model is often read to mean the requirements for the entire product are written and passed down to the next activity on the left leg of the V, and when that activity is completed then its output is passed along until eventually all the activities on the right side are performed in their turn. We do not mean that here. Instead, look at the flows that pass horizontally across the open jaws of the V. If these exist in small increments, then the testing people have time to prepare correct test cases and are also able to test in small increments.

The other effect of an iterative process is almost all activities on the V are active at the same time. This makes your staffing somewhat easier, as most of the activities are more or less constant. However, it does require more attention to managing the dependencies among the iterations.

Your other responsibility is to ensure all activities are capable of producing the appropriate feedback, and that each of them is also capable of accepting the feedback and adjusting itself accordingly.

This leads us to look at the organizational nature of the process. You must ensure that any process either fits into your organization or you must partition it further. This may be necessary because parts of the process are carried out in different locations and a need exists to monitor the progress of the interfaces among the locations. As much as possible it is preferable (provided the external interfaces are defined and agreed upon as above) for the people inside a process to decide how they will accomplish the work of the process.

The Volere Process Model

In our previous book *Mastering the Requirements Process* we described a generic requirements process in quite some detail. While we are not suggesting you adopt this process wholesale, it does specify many of the activities your team needs to carry out in order to successfully gather and verify the requirements. We mention the Volere process here because it has been adopted (and adapted) by thousands of projects, and it may well serve as part of your project roadmap. The Volere process includes

- Project Blastoff—Establishing scope, stakeholders, and goals
- Trawling for requirements—Techniques for gathering and discovering requirements
- Writing requirements—How to write unambiguous and testable requirements
- Quality gateway—How to test requirements for defined qualities
- Requirements review—How to deal with conflicts and how to prioritize

Most of the activities in the Volere process belong within the processes *Define Business Requirements* and *Test Requirements* on the V model. There are also some parts of the Volere process (specifically the defining of constraints and product boundary) that provide input for *Design Solution Architecture* and *Design Systems*.

In this as in any process interfaces exist among the activities. Most of the time humans perform these activities, which means the interfaces need to be in some written or diagrammatic form. For example, on the V model, the *Test Requirements* activity sends *Requirements Acceptance Tests* to the *Acceptance Testing* activity. As the latter activity may not take place for some time after the former, there is a need to have a persistent record of the acceptance tests.

This leads us to documentation.

Documentation—What Is It For?

What is it for? To help the business analysts discover the real requirement, to record the decision process that leads to the requirement, to transmit the requirement in an unambiguous way to the downstream activities, to enable testers to determine if the requirements have been correctly implemented. Apart from that, little else.

Using your code as the documentation of the current state of a requirement is, unfortunately, not going to work. The code is, after all, the implementation and gives little indication of its underlying requirement. For example, consider this:

"I want the monthly sales figures on the screen."

This is not a requirement—far from it. It is firstly a perceived solution to the problem (the screen is a technological artifact) and "monthly sales figures" are the requirer's first thoughts on what he wants. Why does the requirer want this? It is obvious the monthly sales figures are part of some larger piece of work being done, and you should understand it before building this alleged requirement. If you rush into implementing this without understanding wider ramification, and along the way discovering the real requirement, you run the risk of implementing something that is merely the idiosyncratic whim of the single requirer. There is a lot more to it. What about the security of this requirement? Does the requirer's management want these figures on a screen where anybody can see them? What does the requirer do with the sales figures? Can you do it for him? Is this to be used by more than one person and if so, what are the usability needs? There are so many unanswered questions it's dangerous to implement this requirement without some better understanding of the larger picture.

Some universally accessible way of writing down the requirement must exist so all interested stakeholders can verify it.

We have found that recording the requirement along with its fit criterion, its customer value, and the other attributes of the requirement, is the best way of correctly understanding the requirement. It is also the best way of communicating it. Some universally accessible way of writing down the requirement must exist so all interested stakeholders can verify it. We somehow think most business users are not all that adept at reading Java.

Models, the Common Language

There are various ways of "writing down" the requirements that help with the gathering and understanding of requirements. Functional requirements are the most obvious, so let's start there. Functionality is two-dimensional: Data is processed and moves to another process, or a data store, or both. Meanwhile, other processes are feeding that data store or retrieving information from it.

This kind of two-dimensional activity lends itself to a two-dimensional model. There are many types of functional model, and we have included several samples to show the kinds of things that are suitable. The notation of the model is not important—and it is supremely important not to get into religious wars as to what kind of functional model is "best"—but it is important that all of your team and as many as possible of the other stakeholders can understand and contribute to the content of the model. The models must also be rigorous enough that developers can get a precise understanding of what is needed, and can use the models as part of their input to constructing the final product.

Take a moment to look at the models shown in Figure 11.5, Figure 11.6, and Figure 11.7. All three show the same piece of work—a DVD rental business—and any are suitable for your analysts to use when determining the functionality of a piece of work.

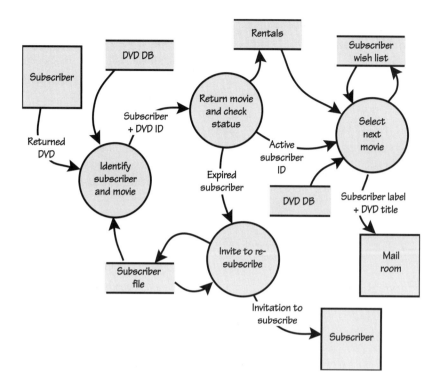

Figure 11.5

A data flow model showing functional requirements. This is a DVD rental service that sends out another movie from the subscriber's wish list whenever a DVD is returned.

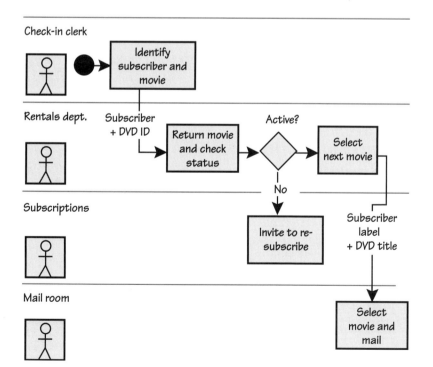

Figure 11.6

A business process workflow model of the same movie rental business as shown in Figure 11.5. This diagram highlights the organizational aspects of the processes. The processes may be automated or manual.

Figure 11.7

A UML activity
diagram. This shows
the processes and
objects involved in
the return of the
movie.

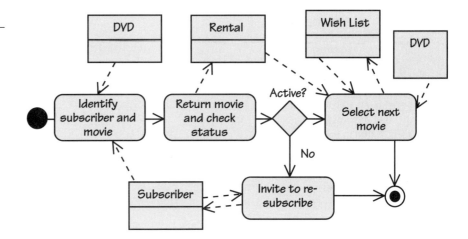

A functional model shows functional processing, and as such you can use it as your way of recording and communicating functional requirements. Keep in mind the model samples shown are not complete—some kind of process specification must be attached, along with a data dictionary. However, once these are in place the models do capture the essence of the functional requirements.

Requirements and Natural Language

If the stakeholders concerned with your functional requirements are not prepared to review functional requirements in the form of models, it is necessary to write the requirements in natural language. In Chapter 4 we describe how to use the Volere requirements shell as a guide to writing the attributes of an atomic requirement.

The more closely your stakeholders are working with the developers the less need you are likely to have to "translate" the functional requirements into natural language. However, given the characteristics of the majority of the projects we work on (large size, many stakeholders, geographical/organizational distribution, multiple technologies, all or partially outsourced), it is usually necessary to write the functional requirements using natural language.

There are of course some attributes of the requirements that are not part of the functional model. For example, attributes like customer value, rationale, and source would need to be captured even if you did decide to use a model as the sole specification for your functional requirements.

See Chapter 4—
Learning What
People Need for more
on how to use the
Volere requirements
shell to write both
functional and non-
functional require-
ments in natural
language.

Nonfunctional Requirements

Functionality is not all there is to a product. A product also has nonfunctional requirements that generally do not show up on a process model. For example:

- Look and feel requirements are best understood and demonstrated using software prototypes and sketches.
- Usability requirements are best completed with a combination of written requirements—the fit criterion is very important with usability requirements—and prototypes.
- Legal requirements are best expressed in text along with references to all the relevant laws, statutes, and legal opinions.
- As are the business rules.
- Data requirements and structures are best modeled with some flavor of class or data model.
- Cultural requirements are expressed in text, but sometimes you can only find them by testing a prototype.
- Constraints are a combination of text and models.
- Operational requirements can be expressed as a combination of text and models.

The point of all this is no single best form exists in which to record requirements. Your process must do it according to its information needs and consistent with having all stakeholders communicate effectively. However, your requirements knowledge model defines what attributes you need to learn about each requirement and how those atomic requirements need to be related to other classes of knowledge.

Size Matters . . . and So Do Other Factors

Having looked at what your business analysts have to learn—the Requirements Knowledge Model—and how this knowledge is distributed—the V model—and suggested a process on which to base your own—the Volere process—we now turn to factors that may make some difference to the way you approach your requirements process.

The size of the product, which has an effect on the size of the project team, makes a difference to the degree of formality your requirements documentation needs. The more people involved the greater the need for requirements to be centrally recorded for access by all stakeholders. It also means you need to write the requirements in a standardized format so each stakeholder receives exactly the same understanding of them.

The type of product influences the process you choose. As an example, if you are to deliver a medical product, the rules of the health authority in your country (FDA, Health Canada, etc.) may actually specify for you the process to be used. Other products that have some safety implication (air traffic control, elevators, emergency dispatching services) require a greater degree of formality in how they are specified, with an emphasis on precise, communicable, testable requirements.

The situation of your project also makes a difference to your plan of attack. If your team is relatively inexperienced, you need to place a greater emphasis on recorded requirements and the fit criterion of each requirement becomes crucial. Your elicitation techniques should tend toward apprenticing and workshops, and a quality gateway becomes essential and helpful. On the other hand, if you have good subject-matter experts and experienced programmers on your team, you can move more toward narrative and prototyping.

RESOURCE NOTE
For sage advice on risk
and how to manage it
we recommend *Waltz-
ing with Bears—Manag-
ing Risk on Software
Projects,* by Tom
DeMarco and Tim Lister,
Dorset House, 2003.

These three factors (size, type, situation) are overlaid by risk. When selecting a process, you assess the risk attached to what you propose to do. By this, we mean what is the likelihood an action—or indeed lack of an action—has a negative effect on your progress? What is the impact or cost of this negative effect? While you cannot avoid all risk—it is not desirable to do so unless you are Spiderman—it is foolish to launch the project if the odds are stacked against you.

Types of Projects

You also have to consider how the type of project you are embarking on makes a difference to your requirements process.

In-House Software

When you are building a product to be used by known users in the same organization that employs you, emphasize apprenticing—working with the hands-on users to learn their work—and use case workshops where the analysts work with the requirers to build models or prototypes of the desired product. Documentation can be less formal, provided that the steps leading to a decision are retained. Quick iterations of the product are encouraged.

Package or COTS

It is of course necessary to determine the requirements before you start buying the package. The requirements should be formalized so they act as part of the contract to buy. We illustrate this in Figure 11.8. The pack-

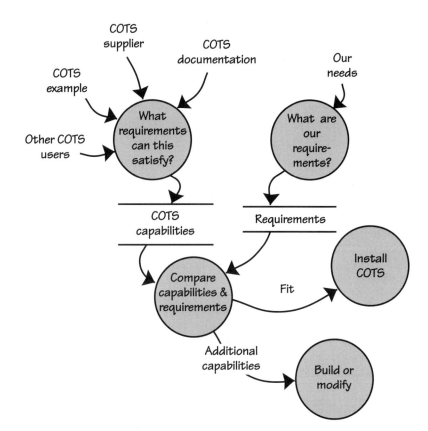

Figure 11.8

Requirements for COTS. When installing a COTS package, you need a process for matching your requirements with the COTS capabilities and identifying the fit and shortfall.

age vendor must be required to demonstrate how the requirements are met by the package and identify the requirements not met. Put emphasis on comparing your context model and the package to establishing how it fits into the organization.

If the package is to be selected and the organization made to change to fit the package, then the requirements role is to identify and specify the work to be done by the requirers. Requirements analysts are the ideal people to produce work flow models of how the package and the re-shaped organization work together.

Commercial Software

This is software for sale to a large number of people, usually but not always aimed at personal computers. The emphasis here must be on innovation and making the product's behavior as close as possible to the mental model of the intended users.

Large Projects

Large projects need some kind of automated tool to provide universal access to the requirements with links from the requirements to the test cases and the code. Also more of a need occurs for a formally implemented link between the requirements and components of the product.

Web Projects

Highlight the need for quality and usability of the Web site. Prototypes, scenarios, and stories help in these situations. These help to understand the requirements for the Web site experience. This means knowing what the intended user wants, and what he finds useful. We have found workshops walking through business use cases to be very useful. Iteration is important in Web projects; the site should be able to be released iteratively within reason.

Major Overhaul

This is a project to redevelop a significant piece of software. The project may involve moving the software from one platform to another or redesigning it and including significant new features. This software will have been used for many years and a major source of requirements is existing code. The requirers are familiar with it but you also want them to think further to what the new product should be doing.

When you are overhauling existing systems have your team concentrate on the essence. This helps to overcome a tendency for the requirers to specify requirements that are almost identical to the current solution.

Newness

For new and innovative products, pay less attention to speed of producing iterations and more to exploration of the product. Concentrate on inventing and brainstorming as many requirements as you can. Then you can choose among them and set priorities.

Looking at the Work, Not Just the Product

The intention of a requirements project is to start by studying some work or business area, then deriving a software product to improve on that work. However, many projects start out with the intention of building a software solution they guessed on day one.

For example, "Let's put stock quotes on a handheld" is a proposed solution. It ignores the concept of work. What are the quotes to be used for? What action does the recipient perform with them? Do the handheld owners want all quotes, or just stocks they are following? Do they want to sell if the stock reaches a predetermined price? And though many more questions exist that can be asked about the work surrounding the handheld, almost none of them get asked if the team is concentrating on "putting those quotes on a handheld." By studying the work and coming to a full understanding of what is really going on, you may come to realize the first guess—and it is rarely more than a guess—of the implementation does not make for the best product.

The work is the important thing to look at. Manchester (England) Airport uses a robot to clean the floors during operating hours. Some analyst was alert to the work surrounding the floor cleaning since, apart from using laser scanners and ultrasonic detectors to keep it from colliding with passengers, the robot also alerts passengers to security and no-smoking rules. Thus by looking at the work and not just the assumed product, a better product has been created.

Stakeholders and Why There Are Lots of Them

The idea of a requirer sitting down with a pair of programmers and describing a product that he wants is very attractive. However, we have yet to work on a project where only one requirer participated, or any single person who could give all the requirements for a feature. The products we build are large and complex, and it is extremely rare for a single stakeholder to be the only person with enough knowledge to be the sole source of requirements (see Figure 11.9). We usually have to consult quite a few stakeholders for each part of the product.

Figure 11.9

A person is able to speak for his part of the work. However, if you use only his version of the work you risk not finding vital requirements that can be supplied by the surrounding workers.

A lone person can only speak for his part of the work. Usually he is not completely aware of the wider issues. He focuses on his own job because naturally he considers this to be the most important thing. While he is well aware of the functionality needed for his part of the work, he is unlikely to be an authoritative voice on other aspects of the requirements. For example, security requirements: the requirer trusts himself, and probably is not aware of wider corporate needs for security. He may have opinions on the look and feel requirements, but you should also hear from the corporate branding office. Cultural requirements are too important to be left to one requirer. Operational requirements may well be beyond his expertise. All of this means you always have to talk to many people before you get a complete picture of one person's work.

You always have to talk to many people before you get a complete picture of one person's work.

We have spoken earlier in this book (Chapter 3) about project sociology. Your project team is made up of humans working to tight deadlines with changing requirements. This, and the need to know who all the interested people are, suggests strongly your process should spend some time exploring your project sociology.

The Difference between Requirements and Design

This causes a lot of debate and a lot of lost time. And it needn't. The requirements activity is about understanding the underlying business problem, of learning what the user's business is about, and then finding a product that will help with that business. The requirements themselves are a description of that product seen from the point of view of the business—you can think about it as an external view of the product.

Design is concerned with crafting a technological solution to the problem stated by the requirements. We show this in Figure 11.10. This

Figure 11.10

When we refer to "requirements" we are talking about a business need that is uncoupled from any technology that may be used to implement it. Requirements are absolute. "Design" on the other hand is making a technological choice on how the requirement might be implemented. Thus design is to some extent, arbitrary.

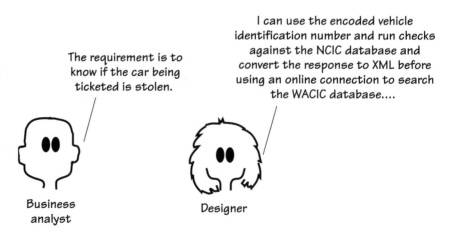

The requirement is to know if the car being ticketed is stolen.

Business analyst

I can use the encoded vehicle identification number and run checks against the NCIC database and convert the response to XML before using an online connection to search the WACIC database....

Designer

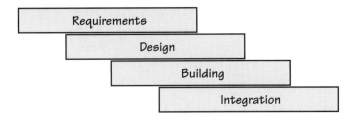

Figure 11.11

The activities of
system development
should overlap. We
suggest your
requirements analysts
get enough of a head
start before the
designers move in.
Similarly, program-
mers can start with
construction before
all of the design is
complete. The
diagram shows
timelines, not
amounts of effort.

difference is often referred to as "what" and "how." Confusingly, some authors refer to activities that precede the implementation as design. For example, Beyer and Holtzblatt called their excellent book *Contextual Design*, but it is about finding out what is needed. In this book, we refer to design as the activity where technology is introduced.

The distinction is important, as it is close to impossible to come up with the correct design if the requirements are not known. For this reason we suggest your team understand at all times whether they are working on requirements or solutions. How many (or how much) of the requirements do you define before starting design? How safe is it to overlap? Except in unusual circumstances, we never advocate establishing all the requirements before starting the design. You generally need to design and even build part of the intended product to prove the concept and get some indication from the business you are in the right ballpark. We show these overlapping activities in Figure 11.11.

It is close to impossible to come up with the correct design if the requirements are not known.

Testing, Testing

The most valuable testing you can do is early in the project. Testing the actual requirements is more cost effective—it finds a greater number of expensive errors earlier—than finding requirements errors by testing the software. And testing what comes before the requirements is even more valuable. We have talked about the need to have clear, agreed-upon, and testable goals for the project. You can only know you have these when the goal is tested. Similarly with scope: The testers test the context model (or whatever model you are using) to verify it is an accurate representation of the work area to be studied. Testing the goals and scope means you are basing your requirements gathering on a proven foundation.

To test the requirements we suggest you set up a *quality gateway*. This tests each requirement for compliance to your requirements standards before recording it in the specification. Apart from ensuring all your requirements are properly written, the effect you see from this is upstream of the gateway. Because requirements analysts understand their requirements are going to be tested, they tend to be more careful in making them clear, unambiguous, testable, and attributed.

Architecture and Design

If we consider the idea of developing a product in several chunks over a period of time, it is clear that in order to make any decisions about the product scope (and hence the delivery chunks) we need to consider the systems architecture early in the project.

One way of doing this in parallel is to go back to your knowledge model and to agree how requirements analysts and technical specialists must work together. Start by considering who is responsible for what parts of each class of knowledge.

For example, a requirements analyst is responsible for defining the work context, the business events, and the business use cases. Before the requirements analyst starts to write detailed atomic requirements, it makes sense to involve people with technical knowledge. The reason is that without some technical guidance a requirements analyst may spend time writing detailed requirements that are not possible within the technical scope. Another reason is that someone with technical knowledge may suggest a business requirement the analyst has missed because he thought it was not possible.

Something that works for us is, before writing atomic requirements, requirements analysts talk through each business use case (remember these could be in the form of models, scenarios, low-fi prototypes . . .) with the technical specialists and together decide on a reasonable boundary for the product use cases. So the association between business use case and product use case—in other words the product use case boundary—becomes the shared responsibility of the requirements analysts and the technical specialists.

Then the business analyst goes ahead and specifies the functional and nonfunctional requirements and the constraints for the product use case. This collaborative approach can save enormous amounts of time because the requirements specified in formal and consistent detail are only those that are included in the product. But the product boundary is realistic because it has been guided by the technical expertise.

One of the authors (Suzanne) did some consulting on a project in which the requirements analysts had worked on the requirements without involving any of the technical specialists until after all the requirements had been specified. The quality of the requirements was very good. But the amount of work that had been done in detailed requirements specification was considerably more than it needed to be. When

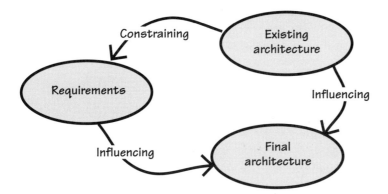

Figure 11.12

Requirements and Architecture. The constraints on the existing systems architecture have an effect on whether and how requirements can be met. However, the requirements themselves can provide ideas for improing the architecture so it can meet more requirements. Hence we suggest you consider requirements and design in parallel.

the analysts handed the requirements over to the technical developers it was clear many of the requirements could not be implemented because of constraints the requirements analysts did not understand.

If the technical specialists (people who understand the details of the systems architecture) had been called in close to the beginning of the project, their input would have been invaluable. They would have been able to advise on the architectural constraints and opportunities available to guide the requirements analysts' efforts. We are not advocating finding the solution before defining the requirements. We are saying that if you consider these things in parallel you will save yourself time by creating early communication with stakeholders who have different skills and priorities.

The influence between requirements and architecture, illustrated in Figure 11.12, works in both directions. We have said that there are constraints on the requirements caused by the systems architecture. The requirements can also influence changes to the architecture by making the technical specialists aware of a requirement that cannot be met by the existing architecture. But maybe, the architecture can be modified to make it possible to implement the requirement. If the requirements and the first-cut design are accomplished in parallel it builds a feedback loop that makes it possible to do more in less time.

A Fundamental Truth

The most successful products we have in this world are those that do what they are supposed to do—are useful for someone to work with or play with—and behave in a manner the user finds attractive.

Nobody cares about the construction of products (expect the people constructing them); everybody cares about what they do. Nobody cares what programming language is used to write a piece of software, or

This then is the role of requirements: to provide useful and usable products, to ensure that what is delivered is in line with what is needed.

(within reason) how long it takes to write it. Everybody cares what it does. Consumers and users do not care if it is object-oriented, uses a database, is open source, is agile, was built by one person or a team, or anything else about its construction.

However, they do care if it does what they want and need it to do. They will use it if it provides useful functionality. They will buy it if it provides value to their organization.

This then is the role of requirements: to provide useful and usable products, to ensure that what is delivered is in line with what is needed. Along the way the requirements will help an on-time delivery and guarantee the client's satisfaction with your product.

What Do I Do Right Now?

The point of considering process is that if you have a reasonable process it increases your chances of getting the right requirements. There are a number of PSIs (listed in Chapter 1) that are affected by having a better requirements process. Positive signals from these PSIs suggest you are in control of your process and your project. Naturally, negative signals indicate the opposite.

We have been discussing process in this chapter and want at this stage to reiterate we do not intend your process to be formal, laborious, or document-heavy. However, there must be some agreed activities and deliverables if the members of your project team are all to move in the same direction and communicate effectively.

Let's look at the success indicators and see what you can do with your process to accommodate them.

The first of the PSIs is

- No excessive schedule pressure

The inference to be taken from this PSI is you include some way of measuring and estimating in your process. We have suggested you use models to help with gathering the requirements and to provide an added attraction of being measurable. Refer to Chapter 8—Measuring Requirements for more on measuring. We have also noted in our consulting work the organizations that have an established process are far more likely to produce accurate estimates. This is on the basis that if the process is established and follows a similar path for each project, then the effort needed each time is more predictable.

The list of PSIs also includes:

- Good quality code/solutions
- No nasty surprises

Our experience has been these are addressed by including an adequate requirements activity as part of your development process. Furthermore, we advocate testing of requirements. This means you involve your testing people early in the cycle and install some kind of quality gateway procedure; these steps ensure all requirements are tested to satisfy agreed-upon quality gateway criteria before they are allowed to proceed to downstream activities.

The PSIs list:

- Adequate productivity
- Good team morale

These are addressed by having clear communications within your group. We have spoken in this chapter about the deliverables of the requirements process and in particular the requirements knowledge model. We suggest you build such a model for your own project. It will be different, but not substantially so, for your own project. A good model gives team members a clear definition of what they are to produce, thus not to waste time discussing (or arguing) about what has to be done.

The happiest teams we have led or consulted with are also the most productive. People generally enjoy their work, and giving them a clear and easily accessible definition of what they have to produce—we're talking about the Requirements Knowledge Model—means adding to that enjoyment by removing ambiguities about their deliverables and the frustration of producing wasted output.

The last of the PSIs we deal with is

- Testing is effective.

In the section on the V model, we looked at the idea of both testing the requirements—the highest-value testing of all—and providing testing input to downstream activities. Your process must include testing. The most effective testing approach includes testing within mainstream activities rather than marginalizing it by having testers work for a separate department with separate culture and separate objectives.

In all cases where we have included the testers as an integral part of the project team and insisted all members provide input to testing, we have found both quality and productivity increase. We have experienced that better requirements lead to improved products and enhance the enjoyment of your projects.

What's the Least I Can Get Away With?

Recognize that having a defined process (most importantly, consistent deliverables) is necessary for all the team to communicate effectively. Also recognize that defining the process does not take weeks of study and produce copious documentation that everybody ignores. Here is the minimalist way of deciding your process:

- Copy our Requirements Knowledge Model.
- Make any obvious changes.
- Give a copy to everyone on the team and ask them to use it to guide their work and to let you know when and if they discover additions or alterations.
- Plan to release your product in cycles.
- Alert your client and potential users this is what will happen.
- Look at the work, not just the product.
- Test, and test early.
- Ask your testers to join your project team and get involved in testing the requirements.

Resources for Your Process

The following sources, in addition to those already referenced, have useful information on creating a solid requirements process.

- Beck, Kent, and Martin Fowler. *Planning Extreme Programming*, Addison-Wesley, 2001—*eXtreme Programming is not hacking, but a defined way of developing software. Martin Fowler and Kent Beck explain how to approach XP. The book is aimed at managers and how they should manage their XP projects.*
- Beyer, Hugh, and Karen Holtzblatt. *Contextual Design—Defining Customer-Centered Systems.* Morgan Kaufmann, 1998—*This book looks at the idea of analyzing the work, and not just the product. It has a lot of excellent material on how your analysts can work with and study the people who use your product.*
- Bragg, Tom. *Designing and Building Software Projects: Lessons from the Building Trades.* Agile Project Management Advisory Service: Executive Report, Vol. 3 No. 10. Cutter Consortium, 2002—*This contains some lovely ideas for staffing projects. Bragg looks at the building industry and compares staffing there with the software field.*
- Brooks, Fred. *The Mythical Man-Month.* Addison-Wesley, 1975—*The classic Brooks management text. He muses on the lessons learned*

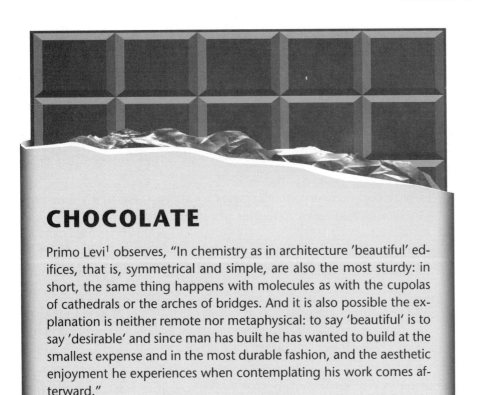

CHOCOLATE

Primo Levi[1] observes, "In chemistry as in architecture 'beautiful' edifices, that is, symmetrical and simple, are also the most sturdy: in short, the same thing happens with molecules as with the cupolas of cathedrals or the arches of bridges. And it is also possible the explanation is neither remote nor metaphysical: to say 'beautiful' is to say 'desirable' and since man has built he has wanted to build at the smallest expense and in the most durable fashion, and the aesthetic enjoyment he experiences when contemplating his work comes afterward."

1. Levi, Primo. *The Periodic Table.* Sphere Books, 1988.

from large projects, and in particular the building of an operating system for IBM.

- DeMarco, Tom and Tim Lister. *Peopleware: Productive Projects and Teams,* 2nd Ed. Dorset House, 1999—*Another classic. DeMarco and Lister look at how to have productive and happy teams. This book is a series of essays, each with several valuable lessons.*

- Highsmith, Jim. *Adaptive Software Development.* Dorset House, 2000—*Valuable advice on how to build an organic development process and to keep changing it to reflect changes in the project.*

- Leffingwell, Dean, and Don Widrig. *Managing Software Requirements—A Unified Approach.* Addison-Wesley, 2000.

- Maiden, N.A.M., and Ncube C. (1998). "Acquiring Requirements for Commercial Off-The-Shelf Package Selection," *IEEE Software,* 15(2), 46–56—*Contains much needed advice on why requirements for COTS are different and how to deal with the differences.*

- Orr, Ken. *Agile Requirements*. Agile Project Management Advisory Service. Executive Report, Vol. 3 No. 12. Cutter Consortium, 2002— *Some wise words on the management of requirements and associated processes.*
- Weinberg, Jerry. *Quality Software Management, Volume 3: Congruent Action*. Dorset House, 1994—*This third book in Weinberg's management quartet (see Bibliography) provides insights in how to take management action that is relevant to what is happening in the real world.*

Requirements Knowledge Model

This model is a representation of the knowledge you gather during the requirements activity. We present it here as a guide to the information and as a tool for communication among the stakeholders on your project. We suggest that you consider this model with regard to who gathers what information and how it is packaged and reviewed.

Note each of the classes on the knowledge model corresponds to one or more sections in the Volere requirements template. What follows defines and describes the classes of knowledge and their associations. We list associations after the classes.

Knowledge Class: Business Event

Purpose:
A *Business Event* is some happening outside the work that is in effect a demand for some service provided by the work. For example, a motorist passes an electronic tollbooth, a customer orders a book, a doctor asks for the scan of a patient, a pilot lowers the landing gear.

Business events can also happen because of the passage of time. For example, if a customer's bill is not paid in 30 days, then it is time for the work to send a reminder. Or, say, it is two months before an insurance policy is due to expire.

Attributes:
Business Event Name
Business Event Adjacent Systems/Actors

Figure A.1

The knowledge model identifies classes of knowledge concerned with requirements and the associations between them. This model is intended as input to designing your own knowledge model and requirements processes as discussed in Chapter 11.

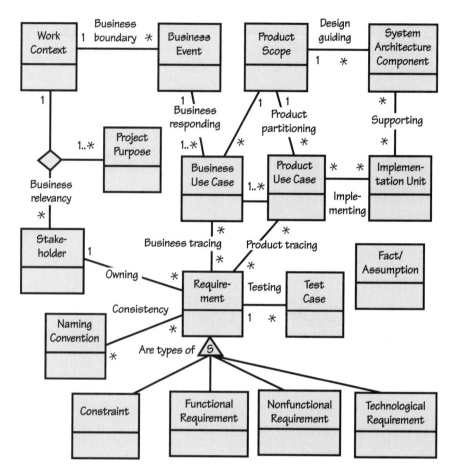

Considerations:

It is important to recognize the business event: Its nature, the circumstances that exist at the time the event happens, and the activity of the adjacent system at the time of the business event are all important indicators of the appropriate response.

Suggested Implementation:

Please refer to Section 7 of the Volere Requirements Specification Template. A list of the business events and their associated input and output flows suffices. It is practical to give each business event a unique identifier.

Knowledge Class: Business Use Case

Purpose:

A *Business Use Case* is the processing done in response to a business event. For example, "policyholder decides to make a claim" is a business event. The business use case is the processing carried out to approve or deny the claim. Also see *Product Use Case.*

Attributes:

Business Use Case Name
Business Use Case Description
Business Use Case Inputs
Business Use Case Outputs
Business Use Case Rationale
Normal Case Scenario
Exception Case Scenarios
Preconditions
Post or Exit Conditions

Considerations:
Business use cases are self-contained portions of the work, and can be studied independently. For this reason they are an important unit that project leaders can use to structure the analytical work.

Suggested Implementation:
Please refer to Section 7 of the Volere Requirements Specification Template. An automated tool that enables sharing of the business use case attributes is advisable.

Knowledge Class: Constraint

Purpose:
A *Constraint* is a type of requirement. It is a preordained design decision for the product; or a restriction on the project itself, such as the budget or time allowed.

Considerations:
We treat constraints as a type of requirement—although not conventionally gathered, they must be met. We highlight them because it is important you and your management are aware of these restrictions on your product and project.

Suggested Implementation:
Section 4 of the template. Design constraints should be recorded in the same manner as the other requirements. See the Knowledge Class: *Requirement* for attributes.

Knowledge Class: Fact/Assumption

Purpose:
An *Assumption* states an expectation on which decisions about the project are based. For example, it might be an assumption that another

project will be finished first, that a particular law will not be changed, or that a particular supplier will reach a specified level of performance. If an assumption turns out to be false, then it will have a detrimental impact on the project. The intention of stating the assumption is to expose the risk that the assumption carries with it. A *Fact* is some knowledge relevant to the project that affects its requirements and design, or information that should be brought to the attention of readers of the requirements documents. A fact can also state some specific exclusion from the product and the reason for that exclusion.

Fact/Assumption is a global class and can have an association with any of the other classes in your knowledge model.

Attributes:
Description of the Assumption

Considerations:
Assumptions indicate a risk. For this reason they should be highlighted and all affected parties made aware of the assumption. You may consider installing a mechanism to resolve all assumptions before implementation starts.

Suggested Implementation:
Section 6 of the template; these can be written in free text. They should be regularly circulated to management and the project team.

Knowledge Class: Functional Requirement

Purpose:
A *Functional Requirement* is an action the product must be capable of accomplishing. For example calculate the fare, analyze the chemical composition, record the change of name, find the new route. Functional requirements are concerned with creating, updating, referencing, and deleting the essential subject matter within the context of the study.

Attributes:
This is a subtype of *Requirement* and inherits its attributes.

Suggested Implementation:
Section 9 of the template. See Knowledge Class: *Requirement* for the attributes.

Knowledge Class: Implementation Unit

Purpose:
The unit for packaging your implementation.

Considerations:
The *Implementation Unit* can be what your customers refer to as a "feature," or if your product is a consumer item it is possibly called a "function." The choice of implementation unit is driven by a combination of your implementation technology and your implementation process. When you tailor this part of the knowledge model you might find you replace implementation unit with several classes. The important issue is you can unambiguously trace your implementation unit back to relevant requirements.

Knowledge Class: Naming Convention

Purpose:
A *Naming Convention* is a glossary that defines the meaning of terms used within the requirements documents. Most projects use specialized terminology—this glossary is the authority for their meaning.

Attributes:
   Name of the Term
   Definition of the Term

Suggested Implementation:
Section 5 of the template; should be in the form of a glossary showing the terms and their meaning for your project.

Knowledge Class: Nonfunctional Requirement

Purpose:
A *Nonfunctional Requirement* is a quality the product must have. For example, it must be fast, attractive, secure, customizable, maintainable, portable, and so on. Nonfunctional requirements types are: *Look and Feel, Usability, Performance and Safety, Operational Environment, Maintainability, Security, Cultural and Political, and Legal.* For more about nonfunctional requirements please refer to the Volere requirements template at http://www.volere.co.uk

Attributes:
This is a subtype of *Requirement* and inherits its attributes.

Considerations:
The nonfunctional properties are important if the user or buyer is to accept the product.

Suggested Implementation:
Sections 10 though 17 of the template. It is vital you give all nonfunctional requirements their correct fit criterion.

Knowledge Class: Product Scope

Purpose:
The *Product Scope* identifies the boundaries of the product to be built. The scope is a summary of the boundaries of all the product use cases.

Attributes:
> User Names
> User Roles
> Other Adjacent Systems
> Interface Descriptions

Suggested Implementation:
Section 8 of the template. This should preferably be a diagram, either a use case diagram or a context model.

Knowledge Class: Product Use Case

Purpose:
A *Product Use Case* is a functional grouping of requirements to be implemented by the product. It is that part of the business use case you decide to implement as your product.

Attributes:
> Product Use Case Name
> Product Use Case Identifier
> Product Use Case Description
> Product Use Case Stories
> Product Use Case Scenarios
> Product Use Case Fit Criterion
> Product Use Case Owner
> Product Use Case Benefit

Suggested Implementation:
Section 8 of the template. The product use cases are a good mechanism for communication within the extended project team.

Knowledge Class: Project Purpose

Purpose:
To understand why the company is making an investment in doing this project.

Attributes:
> Project Goal Description
> Business Advantage
> Measure of Success

Suggested Implementation:
Section 1 of the template. This is the basis for making decisions about scope, relevance, and priority. *Project purpose* is the guiding light for the project. Ideally this should be defined as part of project initiation. The project purpose must be unambiguously defined and agreed upon before gathering detailed requirements.

Knowledge Class: Requirement

Purpose:
A *Requirement* specifies a business need or want to be included in the product.

Attributes:
   Requirement Number
   Requirement Description
   Requirement Rationale
   Requirement Type
   Requirement Fit Criterion
   Requirement Source
   Customer Satisfaction
   Customer Dissatisfaction
   Conflicting Requirements
   Dependent Requirements
   Supporting Material
   Version Number

Considerations:
Also see the subtypes of requirement, namely *Constraint, Functional Requirement, Nonfunctional Requirement, Technological Requirement.*

Suggested Implementation:
Sections 9 through 17 of the template. Various automated tools are available; these allow team access to the requirements.

Knowledge Class: Stakeholder

Purpose:
Stakeholder identifies all the people, roles, organizations who have an interest in the project. This covers the project team, direct users of the product, other indirect beneficiaries of the product, specialists with technical skills needed to build the product, external organizations with rules or laws pertaining to the product, external organizations with specialist knowledge about the product's domain, opponents of the product, producers of competitive products.

Attributes:
    Stakeholder Role
    Stakeholder Name
    Types of Knowledge
    Contact Information (e.g., email address)

Suggested Implementation:
Section 2 of the Template. Use the stakeholder map and stakeholder template to define the attributes for each stakeholder.

Knowledge Class: System Architecture Component

Purpose:
A piece of technology, software, hardware, or abstract container that influences, facilitates, and/or places constraints on the design.

Knowledge Class: Technological Requirement

Purpose:
A *Technological Requirement* exists because of the technology chosen for the implementation. These requirements exist to serve the purposes of the technology, and are not originated by the business.

Considerations:
The technological requirements should only be considered when you know the technological environment. They can be recorded alongside the business requirements, but it must be clear which is which.

Knowledge Class: Test Case

Purpose:
The design for test is the result of a tester reviewing a requirement's fit criterion (precise measure) and designing a cost-effective test to prove whether or not a solution meets the requirement.

Considerations:
You might consider having your testing people write the test cases as the requirements are being written. Also consider replacing a functional requirement's fit criterion with the appropriate test case.

Knowledge Class: Work Context

Purpose:
Defines the boundary of the business area that is to be affected by the installation of the product. The work context is thus describing the scope of the investigation necessary to discover, invent, understand, and identify requirements for the product.

Attributes:
    Adjacent Systems
    Input Dataflows
    Output Dataflows
    Work Context Description

Considerations:
This should be recorded publicly as our experience shows it is the most widely referenced document. A context model is an effective communication tool for defining the work context.

Suggested Implementation:
Section 7 of the template. This is best illustrated with a context model or a use case model.

Association: Business Boundary

Purpose:
To partition the work context according to the functional reality of the business.

Multiplicity:
For each *Business Event* there is one *Work Context.*
    For each *Work Context* there are potentially many *Business Events.*

Association: Business Relevancy

Purpose:
To ensure relevant business connections among the scope of the investigation, the project purpose, and the stakeholders

Multiplicity:
The trinary association is as follows:
    For each instance of
        one *Work Context* and
        one *Stakeholder* there are one or more *Project Purposes.*
    For each instance of
        one *Project Purpose* and
        one *Stakeholder* there is one *Work Context.*
    For each instance of
        one *Project Purpose* and
        one *Work Context* there are potentially many *Stakeholders.*

Association: Business Responding

Purpose:
To reveal what business use cases are used to respond to the business event.

Multiplicity:
For each *Business Event* there is usually one, but could be more than one, *Business Use Case.*

For each *Business Use Case* there can only be one triggering *Business Event.*

Association: Business Tracing

Purpose:
To keep track of the requirements generated by each business use case. Note this is a many to many association because a given requirement may exist in more than one business use case.

Multiplicity:
For each *Business Use Case* there are potentially many Requirements.

For each *Requirement* there are potentially many *Business Use Cases.*

Association: Consistency

Purpose:
To keep track of the requirements use that defines naming conventions so you can check consistency and assess the effect of change.

Multiplicity:
For each *Requirement* there are potentially many *Naming Conventions.*

For each *Naming Convention* there are potentially many *Requirements.*

Association: Design Guiding

Purpose:
Some of the design decisions about product use cases are influenced or driven by characteristics of components of the systems architecture. Keeping track of these associations helps in reviewing and revising design decisions.

Multiplicity:
For each *Product Scope* there are potentially many *System Architecture Components*

For each *System Architecture Component* (in a particular project) there is one *Product Scope.*

Association: Implementing

Purpose:
To keep track of which product use cases are implemented in which implementation units.

Multiplicity:
For each *Product Use Case* there are potentially many *Implementation Units*.
  For each *Implementation Unit* there are potentially many *Product Use Cases*.

Association: Owning

Purpose:
To keep track of what stakeholders are the source of what requirements. The idea of "ownership" is to identify a person who takes the responsibility for helping to get answers to questions about the requirement.

Multiplicity:
For each *Requirement* there is one *Stakeholder*.
  For each *Stakeholder* there are potentially many *Requirements*.

Association: Product Partitioning

Purpose:
All the product use cases together form the complete scope of the product. The product scope is partitioned into a number of product use cases.

Multiplicity:
For each *Product Use Case* there is one *Product Scope*.
  For each *Product Scope* there are potentially many *Product Use Cases*.

Association: Product Tracing

Purpose:
To keep track of what requirements are contained in what product use cases for the purpose of traceability and dealing with change.

Multiplicity:
For each *Requirement* there are potentially many *Product Use Cases*.
  For each *Product Use Case* there are potentially many *Requirements*.

Association: Supporting

Purpose:
To keep track of what systems architecture components support what implementation units for the purpose of tracking tests and assessing impact of change.

Multiplicity:
For each *System Architecture Component* there are potentially many *Implementation Units*.
  For each *Implementation Unit* there are potentially many *System Architecture Components*.

Volere Requirements Specification Template

This template can be used as the foundation for any requirements specification document. We have referred to it a number of times in this book and present an outline version of it here. The complete template is downloadable from www.volere.co.uk.

Project Drivers

1. The Purpose of the Product
   1a. User problem or background of the project effort.
   1b. Goals of the project.
2. Client, Customer, and other Stakeholders
   2a. Client—the person who authorizes the development, and/or is paying for it.
   2b. Customer—the person(s) who will buy the product.
   2c. Other stakeholders. (See Chapter 3—Project Sociology for lists of potential stakeholders.)
3. Users of the Product
   3a. Hands-on users—people who operate the product.
   3b. Priorities assigned to users.
   3c. User participation—an estimate of needed involvement in the project.

Project Constraints

4. Mandated Constraints
    4a. Solution design constraints.
    4b. Implementation environment of the current system.
    4c. Partner or collaborative applications to be used by the product.
    4d. Off-the-shelf software used within the product.
    4e. Anticipated workplace environment.
    4f. Project duration budget.
    4g. Financial budget for the project?
5. Naming Conventions and Definitions
6. Relevant Facts and Assumptions
    6a. Factors that have an effect on the product but are not mandated requirements constraints.
    6b. Assumptions the team is making about the project.

Functional Requirements

7. Scope of the Work
    7a. Context of the work.
    7b. Work partitioning or business use case list.
8. The Scope of the Product
    8a. Product boundary.
    8b. Product use case list.
9. Functional and Data Requirements
    9a. Functional requirements.
    9b. Data requirements.

Nonfunctional Requirements

10. Look and Feel Requirements
    10a. Interface appearance.
    10b. Style of the product.
11. Usability and Humanity Requirements
    11a. Ease of use.
    11b. Personalization and internationalization requirements.
    11c. Ease of learning.
    11d. Understandability Requirements
    11e. Accessibility requirements.
12. Performance Requirements
    12a. Speed and latency requirements.
    12b. Safety critical requirements.
    12c. Precision requirements.

12d. Reliability and availability requirements.

12e. Robustness requirements.

12f. Capacity requirements.

12g. Scalability or extensibility requirements.

13. Operational Requirements

13a. Expected physical environment.

13b. Expected technological environment.

13c. Partner applications.

13d. Productization requirements.

14. Maintainability and Support Requirements

14a. Maintenance requirements.

14b. Special conditions for maintenance.

14c. Supportability.

14d. Adaptability requirements.

15. Security Requirements

15a. Access requirements.

15b. Integrity requirements.

15c. Privacy requirements.

15d. Audit requirements.

15e. Immunity requirements.

16. Cultural and Political Requirements

17. Legal Requirements

17a. Compliance requirements.

17b. Standards requirements.

Project Issues

18. Open Issues

19. Off-the-Shelf Solutions

19a. Ready-made products that can be bought.

19b. Ready-made components suitable for this product.

19c. Other products than can be copied.

20. New Problems

20a. New problems caused by installing the product in the current environment.

20b. Affects on the installed system.

20c. Adverse effects on existing users.

20d. Limitations of the anticipated implementation environment.

20e. Other problems.

21. Tasks

21a. Steps to be taken to deliver the product.

21b. Development phases.

22. Cutover

    22a. Special requirements to have the existing data and procedures work in conjunction with the new product.

    22b. Data to be modified/translated for the new product.

23. Risks

24. Costs

25. User Documentation and Training

26. Waiting Room

27. Ideas for Solutions

Glossary

ACM Association for Computing Machinery

adjacent system a system that provides information to or receives information from the work you are studying.

apprenticing the requirements analyst learns the work or business that the end-user does by doing the work under the end-user's supervision.

association a business link between classes. Also known as a relationship.

attribute an element of stored data. *Also see* data element.

brainstorming a group of interested, bright people who try to generate as many ideas as possible for the product by feeding off one another's ideas.

business analyst the person in most organizations responsible for collecting and recording the requirements.

business event something that happens and causes the work to respond. Business events happen either outside the work in the adjacent systems, or because it is time for the work to produce some service.

business use case the response the work or business makes to a business event. Think of this as a self-contained amount of functions and data that happens in its own discrete time frame.

class a collection of data attributes about a single subject. In this book we use this term to mean only the data, and are ignoring the processes attached to classes in object models.

client the person who pays for the development of the product. This can be someone in your organization, or someone outside for whom you are building the product.

constraint   a preexisting restriction that limits the solution you can provide. This can be a design constraint (the product shall run on a mobile telephone) or a project constraint (the product shall be available three months from now).

context diagram   a diagram showing the work to be studied encapsulated as one process, and the data connections to the outside world represented as adjacent systems.

cooperative adjacent system   one that provides an immediate and predictable service to the work or product. It is usually an automated system with a database containing information used by the work.

COTS   commercial off the shelf

CRM   customer relationship management

customer   the person who buys the product. *See also* client.

data element   an individual item of data that is not subdivided for requirements purposes.

data flow   data that moves from one process to another. Usually represented by a named arrow.

data store   a repository of data. Used as a generic name for file, database, and so forth.

design   the act of crafting a technological solution to fit the requirements.

entity   *see* class.

fit criterion   a quantification or measurement of the requirement such that you are able to determine if the delivered product satisfies the requirement.

function points   a measure of functionality. This is used in requirements projects to measure the work area in order to project the amount of effort needed to study it and write the requirements.

functional requirement   Something that the product must do. Functional requirements are part of the fundamental processes of the product.

IEEE   Institute of Electronics and Electrical Engineers

IFPUG   International Function Point Users Group

KLOC   thousands of lines of code

knowledge model   a class diagram showing the information that is typically gathered by the requirements activity.

nonfunctional requirement   a property or quality the product must have such as an appearance, a speed, or an accuracy property.

product   the thing that your project is to build. You write the requirements for the product.

product use case   part or all of a business use case. The product use case is an amount of functionality allocated to the product. We write requirements for the product use case.

project sociology   the act of identifying all the stakeholders for the requirements project.

prototype   a simulation of the product. In the context of this book it will be a prototype to aid the gathering of requirements and not a design prototype.

PSI   project success indicator

requirement   something the product must do or a property that the product must have.

requirements specification   a document that contains the requirements. The specification defines the product, and may be used as a contract to build the product.

requirer   anyone who has requirements. This is also referred to as a stakeholder.

ROI   return on investment

SME   subject-matter expert

snow card   an 8 by 5 inch card with the components of the requirement printed on it. It is used as a low-tech way of writing requirements.

stakeholder   anybody who has some interest in the product. Stakeholders are not in this sense financial stakeholders.

SWEBOK   software engineering body of knowledge

system   any combination of humans, hardware technology, software technology or materials that carries out a defined purpose. It is best qualified to explain the type of system under discussion. This could be a socio-technical system that involves people and technology, a computer system that involves a mixture of hard and soft technology, a software system that involves soft technology, or a social system that just involves human beings.

UML   unified modeling language

use case   we prefer not to use this alone, but correctly identify it as a business use case or a product use case.

work   the business area that eventually will include the product. The work is the area surrounding the product, and is usually affected by the introduction of the product.

Bibliography

Alexander, Ian and Neil Maiden (eds.) *Scenarios, Stories, and Use Cases—Through the System Life-Cycle*. Scheduled to be published by John Wiley & Sons, 2004.

Alexander, Ian, and Richard Stevens. *Writing Better Requirements*. Addison-Wesley, 2002.

Beck, Kent, and Martin Fowler. *Planning Extreme Programming*. Addison-Wesley, 2001.

Beck, Kent. *eXtreme Programming Explained*. Addison-Wesley, 2000.

Belbin, R. Meredith. *Team Roles at Work*. Butterworth-Heinemann, 2001.

Beyer, Hugh, and Karen Holtzblatt. *Contextual Design—Defining Customer-Centered Systems*. Morgan Kaufmann, 1998.

Brealey, R., and S.C. Myers. *Principles of Corporate Finance*. Sixth Edition, McGraw-Hill, 2000.

Brooks, Fred. *The Mythical Man-Month*. Addison-Wesley, 1975.

Checkland, Peter. *Systems Thinking, Systems Practice*. John Wiley & Sons, 1993.

Christensen, Clayton. *The Innovator's Dilemma—When New Technologies Cause Great Firms to Fail*. Harvard Business School Press, 1997.

Cockburn, Alistair. *Writing Effective Use Cases*. Addison-Wesley, 2001.

Constantine, Larry, and Lucy Lockwood. *Software for Use—A Practical Guide to the Models and Methods of Usage-Centered Design*. Addison-Wesley, 1999.

Davis, Alan. *Software Requirements—Objects, Functions and States*. Prentice Hall, 1990.

De Liefde, Willem. *African tribal leadership voor managers van dialoog tot besluit* (from dialog till decision) Kluwer-Deventer, the Netherlands, 2002.

DeMarco, Tom, and Tim Lister. *Waltzing with Bears: Managing Risk on Software Projects*. Dorset House, 2003.

DeMarco, Tom, and Tim Lister: *Peopleware: Productive Projects and Teams*, 2nd edition. Dorset House, 1999.

Favaro, John and Kenneth. "Strategic Analysis of Application Framework Investments." In B*uilding Application Frameworks: Object-Oriented Foundations of Framework Design*. M. Fayad, R. Johnson, eds. John Wiley & Sons, 1999.

Garmus, David, and David Herron. *Function Point Analysis: Measurement Practices for Successful Software Projects*. Addison-Wesley, 2000.

Gause, Donald, and Gerald Weinberg. *Are Your Lights On? How to Figure Out What the Problem Really Is*. Dorset House, 1990.

———. *Exploring Requirements: Quality Before Design*. Dorset House, 1989.

Gershenfeld, Neil. *When Things Start to Think*. Henry Holt & Company, 1999.

Gilb, Tom, and Dorothy Graham. *Software Inspection*. Addison-Wesley, 1993.

Gottesdiener, Ellen. *Requirements by Collaboration—Workshops for Defining Needs*. Addison-Wesley, 2002.

Hatley, Derek, Peter Hruschka, and Imtiaz Pirbhai. *Process for System Architecture and Requirements Engineering*. Dorset House, 2000.

Highsmith, Jim. *Adaptive Software Development: A Collaborative Approach to Managing Complex Systems*. Dorset House, 2000.

Hoffman. Lynn. *Foundations of Family Therapy: A Conceptual Framework for Systems Change*. Basic Books, 1981.

Hooks, Ivy, and Kristin Farry. *Customer-Centered Products—Creating Successful Products through Smart Requirements Management*. American Management Association, 2001.

Jackson, Michael. *Problem Frames—Analyzing and Structuring Software Development Problems*. Addison-Wesley, 2001.

———. *Software Requirements and Specifications—A Lexicon of Practice, Principles and Prejudices*. Addison-Wesley, 1995.

Jacobson, Ivar, Grady Booch, and James Rhumbaugh. *The Unified Software Development Process*. Addison-Wesley, 1999.

Jones, Capers. *Conflict and Litigation between Software Clients and Developers*. Software Productivity Research, 2001.

———. *Software Quality—Analysis and Guidelines for Success*. Thomson Computer Press, 1997.

Kelley, Tom. *The Art of Innovation—Lessons in Creativity from IDEO, America's Leading Design Firm*. Doubleday, 2001.

Kovitz, Benjamin. *Practical Software Requirements—A Manual of Content and Style*. Manning Publications 1999.

Kruchen, Phillippe. *The Rational Unified Process—An Introduction*. Addison-Wesley, 1999.

Lauesen, Soren. *Software Requirements—Styles and Techniques*. Addison-Wesley, 2002.

Leffingwell, Dean, and Don Widrig. *Managing Software Requirements—A Unified Approach*. Addison-Wesley, 2000.

Levine, Rick, et al. *The Cluetrain Manifesto—The End of Business as Usual*. Pearson Education, 2000.

McConnell, Steve. *Professional Software Development*. Addison-Wesley, 2004.

McMenamin, Steve, and John Palmer. *Essential Systems Analysis*. Yourdon Press, 1984.

Norman, Donald. *The Design of Everyday Things*. Doubleday, 1988.

———. *The Invisible Computer*. MIT Press, 1999.

Pardee, William. *To Satisfy and Delight Your Customer*. Dorset House, 1996.

Peters, Tom. *The Circle of Innovation*. Alfred A. Knopf, 1997.

Pfleeger, Shari Lawrence, Les Hatton, and Charles Howell. *Solid Software*. Prentice Hall, 2002.

Poundstone, William. *How Would You Move Mount Fuji? Microsoft's Cult of the Puzzle—How the World's Smartest Company Selects the Most Creative Thinkers*. Little Brown, 2003.

Robertson, James and Suzanne. *Mastering the Requirements Process*. Addison-Wesley, 1999.

Robertson, Suzanne and James. *Complete Systems Analysis—The Workbook, The Textbook, The Answers*. Dorset House, 1998.

Rupp, Chris. *Requirements-Engineering und –Management*. Professionelle, iterative Anforderungsanalyse für IT-Systeme. Carl Hanser Verlag, 2001.

Schank, Roger. *Tell Me a Story*. Northwestern University Press, 1998.

Schrage, Michael. *Serious Play: How the World's Best Companies Simulate to Innovate*. Harvard Business School Press, 2000.

Senge, Peter M. *The Fifth Discipline. The Art and Practice of the Learning Organization*. Doubleday, 1990.

Senge, Peter M., et al. *The Fifth Discipline Fieldbook, Strategies and Tools for Building a Learning Organization*. Doubleday, 1994.

Sommerville, Ian, and Pete Sawyer. *Requirements Engineering—A Good Practice Guide*. John Wiley & Sons, 1997.

Thayer, Richard, and Merlin Dorfman (eds.). *Software Requirements Engineering*, Second Edition. IEEE Computer Society Press, 1987.

Thomsett, Robb. *Radical Project Management*. Prentice Hall, 2002.

Trompenaars, Fons, and Charles Hampden-Turner. *Riding the Waves of Culture—Understanding Cultural Diversity in Business*. Nicholas Brearly Publishing, 1997.

Tufte, Edward, R. *The Visual Display of Quantitative Information*. Graphics Press, 1983.

———. *Envisioning Information*. Graphics Press, 1990.

———. *Visual Explanations*. Graphics Press, 1997.

United States Marine Corps. *Warfighting*. Currency Doubleday, 1994.

von Oech, Roger. *A Kick in the Seat of the Pants. Using Your Explorer, Artist, Judge and Warrior to Be More Creative*. Harper & Row, 1986.

———. *A Whack on the Side of the Head. How to Unlock Your Mind for Innovation*. Creative Think, 1982.

Weinberg, Jerry. *An Introduction to General Systems Thinking, Silver Anniversary Edition*. Dorset House, 2001.

———. *Quality Software Management*, Volume 1—Systems Thinking. Dorset House, 1992.

———. *Quality Software Management, Volume 2—First-Order Measurement*. Dorset House, 1993.

———. *Quality Software Management, Volume 3—Congruent Action*. Dorset House, 1994.

———. *Quality Software Management, Volume 4—Anticipating Change*. Dorset House Publishing, 1997.

Wiegers, Karl. *Software Requirements*, Second Edition. Microsoft Press, 2003.

Index